Praise for

I Must Not Think Bad Thoughts

"These short, sharp, well-turned pieces will make you look at the world in a new and rewardingly disturbing way. What makes Mark Dery such an appealing tour guide through all these bad thoughts of his is that he's right there with us, trying to answer the tough questions, and willing to turn his probing mind and eye on himself, too." —*Phoenix New Times*

"More relevant than *Mythologies,* funnier than *Travels in Hyperreality,* more readable than *Simulacra,* less gloomy than *Living in the End Times,* smarter than Hitchens and without the pomposity, Mark Dery's dazzling collection will, I unhesitatingly predict, become a classic of cultural criticism."
—**Jim Lawrence,** *Words, Noises, and Other Stuff*

"Do not turn squeamish from the many considerations of death that lurk within—vampires, tombs, disease, corruption of many varieties. Dery's restless and stylish essay is concerned with one thing only: what it means to be alive in America."
—**Richard Rodriguez,** author of *Brown: The Last Discovery of America*

"A long-awaited compendium of his oft-brutal, usually funny, and always-brilliant writings on the curious, bizarre, and downright dark crevices of our culture. Look no further than this new book for your next monstrous dose of Mark Dery." —*Boing Boing*

"Dery is willing to tackle some tough and controversial subject matter—the Holocaust 'industry,' for example—and examine it with rigor and a willingness to upset conventional or comfortable opinion and piety."   —*PopMatters*

"No critic delves into the dark recesses of American consciousness quite like Dery. And perhaps at no time in recent history has national disillusionment been so primed for such critique."
          —*The Verge*

"The best cultural commentators strip through whatever position is intellectually fashionable at any given moment and attempt to place their subject in the greater context of everything that's come before and that's happening now. Dery does this as well as anyone ever has, and better than most; at his best he brings to mind a more disciplined and educated Lester Bangs, or Tom Wolfe without the white suit and the bullshit mannerisms."   —*Las Vegas CityLife*

"A dazzling performance, with Mark Dery compulsively trawling the garbage-strewn shorelines of the United States to examine its dark and rancid center ... He writes in a breathless and witty style, engagingly full of glib word play."   —**David Lida,** author of *First Stop in the New World: Mexico City, the Capital of the 21st Century*

I MUST NOT THINK BAD THOUGHTS

I Must Not Think Bad Thoughts

DRIVE-BY ESSAYS
ON AMERICAN DREAD, AMERICAN DREAMS

MARK DERY

FOREWORD BY BRUCE STERLING

University of Minnesota Press

Minneapolis

London

Published by the University of Minnesota Press
111 Third Avenue South, Suite 290
Minneapolis, MN 55401-2520
http://www.upress.umn.edu

LIBRARY OF CONGRESS CATALOGING-IN-PUBLICATION DATA
Dery, Mark, 1959–
   I must not think bad thoughts : drive-by essays on American dread, American dreams / Mark Dery ; foreword by Bruce Sterling.
   Includes bibliographical references.
   ISBN 978-0-8166-7773-3 (hc : acid-free paper)
   ISBN 978-0-8166-7774-0 (pb : acid-free paper)
1. Popular culture—United States. 2. United States—Civilization—1970– I. Title.
   NX180.S6D477 2012
   306'.0973—dc23   2011050383

Printed in the United States of America on acid-free paper

The University of Minnesota is an equal-opportunity educator and employer.

21 20 19 18 17 16 15 14   10 9 8 7 6 5 4 3 2 1

TO J. G. BALLARD

Pathologist of the postmodern,
astronaut of inner space,
matchless stylist, generous mentor.

He sought the gold of time.

Cadillacs, Coca-Cola, and cocaine, presidents and psychopaths, Norman Rockwell and the mafia . . . the dream of
America endlessly unravels its codes, like the helix of some
ideological DNA.

J. G. BALLARD, Introduction to *Hello America*

I want to immerse myself in American magic and dread.

MURRAY JAY SUSKIND, the professor of Elvis studies
in Don DeLillo's *White Noise*

Contents

Foreword: I Must Not Read Bad Thoughts *Bruce Sterling*   xiii

Introduction   1

AMERICAN MAGIC, AMERICAN DREAD

Dead Man Walking *What Do Zombies Mean?*   11

Gun Play *An American Tragedy in Three Acts*   18

Mysterious Stranger *Grandpa Twain's Dark Side*   27

Aladdin Sane Called. He Wants His Lightning Bolt Back.
On Lady Gaga   35

Jocko Homo *How Gay Is the Super Bowl?*   48

Wimps, Wussies, and W. *Masculinity, American Style*   57

Stardust Memories *How David Bowie Killed the '60s, Ushered in the '70s, and, for One Brief Shining Moment, Made the Mullet Hip*   64

When Animals Attack! *An Aesop's Fable about Anthropomorphism*   71

Toe *Fou Subliminally Seduced by Madonna's Big Toe*   81

Shoah Business   87

The Triumph of the Shill *Fascist Branding*   94

Endtime for Hitler *On the* Downfall *Parodies and the Inglorious Return of Der Führer*   101

MYTHS OF THE NEAR FUTURE
Making Sense of the Digital Age

World Wide Wonder Closet *On Blogging*   115

(Face)Book of the Dead   122

Straight, Gay, or Binary? *HAL Comes Out of the Cybernetic Closet* 135

Word Salad Surgery *Spam, Deconstructed* 146

Slashing the Borg *Resistance Is Fertile* 151

Things to Come *Xtreme Kink and the Future of Porn* 159

TRIPE SOUP FOR THE SOUL
Religion and All Its Works and Ways

Tripe Soup for the Soul *The Daily Affirmation* 169

Pontification *On the Death of the Pope* 175

The Prophet Margin *Jack Chick's Comic-Book Apocalypse* 182

2012 *Carnival of Bunkum* 188

The Vast Santanic Conspiracy 193

ANATOMY LESSON
The Grotesque, the Gothic, and Other Dark Matters

Open Wide *Dental Horror* 205

Gray Matter *The Obscure Pleasures of Medical Libraries* 212

Thirteen Ways of Looking at a Severed Head 219

Been There, Pierced That *Apocalypse Culture and the Escalation of Subcultural Hostilities* 234

Death to All Humans! *The Church of Euthanasia's Modest Proposal* 240

Great Caesar's Ghost *On the Crypt of the Capuchins* 245

Aphrodites of the Operating Theater *On La Specola's Anatomical Venuses* 252

Goodbye, Cruel Words *On the Suicide Note as a Literary Genre* 260

Cortex Envy *Bringing Up Baby Einstein* 265

Acknowledgments 279

Notes 281

Publication History 315

I Must Not Read Bad Thoughts

BRUCE STERLING

I HAVE READ EVERY MARK DERY BOOK EVER WRITTEN, INCLUD-
ing, of course, this one. I find them exceedingly practical, concrete,
and useful works. Mark is always willing to venture to the fringes, the edges, the
frontiers. He marinates himself in the sensibility of the locals. He
never lies about what he finds. He performs a great service.
He scorns all candy wrapping. He abjures branding and triangula-
tion. He makes the unthinkable lucid.

Since I'm a novelist, and an entertainer by nature, I rather enjoy
some good fantastic flimflam. I've got a soft spot for sense-of-won-
der razzle-dazzle. However, there are some fetid marshes of contemporary life that can't repay an investment of creative effort. They are
witchlights and will-o'-the-wisps. You can't sink pilings and construct
a foundation there; they're hokum all the way down. Mark Dery is
willing to tell you about that. He's even eager to tell you.

Mark has exotic tastes, but he's a thinker of consequence, ever keen
to deflate fraud and to combat superstition. He scouts the terrain
of counterculture—he's a botanist of countercultures, really, always
unearthing new species in unlikely niches—and he takes careful notes.

Having found the cult, he judiciously sips the Kool-Aid. He's an
oenophile in those matters: you can witness him sniffing the Kool-
Aid, rinsing his molars, extracting the full bouquet. Then he spits.

In simpler, more linear times, Mark's social role would have been
clearer. He would have been an avid, left-wing progressive avant-

gardiste. He would have been some raffish Greenwich Village ally of Hannah Arendt or Mary McCarthy, an ideological philosophe with positions staked out all along the front line. He would have been some colossally erudite fringe character who ended up teaching at NYU—and in fact Mark Dery *is* a colossally erudite fringe character who taught at NYU. But these aren't simple, linear times.

These are dark, networked, baroque times dominated by massive fraud and rank political delusion, a Gothic high-tech period. Furthermore, conventional publishing is collapsing, and with it all previous roles for the public intellectual. In these twisted circumstances, Mark Dery has to flourish rhizomatically, and he writes about practically anything.

There's a signature essay in this collection, "World Wide Wonder Closet," where one can see Dery realizing, with an existential horror, that a Gothic network culture has arisen. Its primary means of expression is the weblog, a baroque *Wunderkammer* jammed together on a zero budget by fanatical autodidacts. Dery instantly recognizes that this apparently harmless and whimsical innovation is a dreadful cultural advent. It is symptomatic of a forthcoming collapse in the establishment of public credibility, an abdication of allegiance to facts. And he says so. In detail, and at length. He is both prescient and correct.

Not that there is much he can do about it. Nowadays, Boing Boing, a weblog whose scatterbrained habits he specifically applauds, is the world's major nexus of Mark Dery appreciation. It would be wrong and facile to call this "ironic." This is prescience in conditions of historical inevitability. I learn useful things like this by paying close attention to Mark Dery—not just to his writings, mind you, but to his career.

For instance: Whatever happened to Mark Dery's two favorite topics, the major insights that first won him his fame? Those would be "culture jamming" and avant-garde musical electronica. Well, the term *culture jamming* implies that postmodern late capitalism is a closely organized, efficient profit machine subject to deft semiotic sabotage. That was once true, but now everybody knows how to do that. So there's nothing left of it; our premiere culture jams today are probably deranged Twitter tweets from Sarah Palin insisting that a once-thriving nation be bankrupted forthwith. And electronica is no longer a wildly inventive musical genre. It's a subset of network culture, the specter that haunts the deathbed of the music industry, the zero-budget soundtrack for globalized piracy. He's a prophet who predicted the past. That's why he wisely doesn't dwell on these things anymore.

In social conditions of this description, Dery isn't "advancing" much; he's not avant any particular garde. Instead, he brandishes a Diogenes lantern as the smoke thickens on every side. He no longer sounds like a hipster at the kitchen table of the "coolest people in America." He has the ruminative tone of a Havel-style dissident living in truth amid ever more brazen lies.

Back in the analog press days, there used to be Bohemian bottles in which Mark could pack the genie of his inspiration; in short, Mark knew who he was talking to and who was publishing him. These contemporary essays are different in character. They arose within network culture, are fully informed by it, and are digital in production and distribution. They read like the contents of bottles pitched into the sea.

Beset with Google erudition, they tackle a dizzying set of topics—even within the essays, within the very sentences, there are dizzying arrays of topics. He has abandoned his preset positions in the previous century's cultural landscape. He gazes back with nostalgia because he knows full well that they are deader than abandoned strip malls.

These new essays are more personal and also more universal than his earlier work. They read less like boho fringe reportage and more like moral philosophy.

Anybody interested in weird extremes of human behavior (and no man alive is more so than Mark Dery) eventually has to come to terms with the Nazis. Generally, in modern times, the term *Nazi* is deployed as a stoplight, hot-button, or demonization tool. Here Mark makes a mature effort to get past the culture-jam shriek of *Nazi* to plumb the nature of real-life Nazis as mortal human beings.

It turns out that Mark doesn't much care for Nazis. But he is closely intrigued by how a shell-shocked postcard artist successfully transformed himself, through controlled media and graphic branding, into a fake Wagnerian demigod. Mark perceives certain parallels here. This study seems a work in progress, but it's quite thought-provoking.

Another third rail of culture study is pornography. Here Mark makes a determined effort to forge out on the Internet and uncover the absolute worst—not just the bad thought, but the baddest possible thought. He is gamely pursuing a kind of El Dorado of erotic degradation, an ultimate porn black hole that would cause Websurfers to implode in their ergonomic chairs. He doesn't find this. He does seem to find enough porn to exhaust his interest in that subject conclusively. This grotesque underworld is demystified. It's reduced to online yard goods. It's like the endless patterns spewed out by a bad screensaver.

So pornography is just not that interesting, which seems a banal conclusion. The idea that pornography could permanently lose its half-mystical cachet through its sheer abundance is, in fact, very interesting. There has never been a culture in history that was dismissive and blasé about porn. "Things to Come: Xtreme Kink and the Future of Porn" is the premonition of a bizarre society in which everyone is a Dorian Gray who posts his portrait on Facebook. I wouldn't call that "progress," and this essay is probably his most disgusting essay ever, but this is where Mark, as a culture critic, truly excels. He's very good at going into areas of culture you wouldn't care to visit yourself and performing autopsies. He assesses each bone and organ in detail. Not in a crowd-pleasing way—he doesn't prettify it, culture-industrialize it, and build a gift shop at the door. Mark is like a Martian probe. He is high-tech. He is way out there, on his own. He came equipped with an onboard set of lenses and abrasion tools. Often, his findings are of interest mostly to specialists.

Throughout his career, Mark has commonly spoken as if time were not on his side. All his works are redolent of doom, brinks, chasms, crevasses, dysfunctions, abandonments, catastrophes, massacres, mortuaries, and 1970s-style No Future punk apocalypses. You'd think that the guy was blazingly keen for a counterculture martyrdom, a kind of Sid Vicious Situationist in his own mind. But he's been at his labors quite a while now. For a doomy *poète maudit,* he sure shows remarkable consistency and staying power. This world now looks a lot more like a Mark Dery world than it looked when he started writing. We live in a very Deryesque world, and there are few public thinkers working today of whom one could properly say such a thing. Take most any glossed-up, bow-tied American television pundit of the '80s and '90s—the "commentators," you know, the pundits with "credibility," on the hot-dial short list for the studio. Be honest, and compare their blinkered ideas with the world that we actually inhabit in 2012. This world of bank collapses, evil moguls, extraordinary renditions, organized denial of scientific fact, crumbling infrastructure, flash-mob guttings of organized political parties, that sort of thing. Commentators of that ilk rarely discussed such matters. They never perceived them, never thought to look for the symptoms. They were way too busy engineering consent.

As for Mark, I wouldn't claim he's happy about it, but he's someone whose sensibility is always firmly based on expecting a world of the kind that we actually have. He has always looked outside the pale, but as time has passed and favored his analysis, he seems to be looking deeper and deeper *within* the pale. He won't receive "vindication," and I doubt he expects that, but to me he offers something rather better: he's someone whose work I will genuinely want to read as we share old age.

He'll be telling it as he sees it, and he'll see things that I need to know. He will be a credible witness to that future era's creative life, and he will understand it on its own terms, probably better than it understands itself. So let's think through the worst, shall we? Even if I'm crotchety, vague, backward-looking, and confused, if I'm yesterday's man, a future-shocked cultural relic, well, I reckon he won't be. And that is a very practical, concrete, and useful thing.

Introduction

From a very early age, perhaps the age of five or six, I knew that
when I grew up I should be a writer. . . . I knew that I had a facility
with words and a power of facing unpleasant facts.

—GEORGE ORWELL, "Why I Write"

I must not think bad thoughts,
I must not think bad thoughts,
The facts we hate.

—x, "I Must Not Think Bad Thoughts"

AT SOME POINT DURING MY LONG MARCH THROUGH *THE DREAM*
of the Rood, *The Faerie Queene*, and the metaphysical poets—a protracted agony relieved, for English majors in the early '80s, by such
thrillingly up-to-the-minute fare as *The Great Gatsby* and, still crack-
ling with the Shock of the New, Allen Ginsberg's "Howl"—I rose to
object, in class, to a curriculum dominated by the Greatest Hits of the
Late Cretaceous.

It was the '80s: Why weren't we reading, say, *Naked Lunch*? After
all, the Burroughs novel was published in the year of my birth (1959)
and written by the grand old man of the Beats; hadn't they insinuated themselves into the canon (albeit by tunneling in through the
drains)? The answer, my professor patiently explained, was that only
an academic with a career death wish would be rash enough to assign
a text that hadn't been rendered safe for classroom dissection by historical distance and scholarly embalming.

It made strange music in my head, this admission of intellectual timidity, given the zeitgeist: I was attending college in L.A., where punk rock was the soundtrack of youth culture, a squall of suburban angst and political disaffection. "I Must Not Think Bad Thoughts" by the band X nailed the apolitical vacuity of the decade, when greed was good and the grandfatherly velociraptor in the Oval Office mused, on *Good Morning America*, that "the people who are sleeping on the grates" must surely be homeless "by choice" in this Best of All Possible Worlds.[1] Up-to-the-minute and in-your-face, punk didn't hesitate to deconstruct the world around it—with a chainsaw.

It occurred to me, with X buzzing in my mind's ear and my professor's words hanging in the air, that it's a writer's job, as well, to Think Bad Thoughts—to wander footloose through the mind's labyrinth, following the thread of any idea that reels you in, no matter how arcane or depraved, obscene or blasphemous, untouchably controversial, irreducibly complex, or preposterous on its face.

The ethos of Thinking Bad Thoughts isn't synonymous with the willful perversity of Christopher Hitchens's contrarianism, or with H. L. Mencken's lifelong devotion to spit-roasting the sacred cows of the booboisie, or with the nothing-is-true, everything-is-permitted libertinism of William S. Burroughs, or with the liberatory cynicism of punk rockers like X, or with Orwell's ability to confront hard truths without flinching. Yet it contains a tincture of each.

Thinking Bad Thoughts is above all else a refusal to recognize intellectual no-fly zones. In America, that translates as the rejection of bred-in-the-bone Puritanism; bourgeois anxieties about taste; the self-censorship routinely practiced by academics, fearful of offending tenure committees and blinkered by elite assumptions about what constitutes "serious" subject matter and "scholarly" style; the craven capitulation of Hollywood and the news media, phobic of *truly* controversial content that might scare off advertisers or upset Middle America's mental digestion. (By "truly controversial content," I mean incendiary *ideas* that challenge the founding assumptions of official fictions or popular pieties. Take your pick, for example, of Noam Chomsky's Top 10 List of Things You Can't Say on *Nightline*: "The biggest international terror operations that are known are the ones that are run out of Washington; if the Nuremberg laws were applied, then every postwar American president would have been hanged; the Bible is one of the most genocidal books in the total canon; education is a system of imposed ignorance . . .").[2] The politics of Thinking Bad Thoughts stands foursquare against the faux-populist demagogues, brownshirt pundits, evangelical know-nothings, and Tea Party lumpen of the anti-intellectual right *and* against the Stalinist thought police of the left at its most inquisitional, scouring every soul for counterrevolutionary tendencies—those ineradicable pockets of racism, sexism, sizeism, ageism, ableism, and lookism lurking in even the most ideologically pure of heart.

When my dreams showed signs
of becoming
politically correct
no unruly images
escaping beyond borders . . .
then I began to wonder
(Adrienne Rich, "North American Time")

Thinking Bad Thoughts is an intellectual insurgency against the friendly fascisms of right *and* left, happy bedfellows in their prohibition, on pain of death, of thoughtcrime. (Exhibit A: Andrea Dworkin, standard-bearer of the penis-is-a-weapon, intercourse-is-rape phalanx of feminism, shoulder to shoulder with the religious right in her jihad against porn and all its works and ways.) It's the unshakable conviction that, while some beliefs may be ethically indefensible, morally repugnant, or universally unpopular, no subject should be ruled out of bounds, no thought forbidden; intellectual freedom is unimaginable without the right to think the unthinkable.

Which is, after all, the point of the book in your hands: to cast a critical eye on the accepted order of things, to read between the lines of the world around us, considered as an ideological text—in short, to Think Bad Thoughts. And to inspire you, my reader, to do so as well.

MY ABIDING SUBJECT, in these essays, is America. Like the neocons
and their devolutionary descendants, the Hoveround hordes of the
Tea Party, I am a devout believer in American exceptionalism, though
not as my friends on the right understand it.

America *is* historically unique in the fervor of its dream of itself
as a shining City upon a Hill, showered in God's grace . . . and in
the pitch-blackness of the dark places in its national psyche. In the
Big-Man-on-Campus swagger of its self-regard, the sachrymose sentimentality of its self-mythologization . . . and in the mocking distance between its patriotic fables and the bred-in-the-bone bigotry
and brutality of its history—a sustained crescendo of violence, official
criminality, and perversions of democracy so grotesque they'd bring a
blush to Caligula's cheek: covert operations, state-sanctioned torture,
extraordinary rendition, the rollback of civil liberties, the rise of the
surveillance state.

The French philosopher Jean Baudrillard, a postmodern de
Tocqueville, put it nicely in his book *America*, in an ironic paean to
New York that is easily repurposed as an ironic paean to the whole
country: "It is a world completely rotten with power, wealth, senil-
ity, indifference, Puritanism and mental hygiene, poverty and waste,
technological futility and aimless violence, and yet I cannot help but
feel it has about it something of the dawning of the universe."[3]

As it happens, Winthrop's homily about the City upon a Hill
sheds light on America's split personality. Exhorting his shipmates
on the *Arabella*, in flight from religious persecution in England, to
turn the Massachusetts Bay Colony into A Model of Christian Charity, the Puritan divine conjured a new Jerusalem in the wilderness:
"We shall find that the God of Israel is among us, when ten of us
shall be able to resist a thousand of our enemies, when he shall make
us a praise and glory that men shall say of succeeding plantations,
'the Lord make it like that of New England.' For we must consider
that we shall be as a city upon a hill. The eyes of all people are upon
us."[4] It's all there, or at least an evil gleam of it: the heady sense of

4

exceptionalism; the kick-ass triumphalism that would one day take shape in the frat-house war chant, *U-S-A, U-S-A!*; the internal tension, held in matter–antimatter balance throughout American history, between Christian values and Enlightenment virtues (Winthrop was Cambridge educated and had practiced law at the Inner Temple); the dreams of Liberty and Justice for All coexisting uneasily with theocratic rule in a Puritan colony. (No sooner had the Puritans built their Shining City than they began busying themselves persecuting *other* religious minorities, such as the Quakers.)

The afterlife of Winthrop's ringing phrase is equally instructive about the false front of the American Dream. In January 1961, in his last formal speech before assuming the presidency, President-Elect John F. Kennedy wove Winthrop's words into his address to the General Court of Massachusetts, noting that "the eyes of all people are truly upon us—and our governments, in every branch, at every level, national, state and local, must be as a city upon a hill—constructed and inhabited by men aware of their great trust and their great responsibilities."[5] Humbly asking God's help and his audience's prayers in fulfilling the nation's sacred trust in him, he hoped history would judge his administration as "men of integrity—men who never ran out on either the principles in which they believed or the people who believed in them," standard-bearers of the American Way, "devoted solely to serving the public good and the national interest," and so on, scaling purple mountain majesties.

As we now know, JFK's Republic of Virtue had some troubling secrets buried in its basement: the Kennedy family's ties to the mob; the plots to assassinate troublesome foreign leaders like Castro; the president's role in the ouster and murder of South Vietnamese president Ngo Dinh Diem, an event that more than any other led to the American nightmare in Vietnam; and, making a mockery of gilt-edged rhetoric about "men of integrity," the Kennedy brothers' compulsive womanizing, so rapacious it stunned the Secret Service agents who were privy to it. As the investigative reporter Seymour M. Hersh reveals, in *The Dark Side of Camelot:*

Jack Kennedy had been living a public lie as the attentive husband of Jacqueline, the glamorous and high-profile first lady. In private Kennedy was consumed with almost daily sexual liaisons and libertine partying, to a degree that shocked many members of his personal Secret Service detail. The sheer number of Kennedy's sexual partners, and the recklessness of his use of them, escalated through his presidency. The women—sometimes paid prostitutes . . . —would be brought to Kennedy's office or his private quarters without any prior Secret Service knowledge or clearance.[6]

Now and again, a Secret Service agent was dispatched to D.C.'s distinguished Mickelson Gallery, charged with the somber responsibility—no doubt in the name of "serving the public good and the national interest"—of delivering for framing "sexually explicit photographs of a naked president with various paramours" in the Lincoln Room.[7] In one image, JFK gambols with two women, all three of them wearing masks. (Cue the original cast recording of the musical *Camelot*, a Kennedy favorite: "I wonder what the king is doing tonight? / What merriment is the king pursuing tonight?")[8]

Ronald Reagan was famously taken with Winthrop's city, too, evoking it in his 1984 acceptance of the Republican Party presidential nomination and again in 1989, in his farewell speech to the nation, in which he gave us the Disney Version, rhapsodizing about "a tall proud city built on rocks stronger than oceans, wind-swept, God-blessed, and teeming with people of all kinds living in harmony and peace."[9]

Peel back the mask of the avuncular Gipper enshrined in conservative myth, however, and you'll find the mendacious schemer who gave Congress the one-fingered salute, green-lighting illegal arms sales to fund the right-wing insurgency against Nicaragua's leftist government; the credulous old ostrich who swallowed his weight in supply-side bunkum, championing tax-slashing economic policies that proved a windfall for the wealthy but helped put the middle class on the endangered species list.

Christopher Hitchens caught a glimpse of the Real Ronnie; he recalls it fondly in his obituary for the man for whom it was always Morning in America:

I only saw him once up close, which happened to be when he got a question he didn't like. Was it true that his staff in the 1980 debates had stolen President Carter's briefing book? (They had.) The famously genial grin turned into a rictus of senile fury: I was looking at a cruel and stupid lizard. His reply was that maybe his staff had, and maybe they hadn't, but what about the leak of the Pentagon Papers? Thus, a secret theft of presidential documents was equated with the public disclosure of needful information. This was a man never short of a cheap jibe or the sort of falsehood that would, however laughable, buy him some time.[10]

I believe the American Gothic is as revealing about who we are, as a nation, as our noblest moments. By the American Gothic, I mean the stomach-plunging drop from reassuring myth to ugly truth—the distance between our dream of ourselves and the face staring back at us from the cultural mirror.

David Lynch's *Blue Velvet* may be *the* quintessential example of the American Gothic. A crime-scene excavation of the crawl space in the American unconscious, as rendered by Norman Rockwell, Lynch's movie reminds us that it's the bedtime stories America likes to tell itself most—the consoling fictions of JFK's Camelot, of Reagan Country, of Disney's Main Street U.S.A., of Frank Capra's *It's a Wonderful Life*, of Mark Twain's boyhood idylls—that inevitably have the darkest undersides. That darkness has always been there, in this New World that has "something of the dawning of the universe" about it, if you know where to look for it.

Lynch's forebear Nathaniel Hawthorne knew this; knew that the Benjamin Franklin side of the American character—scientific, pragmatic, ingeniously inventive, infatuated with the new, turned to face the future—is countervailed by the nation's inner Cotton Mather, reactionary, self-righteous, his god-haunted mind cobwebbed by superstition: witchcraft, demonic possession, and other Wonders of the Invisible World, as Mather called them.

Hawthorne's short story "Young Goodman Brown" does for Winthrop's Puritan America what *Blue Velvet* did for the Reagan '80s. Like Jeffrey Beaumont, the all-American college kid in Lynch's movie, Brown is drawn to the depravity behind the rickrack and gingerbread

of small-town America. Sneaking off to a witches' Sabbath in the wild
wood, he is horrified to see, among the "fiend-worshippers" giving
the devil his due,

> faces that would be seen next day at the council board of the province,
> and others which, Sabbath after Sabbath, looked devoutly heavenward, and
> benignantly over the crowded pews, from the holiest pulpits in the land.[11]

In his analysis of *Blue Velvet,* the film critic Robert Sklar offers as
profound a definition of the American Gothic as any: "'I like the idea
that everything has a surface, which hides much more underneath,'
Lynch has said. 'I go down in that darkness and see what's there.'
Beneath the surface of this quotidian American dreamworld lies voy-
eurism, violence, sadomasochism, sexual aggression—perhaps only a
sleeping character's nightmare, or perhaps, for Lynch, the authentic
American dream."[12]

Like Lynch, I want to peer down, into that darkness, and see
what's there—to immerse myself in American magic and dread, as
the professor of Elvis studies says in Don DeLillo's *White Noise.* And,
equally, to induce in my readers the vertigo that comes from gazing too long into the cultural abyss—then give them a loving shove,
right over the edge.

American Magic, American Dread

Dead Man Walking

IN OUR DAY OF THE (LIVING) DEAD, THE REANIMATED ARE everywhere, from *Pride and Prejudice and Zombies*, Seth Grahame-Smith's inspired mash-up of the zombie myth and Jane Austen's Regency novel of manners, to *The Walking Dead*, a graphic novel about humanity reduced to Hobbesian brutishness in a postapocalyptic America overrun by the undead, to the splatterpunk video game *Left 4 Dead*.

The zombie is a polyvalent revenant, a bloating signifier that has given shape, alternately, to repressed memories of slavery's horrors; white alienation from the darker Other; Cold War nightmares of mushroom clouds and megadeaths; the posttraumatic fallout of the AIDS pandemic; and, in movies like *28 Days Later* and books like Max Brooks's faux-historical *World War Z: An Oral History of the Zombie War*, free-floating anxieties about viral plagues and bioengineered outbreaks. These days, visions of a zombie apocalypse look a lot like the troubled dreams of an age of terrorism, avian flu, and H1N1, when viruses leap the species barrier and spread, via jet travel, into global pandemics seemingly overnight (which may be why the Infected, as they're called in both *28 Days Later* and *Left 4 Dead*, move at terrifying, jump-cut speed, unlike their lumbering, stuporous predecessors).

In the postwar decades, as suburban sprawl and mall culture metastasized across America, Hollywood cast the zombie as the decaying face of popular ambivalence toward amok consumerism. Implacable consumption machines, the mall-crawling dead of George Romero's *Dawn of the Dead* (1978) literalized the infantile psychology of consumer culture, with its oral fixation, insistence on instant gratification, and I-shop-therefore-I-am sense of self-worth, indexed to how pricey your status totems are—the sheer bodaciousness of your McMansion and your Super Duty Ford F-150 long-bed pickup. The insatiable orality implied by market capitalism's redefinition of citizens as consumers—"wallets with mouths," in the cynical parlance of Madison Avenue—is instructive.

Now that the econopocalypse has thrown millions out of work, triggered an upspike in homelessness, and eaten the *braaains* of consumer confidence, the zombie has undergone a role reversal, incarnating American fears that the republic is a shambling shadow of its former glory, Left 4 Dead by the near meltdown of the financial system.[1] Zombies are the Resident Evil of an economy whose moribund state confronts us everywhere we look in a landscape littered with dead malls, "ghost boxes" (dark, shuttered big-box outlets), and "zombie stores"—retailers forced by dismal sales to reduce their inventory to its bare bones, with the ironic consequence that their emaciated stock and empty floor space scare customers away, accelerating their death spiral.

"Zombies represent America hitting a very low bottom, as we witness the spectacle of consumer capitalism transforming itself into a feudalistic dance of death," the cultural critic and horror-movie historian David J. Skal told me. "During the summer of 2009, politicians and political pundits alike started hurling the z-word as an all-purpose epithet while the economy collapsed and health care reform sputtered. Zombies are, in essence, creatures who have already faced Sarah Palin's death panels, the better to escape brain-dead politics and faceless corporatism. Having cannibalized all their home equity, and foreclosed our future, zombies have become everyman avatars that have traded in the forward-looking, if audacious, message 'I must eat you to live,' settling for 'I must eat you just to stay dead.'

"In recent decades, the zombie has been a cartoonish lampoon of consumer capitalism, but in the current economic mess, all the gathering themes of depersonalization and disenfranchisement have come to a critical mass. The image of real estate (representing the living, or the haves) besieged by the ravenous dead (the ultimate have-nots) has long been a staple of zombie narratives and never a more concise cultural statement than at the present. In the 1930s, at least one reviewer of the film *White Zombie* saw reflections of breadlines and displaced workers. Today's zombies have an unprecedented, in-your-face rawness that seems to embody displaced rage about gut issues like food, shelter, and health care—the denial of any of these leading to living death, or death itself."[2]

Every age has its totemic monsters. Because he lived in an era of premature burials, "resurrectionists" (grave robbers), postmortem daguerreotypes, table rappers, and spirit photography, when the air was thick with ectoplasm, Marx—the unparalleled master of the political gothic—opened his *Communist Manifesto* in a dry-ice fog: "A specter is haunting Europe: the specter of Communism." In *Karl Marx: A Life*, Francis Wheen suggests that "more use-value . . . can be derived from *Capital* if it is read as a work of the imagination: a Victorian melodrama, or a vast gothic novel whose heroes are enslaved and consumed by the monster they created ('Capital which comes into the world soiled with mire from top to toe and oozing blood from every pore')." Indeed, Marx's political economics teems with imagery straight out of Victorian penny dreadfuls like *Varney the Vampire* (1847): capital that, "vampire-like, lives only by sucking living labor" *(Capital)*; bourgeoisie that "has become a vampire that sucks out [wage laborers'] blood and brains" *(The Eighteenth Brumaire)* and whose "prolongation of the working day beyond the limits of the natural day, into the night . . . only slightly quenches the vampire thirst for the living blood of labor" *(Capital)*.

Today, gonzo economic commentators like Matt Taibbi take up Marx's tune, describing the investment bank Goldman Sachs as "a great vampire squid wrapped around the face of humanity, relentlessly jamming its blood funnel into anything that smells like money."[3] As befits a nation whose haves and have-nots regard each other across a Grand Canyon–sized income gap that's yawning wider by the minute,[4] America's nightmares are haunted by vampires and zombies—the bloodsucking Wall Street elite, drunk on seven-figure bonuses, and the dead-eyed, bone-gnawing underclass.

The vampire as symbol of a parasitic plutocracy, battening on the tears and toil of wage labor, has been a stock character in the demonology of class war at least since Marx. With predictable perversity, America's winner-take-all culture has embraced the vampire as an aspirational figure. And why not? Whether a scion of old money with a Continental accent or a conscienceless monster in tasseled loafers, chainsawing workers to bolster quarterly earnings, the vampire has perfect hair, a sommelier's taste in type O, and more money than God or, for that matter, Lloyd Blankfein. He's a photogenic poster boy for the new social Darwinism. Here, where neoliberal capitalism is the official religion, on par with *juche* in North Korea, and where the Myth of the Level Playing Field is impervious to fact—for example, that 80 percent of the nation's wealth is held by those in the top 20 percent of the income pyramid, or that the CEO who, a decade ago, raked in 30 times the average worker's salary now makes 116 times that worker's income—nobody wants to be a zombie.[5]

Dead on their feet, zombies began as a glassy-eyed metaphor for the plight of Haiti's human chattel, forced to do the boss's bidding even in death. In his classic ethnographic study *Voodoo in Haiti*, Alfred Metraux underscores the parallels between the living dead and Haitian blacks under the colonial whip: "The zombie is a beast of burden, which his master exploits without mercy, making him work in the fields, weighing him down with labor, whipping him freely and feeding him on meager, tasteless food."[6] Like Frankenstein, a working stiff with neckbolts, ready-made for the Fordist factory, zombies are wage slaves. A solitary hunter, the vampire is well suited to Ayn Randian fantasies of Promethean captains of industry; self-made masters of their own destiny, they need no convincing on the Virtues of Selfishness. Zombies, by contrast, are trade unionists from beyond the grave, a Heritage Foundation wonk's worst nightmare of collectivism on the march, the downsized and the disenfranchised jolted into action by class consciousness.

At the same time, the circular firing squad of Angry White Lumpen, emptying their political ammo clips at illegal immigrants, Nancy Pelosi, and the Red Menace at 1600 Pennsylvania Avenue—everything, in other words, but the structural injustices behind their economic woes—sees zombies as harbingers of a postapocalyptic landscape, overrun by Obamaniacs, where the embattled vestiges of what Sarah Palin likes to call "Real America" make their last stand against an engulfing tide of border-jumping aliens, left-wing academics, and brain-eating libtards. Stockpiling MREs and heavy weaponry, the survivalist fringe can't wait to live in the America of *I Am Legend*. When our unwieldy, duct-tape democracy collapses into anarchy, we'll revert to the sociopathic utopia of the western frontier, a happily uncomplicated time when every man—every well-armed white man, at least—was a law unto himself, free from governmental meddling and moral ambiguities.

Over at SurvivalBlog.com, author Jim Rawles and his fellow survivalists are digging in for an apocalypse straight out of *Left 4 Dead*. There is much talk of "hordes of zombies running rampant" when "the government fails."[7] Contributor Michael Z. Williamson thinks a wicked-looking implement called the Dead On Tools Annihilator Demolition Hammer will come in handy when the system crashes: "Anyone with bayonet training can grip this appropriately and hack through a crowd of zombies, or heft it like an axe and use it on single opponents."[8] An anxious reader with "a heavily supplied, fairly secluded and defensible, and very well-armed suburban outpost with several highly skilled sons for fire support" wonders if he should secure "a secondary retreat for when it looks as if our ammo is exceeded by the number of urban zombies (or, police-state drones, same thing) invading the 'burbs."[9]

By "zombies," a.k.a. the "golden horde" in SurvivalBlog parlance, Rawles and his survivalist brethren mean "the anticipated large mixed horde of refugees and looters that will pour out of the metropolitan regions."[10] The "horde" trope has a familiar ring, especially when coupled with the suggestive adjective "golden," with its echoes of Yellow Peril. We've heard it before, in colonial whispers of rebellious coolies, out on the edge of empire, and in *The Turner Diaries'* revulsion at the mongrel metropolis, that polymorphous horror of miscegenation and moral relativism. "The foundational morality of the civilized world is best summarized in the Ten Commandments," writes Rawles, in his "Precepts of Rawlesian Survivalist Philosophy." "Moral relativism and secular humanism are slippery slopes. The terminal moraine at the base of these slopes is a rubble pile consisting of either despotism and pillage, or anarchy and the depths of depravity."[11] Better to arm ourselves to the teeth, light out for the territories, and rebuild society in a blast-proof City upon a Hill, populated with People Like Us.

To "Browning 35" and the rest of the race warriors on the white-supremacist website Stormfront.org, the zombie apocalypse is a premonition of race war:

I've noticed recently that alot of survivalists and preparedness freaks are big fans of Zombie movies . . . where . . . a small group of people test their skills against an onslaught of blood sucking and brain eating ghouls. For White Nationalists it's easy to translate Non-Whites into the role of the Zombies as they're certainly blood sucking leeches who are overrunning and ruining our countries and who in some cases are literally trying to prey on us and eat us (remember that case a little while ago where that Black guy in East Texas killed and ate his White girlfriend? I'll bet she didn't foresee him turning into a Zombie and eating her.)[12]

"Chrispy"—a participant, like Browning 35, in Stormfront's discussion threads—is locked and loaded for racial Armageddon:

I'm a big fan of the zombie survival stuff. I've read the *Zombie Survival Guide* by Max Brooks as well as his novel *World War Z*. Both were fun reads but certainly lacking as far as hardcore survival goes. One must always remember that in a more realistic SHTF [Shit Hits the Fans] situation we will be facing armed opposition not some mindless shambling horde, but it's still nice to imagine sitting on a rooftop all day with a boomstick popping zombie skulls.[13]

Seriously, guys: "Son of the Mist" reminds the assembled White Nationalists that World War Z isn't any laughing matter:

> All fun stuff aside (I've always been a sci-fi fan and the *Day of the Dead* was a great [semi-comedy] movie except for the race mixing crap), the non whites ARE the "zombies" complete with man eating and crazed, brutal behavior. . . . it will be unleashed full bore when the economy collapses and the Super Depression starts. Just as zombies do what they do, the non whites will show their DNA when the time comes. Count on it, they cannot do anything else!
>
> The wise are getting out of the multi cult cities and setting themselves up with dependable compatriots, well thought out, hardened retreats and lots of supplies.[14]

Unfortunately for the blood-and-soil gang, history teaches us that the war of all against all doesn't end at the barred gates of the *Führerbunker*. It's only a matter of time, after the chairs are jammed against the doors and the windows are nailed shut, before the survivors succumb to power struggles and paranoia. Twenty-eight days later, they're eating each other. Worse yet, you can't always tell Us from Them. "Eyewitness accounts described the assassins as ordinary-looking people," says a radio announcer in *Night of the Living Dead*. Aren't they always?

(2010)

Gun Play

ACT I

A WEEK AFTER JARED LEE LOUGHNER—ACCUSED MULTIPLE murderer and, in the words of the *New York Times*, "curious teenager and talented saxophonist"—went on one of those shooting sprees that Americans seem to regard as the price we pay for our god-given right to an armamentarium straight out of the NRA–wet-dream gun showroom in *The Matrix*, it was business as usual at the Crossroads of the West gun show at the Pima County Fairgrounds.[1]

The seat of Pima County, as irony would have it, is Tucson.

Tucson: where, on January 8, 2011, at a meet-and-greet outside a supermarket featuring Representative Gabrielle Giffords, Loughner emptied thirty-one rounds from his Glock semiautomatic pistol into the crowd, wounding thirteen and killing six, a nine-year-old girl among them.

The Johnny Seven O.M.A. (One Man Army), Topper Toys' multifunction killing machine: the best-selling boys' toy of 1964.

At Crossroads of the West, forty-round magazines for AK-47s could be had for the recession-friendly sum of $19.99, because ... because why?

Because our founding myth of rugged individualism demands it. As does the rough-justice ethos of our frontier heritage. And the Don't-Tread-on-Me antifederalism of our racist past. And the deepening distrust of Big Government, ginned up by Reagan in the '80s and taken to its logical conclusion by the militia movement of the '90s and today's Tea Partiers.

What few mainstream pundits seem willing to discuss is the role, in America's gun violence, of the radically deregulated capitalism championed for decades by neoliberal economists and conservative ideologues. What Ayn Rand would call the virtuous selfishness of winner-take-all capitalism insists on profit maximization at any cost. What better explanation for the millions the gun industry spends in lobbying, campaign contributions, and issue ads to thwart gun control in *any* form, from the right to own assault weapons to background checks?[2] Isn't it all about selling *more* guns in a nation where the ratio of guns to people already stands at about eighty-five guns for every one hundred Americans?[3]

Of course, the paranoid style in American politics is part of the psychotic equation of gun culture, too: these days, too many Tea Partiers, Palinistas, and dug-in survivalists see themselves as Armies of One—lone-man militias standing between angry white Middle America and the zombie apocalypse of Obamaniac socialism. And as everyone in Palin's "Real America" knows, "a well regulated Militia, being necessary to the security of a free State, the right of the people to keep and bear Arms, shall not be infringed."[4] Did I mention that anti-Obama bumper stickers were on sale at Crossroads of the West?

Point taken that the coat-hanger antennae on Loughner's tinfoil helmet were not, in all likelihood, receiving transmissions from some ideological NORAD in Roger Ailes's basement. The accumulating evidence suggests the shooter was crazier than a pair of waltzing mice. A Crossroads of the West attendee was thoughtful on that point, citing scripture—the gun lobby's bumper-sticker refrain—to argue his case: "It's not guns that kill people," said a fifty-eight-year-old mental health worker. "People kill people."[5]

Which would explain why America leads the industrialized world in gun violence, and why American children are eleven times more likely than children in other developed countries to die in a gun accident. Only a card-carrying libtard would link such stats to the fact that our gun laws are obscenely lax, as opposed to, say, those of Japan, whose gun regulation is among the world's strictest and whose rate of gun-related fatalities, incalculably, is among the world's lowest: 1 death for every 2 million people, versus our 14.24 gun deaths for every 100,000.[6]

But if it's people who kill people, not guns, then our off-the-charts gun violence would seem to indicate that a disproportionate percentage of the planet's people-killing people are Americans. What to do about it? The spin-alley response, in some corners of our great republic, is to lay the blame for the Tucson bloodbath on our mental health care industry. Curiously, some of those eager to deflect attention away from gun regulation and onto society's neglect of the mentally ill were decrying, not long ago, universal health care as a budget-busting indulgence of the Nanny State or a federalist plot to Kevork the elderly (death panels!).

Some of their number continue to insist, in a nation whose citizens are the world's most statistically likely people to kill people, that every American should nonetheless have the right to buy an AK-47 with a forty-round magazine—preferably, without that affront to personal liberty known as a background check.

After all, the Tree of Insanity must be refreshed from time to time with the blood of innocent bystanders.

ACT II

Even so, no one can truly understand the land that inspired Dorothy Parker's mordant one-liner "American as a sawed-off shotgun" unless he has held—preferably, fired—a gun, felt the perverse sensuality of the way it fits your grip, thrilled to the queasy buzz of knowing that a twitch of your finger can kill.

In a country where the gap between the power elite and the politically impotent millions, frantically bailing out their underwater mortgages, yawns wider by the minute; a country where the consoling fiction of the level playing field and the aspirational fantasies fanned by celebrity culture parry any hint of class consciousness, owning a gun is the closest many downwardly mobile Americans will ever come to any sense of immediate empowerment.

To be American is to feel that handgun ownership is your birthright; that you're somehow incomplete, nagged by an itchy phantom limb, without a gun.

If you're a boomer, growing up American meant growing up with the ricochet of gunshots—Dealey Plaza, the Audubon Ballroom, the Lorraine Motel, the Ambassador Hotel, My Lai, the Zodiac Killer, Kent State, Son of Sam, the Dakota—as the soundtrack to your restless sleep.

Paradoxically, it also meant growing up in a country that embraces a perverse faith in "regeneration through violence," to borrow the historian Richard Slotkin's unforgettable phrase.[7] In American myth, the act of pulling the trigger is reimagined as an exuberant, youthful nation's verdict on the dead weight of the past, reinventing yourself and remaking the world in a split second. On the big screen of the American unconscious, guilt-free sociopaths like Charlie Starkweather merge with perpetual adolescents like Huckleberry Finn and Dean Moriarty, yielding the devil-may-care thrill killers of *Bonnie and Clyde*, *Badlands*, *True Romance*, and *Natural Born Killers*. Lighting out for the territories, they're fired by a kind of *joie de tuer* that is a gunfighter nation's idea of *joie de vivre*. "Sirhan Sirhan shot Robert F. Kennedy. And Ethel M. Kennedy shot Judith Birnbaum. And Judith Birnbaum shot Elizabeth Bochnak. And Elizabeth Bochnak shot Andrew Witwer," writes J. G. Ballard, in the endless, lunatic genealogy of his "Generations of America," a Swiftian satire of our pathological faith in the promise of violence to Make It New.[8]

1967 advertisement for Mattel's M-16 Marauder, a life-sized replica of the gun American troops were using in Vietnam.

Growing up in '6os America meant reliving the tragedy of the Native American genocide as farce while shoveling in your Swanson Salisbury Steak TV dinner: *Gunsmoke, Bonanza, Death Valley Days, The Rifleman, The Virginian, The Big Valley, Branded, Have Gun–Will Travel, The High Chaparral, Rawhide, Wagon Train*—the list of prime-time westerns seems endless, in hindsight. These and dozens of shows like them schooled Americans in the lesson that there's no problem so complex it can't be resolved with violence. (A lesson taken to heart

by cheerleaders for American exceptionalism and architects of imaginary empire like Paul Wolfowitz and Donald Rumsfeld and William
Kristol, who wrote in their manifesto for a "new American century"
that the United States must assume its rightful "constabulary" role in
global affairs, capable of outgunning the best-armed posse in town.)[9]
PTSD'd by race riots and Vietnam War protests, the America of the
'60s rejuvenated its dream of itself by returning nightly to a Disneyfied version of its frontier youth.

For boys—even boys like this author, whose liberal-ish parents ful-
minated against the soul-scarring effects of "violent toys"—growing
up in that America meant dreaming of guns. Cap guns, whose sweetly
acrid smell is a grace note in memories of my boyhood summers. The
impressively realistic toy Peacemaker in the Sears Roebuck catalog,
with the tie that lashed its holster to your thigh for gunslinger cool
and those little pellets that made smoke wisp convincingly from the
gun's barrel after you'd fired it. The Johnny Seven One-Man Army,
a supergun whose sheer overkill—it rolled a grenade launcher, anti-
tank rocket, antibunker missile, rifle, machine gun, and automatic
pistol into one megaweapon—launched a million power fantasies,
making it the best-selling boys' toy of 1964. Daisy BB rifles, like the
one my friend came within a whisker of blinding his kid brother
with one languid, directionless afternoon when his parents weren't
home. (Why weren't the parents ever home, in '60s Southern California?) And of course real guns, like the .22 my older buddies, long-
haired brothers who embodied cool itself, used to obliterate beer
cans. Later, when their father died by his own hand, I thought of his
locked gun case in their family room, a shrine to quiet menace, and
of cans lined up for execution in the summer sun, jumping to life at
the instant of impact.

So constant a presence was the sound of gunplay in the dream
life of that era that the image of rapt little faces, lit by the flicker of
the cathode-ray tube and accompanied by the *bang! zing!* of gunplay, is now iconic, triggering boomer nostalgia for the days before
social and technological change blew mass culture into a million

little microniches— a time when America was One Nation Under Nielsen, tuning in for the same shows at the same time.

The media-collage band Negativland captures—and critiques— the vibe of the times in *Guns*, an eight-minute welter of sound effects and snippets of dialogue from '60s westerns and toy-gun commercials, set against a darkly atmospheric backdrop of windswept synths and thudding electro beats. All-American tykes in wild-west outfits slap leather, fill their hands, draw a bead on outlaws. A scruffy cowpoke falls dead with his harmonica still in his mouth, a newscaster announces the death of Martin Luther King, Jack Ruby shoots Oswald live on TV. "Very good shooting," drawls a voice lifted from some nameless western, just before JFK crumples in the presidential limousine. Pennsylvania State Treasurer R. Budd Dwyer puts a pistol in his mouth and commits suicide on camera. A commercial voice-over chirps, *"Quaker Puffed Rice Sparkys . . . and Quaker Puffed Wheat Sparkys! Those delicious, nutritious breakfast cereals . . . shot from guns!!!"*[10]

ACT III

There is, of course, no proven link between exposure to fictional violence at a tender age and sociopathic behavior as an adult; the copycat crimes routinely cited by the shoot-your-TV school of media criticism are the exceptions that prove the rule. Rather, as argued earlier, it's the tidal wave of cheap, readily available guns inundating our culture that accounts for our unenviable first-place status, among industrialized nations, in gun violence: homicides, suicides, accidental shootings.

Still, the blood tide of fantasy gunplay washing over the American mind, practically from birth, must have *some* effect, if only to implant in our collective consciousness the seductive lie that, if all else fails— if you're suicidally despondent, like my friends' father; or a demented nonentity, like Mark David Chapman; or a grinning paranoiac, like Jared Lee Loughner, mind swirling with the free-floating fears of the lunatic fringe—there's always a magic bullet.

The Daisy Air Rifle: ballistic fun for the whole family!

EPILOGUE

Leaving the house one day, I hear a voice accosting me from midair. It's the neighbor boy, straddling a bough midway up a tree near our property line.

An intense kid, by turns glumly uncommunicative, then voluble, at times almost manic, he's obsessed with guns, occasionally regaling me with exhaustive plot summaries of bullet-splattered action movies he's seen. His enthusiasm for a film correlates tightly to body count. But he's a purist: deaths inflicted by anything other than bullets are of virtually no interest. Thus, the martial-arts tour de force *Crouching Tiger, Hidden Dragon* rated a yawn because, although it includes at

GUN PLAY

least six killings (one of which involves a bandit skewered on a spear, which is then yanked out of his heart, dispatching him with suitably melodramatic messiness), the movie is ... gunless.

The kid's matter-of-fact, unreflective rhapsodies about on-screen bloodbaths always leave me at a loss for words. On occasion, I ask him what he makes of his monomaniacal fixation on guns. What does it *mean?*, I wonder. Unsurprisingly, for a grade-school kid, he just shrugs and smiles a secretive smile, the universal sign for "whatever."

Again, the voice in the sky calls out. I look up. He's aiming a toy gun at me. Don't ever do that, I growl, nonplussed. He stares me dead in the eye, unblinking. Bang, he says. *Bang bang. You're dead.*

(2011)

Mysterious Stranger

REPORTS OF MARK TWAIN'S RESURRECTION ARE GREATLY exaggerated.

Still, with luck, the publication of the three-volume, 500,000-word, unexpurgated edition of Twain's autobiography will revise the Twain enshrined in the popular imagination—the twinkly-eyed rapscallion with a gently pricking wit—along more accurate, which is to say more mordant, lines: Grandpa Walton as Gawker blogger.

In the four years leading up to his death at seventy-four on April 21, 1910, Twain unburdened himself of his unvarnished opinions on God and country and the human ape, dictating to a stenographer. Fearful that too much blunt truth would blow a sawed-off shotgun blast in his reputation, Twain directed that "all sound and sane expressions of opinion" be purged from his autobiography for a hundred years after his death. "There may be a market for that kind of wares a century from now," he said, in 1906. "There is no hurry. Wait and see."[1] Now, we will.

That Twain the Sage of Pepperidge Farm is a sentimental caricature has been obvious since at least 1917, when H. L. Mencken published his thoughts on the subject in the *New York Evening Mail*. Twain had been in the ground only seven years, but already Mencken felt the need to set the record straight, inspired by the posthumous publication of books Twain had suppressed during his lifetime on the assumption that they would demolish, in one blow, his reputation as a lovable curmudgeon. Twain's misgivings were well-founded:

The Mysterious Stranger and "What Is Man?" are sardonic meditations, respectively, on the hypocrisies and fatuities of religion, and on the moral depravity and brutish self-interest of the species. "Mark Twain dead is beginning to show far different and more brilliant colors than those he seemed to wear during life," writes Mencken, "and the one thing no sane critic would say of him today is that he was the harmless fireside jester, the mellow Chautauquan, the amiable old grandpa of letters that he was once so widely thought to be."[2] He goes on:

> The truth is that Mark was almost exactly the reverse. Instead of being a mere entertainer of the mob, he was . . . a destructive satirist of the utmost pungency and relentlessness, and the most bitter critic of American platitude and delusion, whether social, political or religious, that ever lived.[3]

The Twain rising from the grave on the centennial of his death lives up to Mencken's press—and just in time for our age of Tea Party know-nothings, head-in-the-sand birthers, and Bible-thumping flatheads, not to mention CEOs like Lloyd Blankfein of Goldman Sachs and Tony Hayward of BP, poster boys for corporate arrogance and unchecked greed.

Twain was vociferously opposed to American imperialism, fulminating in suppressed passages in the *Autobiography* against "the iniquitous Cuban-Spanish War" and pouring scorn on a U.S. attack on unarmed tribal peoples in the Philippines, a "long and happy picnic" for "our uniformed assassins" who have "nothing to do but sit in comfort and fire the Golden Rule into those people down there and imagine letters to write home to the admiring families, and pile glory upon glory."[4] As the *New York Times* points out, "The uncensored autobiography . . . includes remarks that, if made today in the context of Iraq or Afghanistan, would probably lead the right wing to question the patriotism of this most American of American writers."[5]

The paper quotes a blast of buckshot aimed, from the distance of a century ago, at the pinstriped swine wallowing in the Wall Street money trough today:

The multimillionaire disciples of Jay Gould—that man who in his brief life rotted the commercial morals of this nation and left them stinking when he died—have quite completely transformed our people from a nation with pretty high and respectable ideals to just the opposite of that; that our people have no ideals now that are worthy of consideration; that our Christianity which we have always been so proud of—not to say vain of—is now nothing but a shell, a sham, a hypocrisy; that we have lost our ancient sympathy with oppressed peoples struggling for life and liberty; that when we are not coldly indifferent to such things we sneer at them, and that the sneer is about the only expression the newspapers and the nation deal in with regard to such things.[6]

And you wondered where the William S. Burroughs of "Roosevelt after Inauguration" and the Hunter Thompson of "The Kentucky Derby Is Decadent and Depraved," not to mention the Matt Taibbi of "The Truth about the Tea Party," learned their close-quarter knife-fighting skills? That's Twain we hear in Burroughs's gleefully perverse caricature of FDR as a latter-day Caligula, filling the nation's highest offices with "hoodlums and riffraff of the vilest caliber," and in Thompson's hangover-blurred vision of the southern "whiskey gentry" as the atavistic result of "too much inbreeding in a closed and ignorant culture," and in Taibbi's joyfully savage beatdown of angry white geriatrics railing against the Nanny State while "propping their giant atrophied glutes on motorized wheelchair-scooters"—paid for by Medicare, naturally.[7]

Nonetheless, the image of Twain as a cigar-puffing wisecracker—George Burns doing a Colonel Sanders impression—will undoubtedly prove tough to uproot, for the simple reason that Americans prefer their history Disneyfied and harbor a constitutional aversion to brow-furrowing, especially about deep, dark things.

Even Camille Paglia, a literary critic of no little energy and no small gifts (when she isn't busy defending the birthers or insisting—no, really—that this Palin gal is an intellectual firecracker), seems to have fallen for the Norman Rockwell school of historical revisionism about Twain.[8]

In her sweeping survey of "art and decadence from Nefertiti to Emily Dickinson," *Sexual Personae*, Paglia dismisses the "Wordsworthian idylls" of *Tom Sawyer* and *Huckleberry Finn* as "completely out of sync with the internal development of major American literature . . . bourgeois fantasies about childhood and lower-class life."[9]

With Paglia, every critical verdict is *deeply personal*; what sets her teeth chattering with rage, in this case, is Twain's "dislike of the witty Jane Austen" (an English major's idea of Blood Libel). Twain, it turns out, is "hateful" not only because he takes Austen down a peg but because "his folksiness and pastoralism are counterfeit, as decadent as Marie Antoinette's masquerades as a shepherdess."[10] (Good line, by the way. Paglia comes to any firefight with a speedloader full of zingers.) Oh, and Twain's late years were characterized by "gloomy negativity" (as opposed to Up with People negativity), which just goes to show that "Wordsworthian benevolence was always false," in the same way that his boys' adventure stories—myth "stripped of chthonian realities" (I *hate* it when they do that)—betray "fear of woman and fear of nature."[11]

The first problem with Paglia's reading of *Tom* and *Huck* is that, while both books do indeed contain rhapsodic set pieces worthy of the term "Wordsworthian," they're hardly outtakes from *Bambi*.

Twain the nature poet is a master of the form, from his Thomas Eakins evocations of the sublime majesty of the big river at night, in *Huckleberry Finn*, to the jeweled miniaturism of his opening description, in chapter 14 of *Tom Sawyer*, of nature coming to life on Jackson's Island, woodpecker by inchworm, catbird by ladybug, to the *Sturm und Drang* of his description in chapter 16 of the storm that drenches the runaway boys, a Caspar David Friedrich painting in prose: "Under the ceaseless conflagration of lightnings that flamed in the skies, everything below stood out in clean-cut and shadowless distinctness: the bending tress, the billowy river white with foam, the driving spray of spume-flakes, the dim outlines of the high bluffs on the other side, glimpsed through the drifting cloud-rack and the slanting veil of rain."[12] This doesn't sound, to me, like a man who fears nature; it sounds like a man who thrills to its gaudiest special effects, cheering on its cannonade of "unflagging thunder-peals" and "booming thunder-blasts."[13] It also sounds like a literary stylist who understands the Burkean sublime and his era's hunger for it, and plays to that appetite with a best-selling novelist's shrewd sense of what sells.

More to the point, Paglia thinks Twain spins "marshmallow myth" because she's looking for the chthonian in the pagan places that matter most to her, notably, sexuality. True child of the free-love '60s that she is, Paglia can't seem to see how ahistorical her analysis is. Yes, *Huckleberry Finn* is weirdly chaste, but it's nominally a children's book and it was published in *1885*, after all. Twain the Swiftian satirist may have had X-ray vision when it came to the social injustices and moral hypocrisies that plagued his age, but that doesn't mean he was immune to the attitudes of the day: he was writing in, and for, Victorian America.

And yes, as Paglia's avowed influence Leslie Fiedler argues in *Love and Death in the American Novel*, *Huckleberry Finn* is a boy's adventure tale, a fantasy of prepubertal innocents who, spared the meddling influence of women (not to mention sexual awakening), will be boys forever.[14] Huck flees "sivilization," a scrubbed and stifling world of schoolmarmish scolding and goody-goody piety run by women—Aunt Polly, Aunt Sally, the Widow Douglas, and the "old maid" Miss Watson—for the carefree lawlessness of life on the run among Men without Women (his drunken father, the runaway slave Jim, Tom Sawyer). At the end of the book, Huck is on the run, once again, from the foster mothers who want to drag him back into civilization's embrace and (s)mother him: "I reckon I got to light out for the territory ahead of the rest, because Aunt Sally she's going to adopt me and sivilize me, and I can't stand it. I been there before."[15] It's an evergreen theme in masculinist fantasies, providing the, er, seed DNA for a literary genre: the male-bonding story, saturated by sublimated (or overt) homoeroticism, that stretches from Huck and Jim to Ishmael and Queequeg in *Moby Dick* to much of Hemingway and Kerouac to the pirate utopias of William S. Burroughs, right up to *Brokeback Mountain*.

But to argue that, because Twain is a sucker for nostalgia, he is therefore all folksiness and pastoralism is to misunderstand him profoundly.

Yes, Twain *is* nostalgic for the distant, drowsy summers of his boyhood, synonymous for him and us with an arcadian America shattered by the Civil War and dragged headlong into modernity by the Industrial Revolution. But *Huckleberry Finn*'s "Wordsworthian idyll" hangs in tense, perfect balance with Twain's scabrous portrait of the herd mentality and mob violence that keep threatening to scuttle our unsteady, sometimes rudderless experiment in mass democracy. Not for Twain Whitman's big-hearted, bear-hug embrace of a mythic American People. He knows what's behind our tear-jerking public homilies about the American Dream, our fulsome Palin-isms about the Real America. Twain has lived in the Real America, and he knows that, at its best—for instance, when a friendless, homeless boy finds the moral courage to help a runaway slave find freedom—it lives up to its myths. But he also knows it at its too-common worst: in the grotesque institution of slavery, of course, but also in the terrifying ignorance of one-horse towns where bored hicks amuse themselves by "putting turpentine on a stray dog and setting fire to him, or tying a tin pan to his tail and see[ing] him run himself to death" or tarring and feathering "some poor friendless cast-out women."[16] He grew up in the age of the lynch mob and the carpetbagger and the jackleg preacher bilking the rubes at a tent-show revival with sanctimonious blather.

Reborn in our time, Twain would probably recognize the America of his antebellum childhood in our Tea Party rallies and subprime-mortgage peddlers and prosperity-gospel televangelists in their stadium-sized megachurches. In *Huckleberry Finn*, he says, across a century, this land is your land, too.

Fiedler, unlike Paglia, understands this, which is why he says, in *Love and Death*, that Huck is the product of "a terrible breakthrough to the undermind of America itself," a figment of the American unconscious as it dreams "the anti-American American dream."[17] Yet something puzzles him:

This thoroughly horrifying book, whose morality is rejection and whose ambiance is terror, is a funny book, at last somehow a children's book after all; and the desperate story it tells is felt as joyous, an innocent experience. This ambiguity, this deep doubleness of *Huckleberry Finn* is its essential riddle. How can it be at once so terrible and so comfortable to read?[18]

My answer to the question Fiedler posed in 1966 is simply that *Huckleberry Finn*'s deep doubleness is *our* doubleness as a nation, and thus feels familiar, terrible though it may be.

Twain dramatizes our essentially double nature—the weird mix of sentimentality and cynicism, idealism and rough justice, gregariousness and loneliness that is an essential part of the American genome. Because he was, as Mencken argues, the most American of American writers, in voice and sensibility and subject, he knows all of our secret places for the simple reason that they're his secret places, too. His mythic portrait of the American psyche is in some ways a self-portrait. He captures our Hallmark sentimentality at odds with our love of violence; our Reaganesque nostalgia tripping over the half-buried bodies in our genocidal history; our lip service to Christian ideals making a jarring noise against the ugly reality of our bigotry. And he manages to conjure a world that is terrible *and* comfortable at the same time because his yearning for a boyhood lost in time is as sincerely felt as his fury at racism and ignorance.

Twain is strangely at home with some of his scoundrels, and even exhibits a perverse fondness for them, because he realizes that he, like all Americans, shares some of their family traits. How many American icons began by reinventing themselves at Ellis Island, their dreams still reverberating with the howl of the mob at their heels? How many American millionaires made their fortunes peddling promises—the dream of home ownership, say, with no money down and no background check?

Like W. C. Fields and William S. Burroughs and Tom Waits, Twain's voice echoes with the cadences and jargon of that archetypal American, the confidence man. A felon with a thousand faces, we see him everywhere in our nation's family photo album: carny barker, riverboat gambler, revival-meeting preacher, traveling salesman, soap-box orator, politician. He may not be the best of Americans, but he just might be the most *American* of Americans, with a silver tongue and something to sell and his cardboard suitcase always packed, ready to light out for the territory if somebody wises up the marks.

> On the road ... I told Tom all about our "Royal Nonesuch" rapscallions, and as much of the raft voyage as I had time to; and as we struck into the town and up through the middle of it—it was as much as half after eight then— here comes a raging rush of people with torches, and an awful whooping and yelling, and banging tin pans and blowing horns, and we jumped to one side to let them go by, and as they went by I see they had the [rapscal-lions] astraddle of a rail—that is, I knowed it was [them], though they was all over tar and feathers, and didn't look like nothing in the world that was human—just a couple of monstrous big soldier-plumes. Well, it made me sick to see it; and I was sorry for them poor pitiful rascals, it seemed like I couldn't ever feel any hardness against them any more in the world. It was a dreadful thing to see. Human beings can be awful cruel to one another.[19]

(2010)

Aladdin Sane Called.
He Wants His Lightning Bolt Back.

"HOW NOT DUMB IS GAGA?" ASKED THE *NEW YORKER* MUSIC critic Sasha Frere-Jones in the first flush of Gagamania in 2009.[1] Years later, well into the Gaga Belle Époque, his question still furrows the American brow. Okay, I'll bite: Not? As in: Not in the least not dumb?

After a close study of Frere-Jones's apologia for Our Lady of Perpetual Pantslessness, I still can't help but read his headline as Protesting Too Much. I *know* it's a textbook example of what lit-crit geeks like to call litotes, a figure of speech in which an affirmative is expressed through the negation of its opposite, but since litotes is usually used as ironic understatement, to drily funny effect (as in "Lady Gaga is not unintelligent"), the headline makes it sound as if Frere-Jones is Damning with Faint Praise. (Reading it, I was reminded of an avant-garde composer I once knew, a hypercerebral Vulcan whose veins ran with antifreeze. When I asked him about some diva on the downtown music scene, he paused for effect, a predatory twinkle in his eye. Then came the headsman's blow: "Not overly burdened with intellect." Which is to say, not not dumb.)

Most of the comment-thread flame wars between Gaga's Kiss Army of "little monsters," as the Lady calls her devout fans, and her no less devout haters are ignited by the Great Debate: Is she a rarified being who has more talent in her clitoral hood than you can even *dream* of, little man? Whose Art for Art's Sake raptures us out of our stonewashed lives, into a disco ball–flecked Bubble World, a Studio 54 in the Sky where gay teens, angsty emo boys, and high school weirdos are waved into the VIP lounge while all the Mean Girls, gay bashers, and weirdophobic frat boys mill outside, crazed with envy?[2] Or is she just some Tisch dropout who watched *Grease* one too many times, pickled her brain in Britney, and now thinks she's some cross between Madonna and Leigh Bowery, just because she forgets to wear pants and name-checks *The Night Porter* (Sontag's "Fascinating Fascism" for people who don't read)? In other words, is Lady Gaga the last, best hope for pop smart enough to beat the Society of the Spectacle at its own game by selling out with a shamelessness that would shock even Andy Warhol (who perfected the concepts of self as brand and art as marketing) yet still snooker cultural-studies profs and nth-wave feminists into a deconstructive swoon about her Judith Butler–approved gender performativity? Or is she something thuddingly dumber: Donatella Versace in the remake of *Blow-Up*? Liza Minnelli in a Vegas revue inspired by *The Reluctant Astronaut*? Perez Hilton singing the Human League songbook? Is she pop, or Pop Art? In on the joke, or just a joke?

One thing is certain: much of the hair pulling about the goggle-eyed vacuity of her music, the self-consciously Warholian Inauthenticity of her persona, her Barbarella-from-*Jersey Shore* getups, and her unashamedly derivative career moves and media poses is really, deep down, a debate about how not dumb—or not not dumb—she is.

Evidence for the prosecution begins with the name, lifted from one of Queen's ditziest tunes: "Radio Ga Ga." Gaga, as in: "Excessively and foolishly enthusiastic: *The public went gaga over the new fashions.*"[3] Or: "Completely absorbed, infatuated, or excited: *They were gaga over the rock group's new album.*"[4] The word's rattlebrained connotations aren't helpful. Nor is Gaga's mouth-breather gape, which combined with her slight overbite gives her a vaguely dumbfounded look. She looks permanently agog, like Paris Hilton after a ministroke.

And then there's the music. Color me rockist, but there is something profoundly, throbbingly *dumb* about Gaga's Fame-Monster Mash of electroclash, bubblegum disco in the Madonna mode, and hair-metal power ballads—an exuberant stupidity that wants to vogue its way into our hearts but makes our minds throw up a little.[5]

Listen to the best songs by her cited influences—Bowie, Queen, Grace Jones—and you'll hear, beneath the virally unforgettable melodies, a percolating intelligence that isn't just a musical sophistication but is equally a cultural literacy. Listen to Gaga and you'll hear the sound of IQ points molting.

Consider "The Fairy Feller's Master-Stroke," from *Queen II*, an object lesson in the cultural distance between 1974 and the superslick android pop of our mashed-up, Auto-Tuned times—and between genius and Gaga. In two and a half glorious minutes, Freddie Mercury reminds us, as all great Aesthetes do, that nothing succeeds like excess: laser-sharp harmonies by robo-seraphim, heavy-breathing glam-metal harpsichord that sounds like Scarlatti shtupping Liberace, guitarist Brian May doing Paganini impersonations, and, to top things off, a gong. (The only thing missing is the ritual sacrifice of an underage hermaphrodite, naked and gilded in gold leaf. And Freddie was just getting to that when management pulled the plug, citing cost overruns.)

BUT THE MUSIC is just the movie soundtrack for the lyrics, which narrate a slow, close-up pan across the painting that inspired the song, the Victorian madman Richard Dadd's obsessively detailed, almost anamorphically distorted rendering of a fairy revel. There's the "politician with senatorial pipe" and the "pedagogue squinting," who "wears a frown," and a "tatterdemalion and a junketer," "a thief and a dragonfly trumpeter," a satyr peering naughtily under a lady's gown.[6] It's all there, rendered with miniaturist precision, right down to "Oberon and Titania watched by a harridan / Mab is the queen and there's a good apothecary-man / come to say hello / fairy dandy tickling the fancy of his lady friend / the nymph in yellow / what a quaere fellow / the ostler stares with hands on his knees / come on, mister feller, crack it open if you please."[7]

In the radio-mandated two and a half minutes, Freddie gave his listeners a whiff of Shakespeare, an introduction to what is now called Outsider art, and some brain-stretchingly arcane vocabulary words. (Queen Builds Word Power!) Gaga gives us *"Rah-rah-ah-ah-ah! Rom-mah-rom-mum-mah! GaGa-oo-la-la!"* ("Bad Romance") and *"Oh, oh, oh, oh, ohhhh, oh-oh-e-oh-oh-oh / I'll get him hot, show him what I've got / Oh, oh, oh, oh, ohhhh, oh-oh-e-oh-oh-oh."* How many electro-disco divas does it take to screw in an ostler? How many could define "harridan" or "junketer," much less weave those words into a narrative rich in literary allusions, historical memory, descriptive detail?

Speaking of which, how many dance-pop singers can tell a story about anything other than themselves? Gaga's infatuation with her own name is revealing. To be sure, "a person's name is to that person the sweetest and most important sound in any language," if you believe Dale Carnegie in *How to Win Friends and Influence People,* the Idiot's Guide to social engineering at its most cynically soft-soapy.[8] But Gaga's jejune insistence on working her (brand) name into seemingly every one of her songs is surely the limit case in adolescent narcissism—either that, or product placement taken to that Jeff Koonsian extreme where art and Advertisement for Myself meet.

Freddie teleported high school pariahs languishing in '70s suburbia into the aesthetic otherworld of the *Yellow Book* Decadents and the Bloomsbury scene, a Bubble World of escapist Victoriana waiting to be explored more deeply if you were an intellectually omnivorous library rat. Gaga is the poet laureate of the supremely banal: porntastic fantasies about riding your disco stick and bluffin' with my muffin, "getting shit wrecked," dry-humping under the disco ball, dreaming of fame, becoming famous, world-wearily lamenting the Faustian bargain of—*yawn*—fame, and popping a wide-on worthy of the *Sex and the City* crew over "Louis, Dolce Gabbana, Alexander McQueen, eh ou," and of course Manolo.[9]

If you're a devout Gagaphile and, improbably, have made it this far, let me channel what you're thinking, right about now: as a Person of a Certain Age and, even more unconscionably, a more or less heteronormative male, I'm incapable of appreciating the gifts of a neo-disco diva whose target audience is—I'm guessing here—girls eight to eighteen (the *Gossip Girl/Sex and the City* demographic), gay teens, and Madonna fans "of every age," as marketers like to say. By rights, I should be femdom'd by the Lady, then thrown to the tender mercies of the butchest of the *Caged Heat* babes in Gaga's *Telephone* video, you're thinking. I'm guilty of rockism, that unbecoming affliction that causes middle-aged, strenuously straight white guys like David Brooks to subject us, periodically, to a column's worth of mawkish, rheumy-eyed cornpone about the irony-free pleasures of the *real* Bruce Almighty (Springsteen, of course), and how it ain't no sin to be—*sob*—glad you're alive, goddammit.[10] (Brooks quotes Springsteen rhapsodist Jon Landau approvingly: "There is no sarcasm in his writing, and not a lot of irony." I *knew* there was a reason I couldn't stand any Springsteen album but *Nebraska*, despite the better angels of my political correctness nagging me—lapsed Marxist that I am—to join the Boss Cult after he released *The Ghost of Tom Joad*. How can an American artist understand the darkness that's always there, on the edge of Disney's Main Street, U.S.A., without recourse to irony? Twain knew that. Bierce knew it. Mencken knew it. Burroughs knew it in his bones. David Lynch is all about it, in his inimitably Zen Eagle Scout way. It's Springsteen's excruciating *earnestness* that makes most of his records unlistenable. Okay, that and those goddamned *sleigh bells*.)

"Rockism means idolizing the authentic old legend (or underground hero) while mocking the latest pop star; lionizing punk while barely tolerating disco; loving the live show and hating the music video; extolling the growling performer while hating the lip-syncher," the music critic Kelefa Sanneh writes in his *New York Times* essay "The Rap Against Rockism."[11] Worse yet, rockism may be a stalking horse for "older, more familiar prejudices," he argues, asking, "The pop star, the disco diva, the lip-syncher, the 'awesomely bad' hit maker: could it really be a coincidence that rockist complaints often pit straight white men against the rest of the world? Like the anti-disco backlash of 25 years ago, the current rockist consensus seems to reflect not just an idea of how music should be made but also an idea about who should be making it."[12]

Actually, Richard Dyer got there long before Sanneh, in his canonical 1979 essay "In Defence of Disco."[13] A gay lefty, Dyer isn't buying the Frankfurt Marxist dismissal of consumer culture's throwaway pleasures as just so many weapons of mass distraction. "The anarchy of capitalism throws up commodities that an oppressed group can take up and use to cobble together its own culture," he writes. "In this respect, disco is very much like another profoundly ambiguous aspect of male gay culture, camp. It is a 'contrary' use of what the dominant culture provides, it is important in forming a gay identity, and it has subversive potential as well as reactionary implications."

True that. Yes, we're all lost in the supermarket of commodity culture, and yes, there *are* pockets of subcultural resistance lurking here and there; the alchemy of audience appropriation can transmute even the most banal or brain-dead pop flotsam into something rich and strange. For all I know, bedroom-wall shrines to Gaga, all over America, are serving as screens for the projection of empowering fantasies by teenage weirdos who will grow up to remake pop in their own, even weirder images. And yes, much of rockism's "Disco Sucks!" contempt for dance-pop's brazen "inauthenticity"—the cyborgian bloodlessness of its machine-driven beats and electro-zap hooks, more sound effect than melody; the "talentlessness" of its button-pushing producers; its social role as the soundtrack of anonymous, drug-wrecked sex in nightclub bathrooms—is often shorthand for homophobia or racism, since disco, ever since it caught the white mainstream's ear in the 1970s, has been associated with the gays, blacks, and Latinos who created it and consume it. For good measure, Gaga defenders might point out the racism inherent in reviewers' stereotyping of the Lady as a skeezy "guidette"—a grenade she catches and lobs back at us in the video for "Eh, Eh (Nothing Else I Can Say)," which features her vamping on a Vespa in front of a bodega called Guido's Meat Market.

All of those points being readily granted, I still say it's disco, and I say the hell with it. It's an error of logic to argue that, simply because some male-menopausal rockists think Gaga is the unholy progeny of Kim Kardashian and Klaus Nomi (a record I'd buy in a heartbeat, by the way), they *must* be homo-Negro-Latino-Italo-phobic, and Gaga *must* be the best thing to happen to pop music since Bowie got his nipples rotated. She isn't, at least not musically. Her songs manage the impossible feat of making craptastic New Romantic clotheshorses like Visage sound inspired. Yes, she's more than modestly gifted as a singer and pianist, but until her music sheds its Madonna-isms and lives up to the mind-shriveling weirdness of her most demented fashion statements and video moments, I mean, who *gives* a disco stick, really?

Frere-Jones thinks Gaga isn't dumb because she "opines in public about whether a certain shade of red is 'Communist' and has dropped Rilke's name more than once," and, uh, because "'Just Dance' is about being drunk in a club, which is a great idea, because songs for drunk people in clubs are rarely sharp enough to be so obvious: a lot gets lost in the quest for the clever."[14] Right, *that's* what's blighting the bumper crop of pop songs and rap tunes about getting shitfaced: too much *cleverness*. In his *Slate* essay "How Smart Is Lady Gaga?" Jonah Weiner suggests that Gaga may be brighter than we know because "she sprinkles her interviews with references to Warhol's 'deeply shallow' aphorism, David Bowie, Leigh Bowery," and she's a master/mistress of "gender sabotage," equal parts Judith Butler and Lady Bunny, as well as "an exquisite horror" who makes American manhood's ball sac retract by coming on like some Weimar Kewpie doll on the cover of *Rolling Stone*.[15]

Talk about defining deviancy down. What beige days we live in, when mentioning Rilke, Warhol, and David Bowie is proof positive of edgy intelligence. Rilke isn't exactly obscure, and Warhol and Bowie are two of the best-known brands in pop history. Gaga isn't all *that* weird, despite her revisionist accounts of growing up feeling "like a *freak*," as she told Barbara Walters.[16] I mean, can we get some context here? Performance artist Leigh Bowery giving himself an enema, onstage, and hosing the front rows at one of his performances with an anal geyser is *weird*.[17] Painter and curiosa collector Joe Coleman adopting a pickled anencephalic fetus as his son and naming it Junior is *weird*.[18] Faking your own hanging at the Video

Music Awards because you "feel that if I can show my demise artistically to the public, I can somehow cure my own legend" isn't weird; it's a time-tested career strategy, straight out of the shock-rock playbook.[19] In his fame-crazed Ziggy days, Bowie worried—in a stage whisper, with all the eager microphones leaning in—about being assassinated onstage and, alternately, fantasized about what it would do for his career. And the staged hanging was vintage Alice Cooper. Of course, we all know where Alice ended up: a born-again Christian, playing golf with Bob Hope.

Of course, Gaga, like Cooper or Bowie, isn't a genuine Outsider, in the Henry Darger sense of the word. Like both, she markets deviance to Middle America, making true transgression safe for prime time (while simultaneously gene splicing a little mutant culture into the mainstream) and, oh yeah, getting richer than Croesus in the process. Which is why she's already justifying her love of the louche to Barbara Walters, earnestly removing her dark glasses and telling Walters she loves her. Babs returned the favor by observing, after the fact, that Gaga impressed her as "quite intelligent," an impression that may or may not have been cemented by the Lady's choice of what Walters called a "serious" Chanel suit, befitting an audience with America's Mother Confessor.[20]

I asked the music critic Simon Reynolds to situate Gaga's megahyped "weirdness" within pop-music history, specifically the glam rock of the '70s—a tradition she consciously aligns herself with, through her frequent invocations of Bowie, Mercury, and T. Rex. "All the ideas are a bit familiar," says Reynolds:

> It's not like this particular iteration of glam is coming in reaction to a period of dowdiness (as with the original glam reacting against blues-bore bands and drab hippies). In fact, it's coming after a period of lowercase-g glamor that's been going on since grunge, really. It's been one long era of bling rap, glitzy R&B/Beyoncé-type fabulousness, slick boy bands and girl bands, *American Idol* pop. Music that's totally about dazzle and theater and choreography and costumes and dance routines. Every year, the Video Music Awards is more and more showbizzy—Pink did her song on a trapeze! And then she topped herself at the Grammies with pure Las Vegas/

Cirque du Soleil-type acrobatics, spinning on a vertical wire thing that I can't even describe.

Even the weird-glamor/arty artifice Gaga's about is all very familiar, after Leigh Bowery ('80s) and Alexander McQueen and Marilyn Manson ('90s) and Fischerspooner (early Noughties). It doesn't have the same impact. The one thing she did that really entertained me and that *did* have a frisson was the whole escapade with the plastic penis, is she a hermaphrodite, etc.

The original [glam-rock movement] was very much using artifice and ambisexuality and aristocracy as subversion *within* rock culture, which at that time was very much on a populist/authenticity/songs-more-important-than-image tip. [Glam] was a dialectical move within rock culture. Gaga's glam is signifying in a context where pop is *already* all about artifice, fantasy, aristocracy/bling, and certainly the gender-bendery [thing] doesn't set off any great shock waves. [21]

Setting Gaga alongside an avowed glam-rock influence like Bowie is instructive. Interviewed by *Melody Maker* for a 1972 profile, Bowie came "on like a swishy queen, a gorgeously effeminate boy ... camp as a row of tents, with his limp hand and trolling vocabulary." In other words, no Chanel suit in sight. Probed about his sexuality, he was quick with his response, dropping the bomb calculated to make him an overnight succès de scandale: "'I'm gay,' he says, 'and always have been, even when I was David Jones.'"[22] Of course, as he confessed in 1993, he was, is, and always has been a "closet heterosexual" who, like, Gaga, was "magnetized by the whole gay scene" because it was "underground"— one of the last forbidden zones, in the wake of the taboo-trashing '60s.[23] But unlike Gaga, who when pointedly asked by Barbara Walters, "Have you had sex with women?" fumfered uncomfortably, "Um, uh, well—my goodness!" Bowie gave as good as he got, without batting a false eyelash.[24] Compare Gaga's tongue-tied attack of Victorian modesty to Bowie's NC-17 response, in a 1976 *Playboy* interview, to the question, "How much of your bisexuality is fact and how much is gimmick?"

BOWIE: It's true—I am a bisexual. . . . when I was 14, sex suddenly became all-important to me. It didn't really matter who or what it was with, as long as it was a sexual experience. So it was some very pretty boy in class in some school or other that I took home and neatly fucked on my bed upstairs. And that was it. My first thought was, "Well, if I ever get sent to prison, I'll know how to keep happy."[25]

For a performer who exults in the fabricated self, Gaga seemed caught in the headlights of fame by Walters's question, as if her inner Stefani Germanotta, the prep-school striver from the Upper West Side, was squirming inside her determinedly scandalous Gaga suit. The retro-pomo angle on Gaga—that she is a self-conscious signifier, a performance artist whose real virtuoso talent lies in constructing and deconstructing her public image—may seem sharp as a tack to undergrads who crib their Baudrillard from *The Matrix*, but we've been there before. "Without any solid or 'real' self, her identity becomes whatever it needs to be, immune to the toxic shock of the incoming century, fully geared up to party in the ruins," writes Jason Louv in his demurely titled essay "Lady Gaga & The Dead Planet Grotesque."[26] Tell it to the French academic Georges-Claude Guilbert, the author of the not at all overreachingly titled *Madonna as Postmodern Myth: How One Star's Self-Construction Rewrites Sex, Gender, Hollywood, and the American Dream.* According to the book's Amazon blurb, Guilbert "examines how Madonna methodically discovered and constructed herself. . . . [He] also details the way in which she organized her own cult (borrowing from the gay community) . . . and cunningly targeted different audiences."[27] Sound familiar? Boundary dissolution, the decentered self, the Body without Organs: it's 1980s *Semiotext(e)* theory, stuck on iPod shuffle. "Is it any wonder that she's provoked the response she has, both adulation and hatred?" Louv wonders. "She's the first non-boring thing to happen in pop music for *almost fifteen years.*"[28]

Actually, not. What's so nonboring about a dance-pop diva who lifts her platinum hair and dark eyebrows from *Who's That Girl?*– era Madonna and her backing tracks from the Human League? About confining your outrageousness to your image while ensuring that your music is safe as milk? About wearing Bauhausian bondage gear that makes you look like Oskar Schlemmer's idea of *Boogie*

Nights but thinking thoughts that a pickled walnut would think, if it could? "I write about what I know: sex, pornography, art, fame obsession, drugs, and alcohol," Gaga told an *Elle* interviewer.[29] Oh, *groan.* "I never heard so many kids talk about just doing anything to be famous," lamented Gaga's household deity, David Bowie, in a 2003 interview. "I mean, yeah, fame is part of the deal when you're a kid and you think, I wanna go into music, but everybody that I knew was really doing it because of their love for it. I don't see so much of that anymore; it's like, 'What should I say so that I can be famous?' It's like the tail wagging the dog, but music's just so accessible and given to us in such awful ways now. It's been devalued tremendously."[30]

Also devalued, as argued earlier, is the currency of freakery—especially brainy outrageousness. Exhibit A: the "meat dress" made of forty pounds of flank steak that Gaga wore to the 2010 Video Music Awards. As a surrealist staged media event in the tradition of Dalí lecturing in a deep-sea diving suit, complete with lead boots and brass helmet, Gaga's prosciutto couture was nutty brilliance; as a departure from the usual awards-show brownnosing and God-thanking it was so radical it caught millions of unprepared viewers right between the eyes. And then she had to go and *rob* the image of its inscrutable power, those *mille-feuille* layers of conflicting meaning that make semioticians go weak in the knees—the sheer USDA-prime *weirdness* of the thing—by Explaining It All for Us, reducing it to a muddled parable about the U.S. military's discriminatory "Don't Ask, Don't Tell" policy . . . or something. Asked what message the meat dress was sending, she told Ellen DeGeneres, "If we don't stand up for what we believe in and if we don't fight for our rights, pretty soon we're going to have as much [sic] rights as the meat on our own bones. And, I am not a piece of meat."[31] (That, of course, is why she went shopping bare-bottomed in Paris and teetered through LAX in little more than a bra and panties, her crotch demurely accessorized with a pair of strategically placed handcuffs.)[32] A true weirdo would have fried the minds of DeGeneres and her audience with, say, a tutorial on the meat dress's intertextual connections to Aztec priests' practice of donning the flayed skins of their sacrificial victims and dancing in them.

Or to body art such as Carolee Schneemann's *Meat Joy,* a 1964 "erotic rite" in which she and others got their Dionysian Frenzy on with sausage, raw fish, and raw chickens. Or whatever. I know, I know: she's *just a pop star.* But don't argue, then, that she's an enfant terrible simply because she takes the noun "skirt steak" literally.

Beneath all that beef beats the heart of a Positive Thinker, steeped in the platitudinous folderol of therapy culture, which teaches that there's no rip in the social fabric or hole in the soul that can't be mended with a dose of self-esteem. Asked by the hosts of the coffee-talk show *The View* what her message to her fans is, she replied, "I would say: be yourself and love who you are and be proud, because you were Born This Way" (the title, not incidentally, of her latest record, released that very day).[33] As a lifeline to teens tormented by high school bullies (as Gaga claims to have been), driven to thoughts of suicide by the acid drip of misogyny and homophobia, Gaga's self-help homilies are all to the good. But, shocked though evangelicals and Palinistas may be by her embrace, like Madonna and Bowie before her, of the fashionably flamboyant drag-queen, leather-bar wing of gay culture, Gaga isn't terribly transgressive. At heart, she's a life coach in megaplatforms, all moral uplift and daily affirmations.

All that said, the "Bad Romance" video shows real promise. The eyeglasses made of razor blades; the gnarled, spastic hand gestures; the mannequinlike dancers in vinyl toques; the wedding dress with the bearskin-rug train (complete with snarling head); Gaga in bed with the charred remains of her lover, her flamethrowing bra having presumably charbroiled him in flagrante delicto: it's Marilyn Manson's *Mechanical Animals,* as reimagined by Matthew Barney. If Gaga can wean herself from the "deeply shallow" referentiality of Artistic Statements like the "Telephone" video, which channels Quentin Tarantino channeling *Caged Heat,* and start to think, *really think,* about her references, rather than just peeling them loose from their cultural contexts and dropping them, plop!, to watch the semiotic ripples spread out, she'll be truly nonboring. Reading a Deeply Silly commentary on the "Telephone" video by "Gaga blogger and doctoral student Meghan Vicks," who wheels out the obligatory reference to

Foucault's *Discipline and Punish* to Explain It All for Us, I'm reminded of a lazy afternoon in L.A., sometime in the '80s, listening to a masseuse to the stars telling me she'd seen Madonna carrying a copy of Foucault's book in her purse to certify her scandalousness.[34] Apparently, my friend chuckled, the poor dear was under the impression—never having *read* the damned thing—that it was a bondage manual.

When Gaga learns that thinking is the most dangerous act of all, she'll really be one scary monster.

(2010)

Jocko Homo

EVERY SUPER BOWL SEASON, THAT GREAT EVENT IN THE HIS-
tory of Our Times is preceded by an interminably drawn-out drum-
roll of breathless speculation, ESPN stat porn, and news-anchor joshing about who's going to be whose daddy. For what seems an eternity
(at least to those of us who would rather undergo a transorbital leu-
kotomy with an ice pick than the protracted brain death of pregame
hype), our cultural conversation is preempted by a live feed from the
jock unconscious of Team America.

It may come as *Piss Christ* blasphemy to many, but there are
some who Truly Do Not Give a Flaming Fuck who finished last in
the league in rushing the ball or who led the league in defending
tight ends or who had a hot flash during red-zone play-action passes
(although that does sound provocative, now that you mention it).

Not that anyone asked us. During the run-up to Super Bowl Sunday, anchorclones, talk-show hosts, politicians, and the rest of the
chattering class act as if we're one big happy congregation gathered
in solemn veneration of the Gipper's jockstrap, displayed in a mon-
strance. It's the sheer presumptuousness of the sports-crazed majority that galls the unbeliever most—an obliviousness to the *possibil-
ity*, even, that not everyone shares the One True Faith. It's the same
genial arrogance that makes evangelical Christians so monumentally
irritating to those of us who prefer a good exfoliating body scrub to
being Washed in the Blood of the Lamb. (The religious reference is
apt: in our national religion, sports is one aspect of the Holy Trinity,

the other two being the Free Market—whose invisible hand, like God's, moves in mysterious ways, but always for the betterment of all—and Christianity, which in the American vernacular is a bizarre amalgam of self-help pep talk, Left Behind doomsaying, and theocratic fascism.) From the gridiron metaphors in your pastor's sermon to the scripted locker-room banter of local TV newsdudes, joshing about who's gonna open a can of whupass on who, to the *Fantasy Games* geek at the office watercooler maundering on about who had six touchdowns and no interceptions in twelve pass attempts this season, posting a 124.3 passer rating, while outside of the red zone his rating on play-action was only 79.7 and his five touchdowns have to be measured, after all, against nine interceptions, the assumption that every red-blooded American—or at least every red-blooded American guy who isn't a wussy—would give his Truck Nutz for Super Bowl tickets is as unconsidered as it is ubiquitous.

Historically, athletic prowess and a consuming passion for sports have been defining aspects of manhood in America. Boys cursed with a congenital ineptitude or, even worse, an indifference to sports tend to end up stuffed into their gym lockers, pitifully bleating for help through the vents. Growing up gay in the South, the humorist David Sedaris "had no interest in football or basketball," he confides, in his essay "Go Carolina," but learned "it was best to pretend otherwise. If a boy didn't care for barbecued chicken or potato chips, people would accept it as a matter of personal taste, saying, 'Oh well, I guess it takes all kinds.' You could turn up your nose at the president or Coke or even God, but there were names for boys who didn't like sports."[1]

Indeed there are—"pussy," "faggot," and "homo" foremost among them.

Recently, over drinks at a bar, I bonded with some friends of mine—all of them intellectually top-heavy ectomorphs who'd ended up in the arts or tech-related industries (code word: geek)—over our mutual sports loathing. (Okay, that and the high-five consensus that *Relayer* is the best Yes album.) One guy reduced his animus to a terse equation: "I hate sports because the guys who beat me up in high school were jocks."

For some men, Super Bowl season stirs memories that won't stay buried—of beatdowns by jocks, some psychological, some literal. Their legacy, in most cases, is inner wounds whose scars still itch, not to mention an undying hatred of sports. In his ESPN essay "Jock Culture," Robert Lipsyte, a former *New York Times* sportswriter and penetrating thinker about the spark gap between sports and masculinity, tallies the societal costs of "jock culture." In a postscript to the article, he recalled:

> The e-mail was overwhelming. It became an Internet forum that wouldn't quit as middle-aged men exposed the emotional scars of high school.
>
> This was typical:
>
>> When I attended high school, I had so much built-up anger from being treated unfairly that, if I had access to guns or explosives, I would have been driven . . . to take revenge on the bastard jocks who dominated the school and made those four years miserable for me. After high school, I was not surprised to hear that a handful of these jocks had either died as a result of drunk driving and drug overdoses, or had spent a little time in jail for violence or drug possession. As for the dead ones, I would probably pee on their graves.
>
> Here's one from a jock:
>
>> We really did get special attention, both from the students and from the teachers. We also did cruel things to other students. I have a twentieth school anniversary this summer and plan on seeking forgiveness from the people I know I helped terrorize.[2]

Reading Lipsyte, I was back in high school P.E. class, in late-'70s Southern California. Gangly and knobby kneed in shorts and T-shirts, we assembled in military formation on the blacktop near the football field, each of us on his number, the number he'd been assigned on Day One, a stenciled number neatly spray-painted on the asphalt. An ex-marine, our coach began every class with a review of his troops, pacing silently along our ranks, staring down any kid cocky enough to meet his gaze. A bullnecked, barrel-chested caricature of Alpha Manhood who regarded us with abiding suspicion from beneath the proverbial low brow, he looked uncannily like the dominant male in a pack of silverback gorillas and could easily have loped along on his knuckles.

Standing smack on your number so that your gym shoes covered it was important. So was standing at attention; only a "numb nuts" slouched, in coach's parlance. Most important of all was ensuring that your jockstrap wasn't hanging out of your shorts, a brazen violation of corps discipline (and the Cosmic Order it implied). Guys who arrived panting on their numbers after the bell rang, guys who wore colored socks rather than the regulation white, and guys whose jockstraps were clearly visible (prima facie evidence of insanity—either that, or a death wish) felt the fateful lightning of coach's terrible swift sword: a goggle-eyed impression of the offender as drooling dorkwad, after which coach pronounced sentence in a drill instructor's bark: "Hit the deck and gimme fifty!" (push-ups, of course). It was boot camp lite; *Full Metal Jacket* meets *Fast Times at Ridgemont High.*

For all that, I had a begrudging respect for coach, maybe even a conflicted affection, somewhere between butt-puckered fear and fond contempt. Despite his simian appearance, the man was articulate and well briefed on his subject. There was a keen intelligence in those beady eyes—and a pathos, too, if you looked hard enough. Sure, he could sink half-court shots like clockwork and kick our asses—all of our asses, simultaneously—and he, and we, knew it. But every year, he'd square off with a busload of new recruits, forever the same age. There would come a time when he'd miss that half-court shot a dozen times for every time he'd swish it, a time when the biggest guy in the class would look him in the eye with the certain knowledge that he could take the old man.

Then, too, I thought I saw a knowing self-parody in coach's überbutch persona, an ironic glint in his eye that translated, in my mind at least, as a winking recognition of the idiocy of masculinity when inflated to extremes. Sure, he modeled a heavily armored masculinity for us and inculcated the militarized mind-set that America confuses with "masculine" virtues—unquestioning obedience (a value diametrically opposed, weirdly enough, to the spirit of skeptical inquiry the rest of our teachers paid lip service to), group cohesion, a Spartan resolve to suck it up, soldier on, Be All You Can Be.

But for those with a functioning irony gland, he seemed, at the same time, to be hinting that real men, men who were truly comfortable with their own masculinity, didn't need to strap on the prosthetic masculinity of the jock (whose very epithet reduces him to a big, swinging dick), the steroid-pumped weightlifter in his thong, the highway cop in mirror shades and jackboots. The fact that all of the above are stock characters in homoerotic fantasy is no accident: their hyperbolized masculinity (what the postmodern theorist Arthur Kroker calls a "hysterical" masculinity, since it fairly screams its anxieties about its manhood) ironically undermines itself, emphasizing not the impregnable masculinity of the man in question but the social constructedness of gender (that is, the extent to which we're all in drag).

Tim Burton's *Batman* offers a ready-made metaphor for the idea that masculinity is not something inherent in us, an act of nature, but something we put on, a figment of culture: the wimpy Michael Keaton becomes Batman only after being sealed in the huge, hulking batsuit. Transformed into an armored phallus with a sculpted six-pack, he speaks through gritted teeth, in the raspy monotone that, in American culture, is a benchmark of Real Manhood, from Duke Wayne to Dirty Harry. (Listen to interviews with icons of masculine power such as law-enforcement officials, Pentagon top brass, or, better yet, football players and coaches, and you'll hear the same terse, tough-talking, g-droppin' tone, almost robotic in its flattened affect; emotional expression is for girls. And girlyboys.) The Batmobile, likewise, is all about masculinity as prosthesis, gender as put-on. It's Darth Vader's idea of a jet-propelled dildo on wheels, an Oscar Meyer Wienermobile retrofitted for the hysterical male. It uses its, er, glans as a battering ram and guards its orifices with heavy-metal shields that sphincter shut when threatened with penetration. (Yeah, sure, sometimes a cigar is just a cigar, but *cum on!*)

Years after the fact, reading the feminist theorist Judith Butler's writings about the "performativity" of gender—her belief that society writes the code for what it means to be a man or a woman, roles we then perform in our everyday lives—I thought of coach and smiled. I thought, too, of his rumored assignations—to play chess, of all geeky things!—with the flinty-eyed, smarter-than-you'll-ever-be English teacher, an unmarried Ms. whose mannish hairdo and steely manner won her everyone's vote for Most Likely to Be a Closeted Lesbian. Somehow, their odd-couple friendship seemed instructive, although none of us knew what it meant, exactly.

During the mind-glazing interludes of game play between the real Super Bowl action—meaning: the commercial breaks—I found my thoughts turning, idly, to coach. And to the bullying jocks of my high school years. And to the question hidden in plain sight, in the middle of the field: What does it mean to be a man in America? Isn't that what the Super Bowl is all about, in a sense? I thought, too, about the Fear of the Inner Queer—of Being a Homo or, worse yet, Being a Pussy—that seems to gnaw, like some infinitely dense, endlessly collapsing black hole, at the heart of American masculinity. I thought about what Robert Lipsyte said during our phone interview, about the blurry line between the homosocial—male bonding, by any other name—and male Eros.

For Lipsyte, the pathologies of American masculinity owe much to jock culture, the "team-sports culture" that "permeates high school" but "starts with Pee Wee and Little League," when "some obscene loudmouth with a whistle around his neck, called coach, creates this little cult around himself, and [the boys] must respond to his authority." Boys learn that "the team comes first, they learn to dominate, to win by any means possible," said Lipsyte, "and to me the key of all of this is: anyone who is not of the team is the Other. This is why it's perfectly okay to garbage-pail a nerd in the lunchroom and why women in particular, unless it's your mother or a cheerleader, must be watched with great wariness, [because women are] the prime Other. So there's your misogyny; beating the shit out of your girlfriend is kind of a jock prerequisite."

But the Queer is an even more unsettling figure, within jock culture, because while women are, at least, reassuringly Other in their undeniable anatomical difference, homosexuals are perilously close to home. If masculinity, in Freudian terms, is a heavily fortified citadel, gay men are inside that fortress, undermining its foundations from within by being male yet violating the official (read: heteronormative) rules of what it means to be a man in America. It's as if you got into the batsuit, only to find that the Joker was in there with you, naked and way too close for comfort.

"I don't think that kids grow up homophobic," Lipsyte told me. "Jocks in particular get called 'sissy' and 'girl' and 'faggot'; even today, in 2010, it's not impossible for a kid who hasn't tried hard enough to find a tampon in his locker. All of this is reinforcing the [notion of] the Other."

As Lipsyte implies, jock culture's hysterical fear and loathing of the Queer is a classic reaction formation, a desperate attempt to draw a bright line between the homosocial and the homosexual. Of course, everyday life is a messy thing, full of gray zones; its haziness has a way of blurring even the brightest lines.

"Football is so homoerotic," said Lipsyte. "I spent a thousand years in locker rooms, and the naked horseplay—the dick-grabbing and the ass-soaping and the slapping in the shower, I mean, come on! I was at a party a couple years ago with John Amaechi. [Amaechi, who played center for five seasons in the NBA, was the first pro basketball player to come out, in 2007—*after* he'd retired, tellingly.—M.D.] He recalled that the first time he went into an NBA locker room, there were all these guys, they were all naked, they were all touching each other, and they were trading jewelry and they were trading shirts and they were looking at each others' musculature, and he said, 'My first thought was, Hey! *I'm* supposed to be queer!'"

In his memoir, *Man in the Middle,* Amaechi is sharply insightful about the wavering borderline between homosociality and homosexuality in jock culture. "Coming out threatens to expose the homoerotic components of what they prefer to think of as simply male bonding," he writes. "And it generally is. It's not so much that there's a repressed homosexuality at play (except for a small minority), only that there's a tremendous fear that the behavior might be labeled as such. Or, as I heard the anti-gay epithets pour forth, that gay men in the locker room would somehow violate this sacred space by sexualizing it."

I thought about these things while watching Super Bowl ads. Calculated showstoppers, the game's commercial breaks (which most viewers find more entertaining than the game itself) target Homo Budweiser, and in so doing offer a borehole into the anxious unconscious of the American male (at least, as imagined by Madison Avenue).

The commercials for the 2010 Super Bowl included an ad for Dockers khakis whose tagline said it all: "Calling all men: it's time to wear the pants." (Dude, if your idea of Alpha-Male wear is a pair of midlife-crisis khakis only George Costanza would be caught dead in, you'd best have "Low Self-Esteem" tattooed on your forehead right now. You'll *never* wear the pants.)

A spot for the Dodge Charger featured a perp walk of hangdog guys staring dejectedly at the camera, their balls broken by the matriarchy's iron heel. (A Manolo Blahnik, no doubt.) A voice-over channels their pain: "I will be civil to your mother. I will put the seat down. I will take my socks off before getting into bed." Then, with a manly vrrrooom, comes the punch line: "And because I do this, I will drive the car I want to drive." Over thrill-cam footage of Ron Burgundy's idea of a bitchen-ass sports car eating up the road, we hear "Charger. Man's. Last. Stand," pounded home with pile-driver clangs—a tagline calculated to reset the clock of gender politics back to one million years B.C., when Raquel Welch wore wooly-mammoth Uggs and men didn't have to take their socks off before going to bed.

But the commercial that spoke volumes about what feminists like to call the Crisis of Masculinity was the metrosexual-friendly ad for Dove "Men + Care" body and face wash. Over Rossini's "William Tell Overture" (a.k.a. the Lone Ranger theme), some opera dude recites—sings, actually—the cultural code for manhood with suitably manly (if winkingly ironic) bravura: "Be good at sports, play hard, run fast ... lift weights, be strong, know how to fight ... be tough, be cool, be full of pride / don't show your sensitive side." In the end, the goateed-white-guy everyman earns the right to chill-ax on his suburban lawn, button-down shirt defiantly undone, necktie cast aside. Bobos of the world, unite; you have nothing to lose but your ties! He's emo's answer to Don Draper. "Now that you're comfortable with who you are," the voice-over asks, "isn't it time for comfortable skin?" Cut to footage of him soaping up in the shower. Like American masculinity itself, caught in the crossfire of the resurgent culture wars, Dove walks a fine line, reinforcing stereotypes of hard-ass manliness yet daring to play drop-the-soap with *Queer Eye for the Straight Guy* definitions of masculinity. Wary of the wussiness implicit in softer, more sensitive skin, the Dove Man is studly enough—comfortable with who he is— to treat himself to a "body wash."

Of course, American men *aren't* comfortable in their skins. Which is why Dove goes to such lengths to reassure us that the guy in the ad isn't, you know, too heteroflexible. Shots of our hero pumping iron, playing football, taking a shot to the head in the boxing ring, and punching some guy's lights out certify his credentials as a bona fide He-Ra, preempting any raised eyebrows about the sort of guy who would use body wash. Clearly, the strenuous life, and sports in particular, is the forge in which Iron Johns are made.

In his own inimitable way, coach helped make me the man I am, even though I'm the furthest thing from a sports fan and cordially loathe jock culture to this day. Now and then, I've wondered what became of him. Some years ago, I got an inkling. To his shock and awe, an old friend, a fellow high school alumnus, ran into coach one day.

In San Francisco.

In the city's Castro district.

In a gay bar.

There's a symmetry to it, if you think about it—a kind of perfection, like the snap coach used to put on a football, sending it spinning through the sky.

(2010)

Wimps, Wussies, and W.

IN APRIL 2007, NBC ANNOUNCED THAT THE SHOCK JOCK DON Imus, whom the network had hired to provide "irreverent" and "controversial" drive-time comedy, was getting the bum's rush because of his irreverent and controversial characterization of the Rutgers University women's basketball team as "nappy-headed hos," a remark that NBC News president Steve Capus deplored as "deeply hurtful to many, many people."[1]

The smoking crater where Imus used to sit afforded a pleasant view for those of us who never understood the appeal of his grizzled-codger shtick, which always sounded, to this writer, like Rooster Cogburn reading *The Turner Diaries*. But amid the camera-ready outrage of pundits and pols (many of whom had, until Imus's nappy-ho moment, been only too happy to laugh along with the irascible old bigot when they were in a book-flogging or vote-grubbing mood), few seemed to notice the situational irony of the thing: in a country where you can't swing a cat without hitting a race-related social problem, we rise up in righteous anger not over the moral obscenity that there are seven times more blacks than whites behind bars, or that black men under twenty-five are fifteen times more likely than whites to be murdered, but over the bigoted fumferings of some "cantankerous old fool" (to quote former Imus newsreader Contessa Brewer).[2]

If we're going to administer a ritual flaying to every shock jock who channels the ugly American id, shouldn't we at least spread the love? How is it that a serial hate-speech offender like Ann Coulter has escaped the skinning knife? She called Democratic presidential candidate John Edwards a "faggot" at a Conservative Political Action Conference; quipped on *Hardball Plaza* that Al Gore is a "total fag"; and wrote, in her syndicated column, that the odds of Hillary Clinton "coming out of the closet" in 2008 are "about even money."[3] Oh, and she managed, by a neat trick of contortionist logic, to argue on the July 25, 2006, episode of *The Big Idea with Donny Deutsch* that Bill Clinton's bodaciously hetero womanizing is proof positive of "latent homosexuality":

> MS. COULTER: I think that sort of rampant promiscuity does show some level of latent homosexuality. . . . I think anyone with that level of promiscuity where, you know, you—I mean, he didn't know Monica's name until their sixth sexual encounter. There is something that is—that is of the bathhouse about that.
>
> [. . .]
>
> DEUTSCH: But where's the—but where's the homosexual part of that? I'm—once again, I'm speechless here.
>
> MS. COULTER: It's reminiscent of a bathhouse. It's just this obsession with your own—with your own essence.
>
> DEUTSCH: But why is that homosexual? You could say narcissistic.
>
> [. . .]
>
> MS. COULTER: Well, there is something narcissistic about homosexuality. Right? Because you're in love with someone who looks like you. I'm not breaking new territory here, why are you looking at me like that?[4]

Did I mention that she mocked a hostile questioner at Indiana University in Bloomington as a "gay boy"?[5]

Coulter's defense is that she's a right-wing wag; humorless liberals who accuse her of gay bashing are just swimming into her gently smiling, Nicorette-scented jaws. Journalists seem to agree: conventional wisdom, among the media elite, holds that nobody takes her homophobic slurs seriously because, like the woman said, she's an insult comic—okay, the kind whose "Reichsminister of Funny Walks" routine would have brought the house down at a Nuremberg rally, but a comic nonetheless.

Another reason she hasn't been Imus-ized is because she's a mouth for hire, not the host of a TV show dependent on controversy-shy advertisers. Most important, racism—slavery, lynching, institutionalized discrimination—has taken a much greater toll, in the history of this country, than homophobia. According to an FBI report on hate crimes committed in 2005, most such attacks (54.7 percent) were racially motivated; only 14.2 percent were inspired by the sexual orientation of the victim.[6]

But there's another reason, closer to home, that the media haven't given Coulter a prime-time waterboarding: her problem is our problem. As a society, we view racial epithets as Class A felonies, whereas homophobic slurs are parking violations, if that. Coulter laughed off her Edwards crack, on *Hannity & Colmes*, saying, "The word I used . . . has nothing to do with gays. It's a schoolyard taunt, meaning wuss."[7] Got that? The slang term "faggot," helpfully defined by the *American Heritage Dictionary* as "offensive slang . . . a disparaging term for a homosexual man," really means "wuss," which is a schoolyard pejorative applied exclusively to guys—guys who are "unmanly," according to the *American Heritage*. In *Fast Times at Ridgemont High*, noted etymologist Mike Damone clarifies matters: "You are a wuss: part wimp, and part pussy." Not that it means you're a fag or anything. Even if you are a fag. Which is just British slang for "cigarette," anyway. *So why are you looking at me like that?*

Seriously, though, Coulter's pretzel logic reminds us that homophobia is so ubiquitous as to be invisible in American society. Only people whose idea of formal attire is a white sheet with eyeholes would dare to use the N-word in public, but homophobic smears reverberate throughout pop culture, where "that's so gay" has become an all-purpose descriptor, routinely used by college students who insist it has no pejorative connotations. "Anti-gay language is still widely condoned by society," says Liz Meyer, a researcher quoted in a *McGill Reporter* article, "Fighting the New F-Word."[8] And little wonder: asked, in a 2003 Pew study, if homosexuality should be accepted by society, only a razor-thin majority (51 percent) of Americans answered yes, in contrast to 83 percent in Germany, 77 percent in France, and 74 percent in Great Britain.

Our long tradition of demonizing our political and ideological opponents is rife with homophobic innuendo. Camille Paglia derided Al Gore for his "prissy, lisping Little Lord Fauntleroy persona," which "borders on epicene."[9] Throughout the 2004 presidential campaign, Republicans dismissed Democratic opponent John Kerry, who spent his childhood summers in France, as too "French" to be presidential timber—a wussy, by any other name. Those French! With their wimpy berets and turtlenecks, maundering on about philosophers like Jean-François Lyotard. (What kind of girlyman is named after a leotard, for chrissakes?) Even their cheese is all soft and runny! And Senator John Edwards was too heteroflexible to be commander in chief; only Straight Guys with a Queer Eye pay $400 for a haircut, right? Me, I just shampoo with a can of Blatz and take a little off the top with a Weed Whacker. Damn straight.

GEORGE W. BUSH LEARNED an unforgettable lesson about the anxious nature of masculinity in America when *Newsweek* tarred his father as a "wimp," a perception Bush 41 never really overcame.[10] Even his Distinguished Flying Cross, earned for bravery under fire as a fighter pilot during World War II, didn't give George H. W. Bush enough juju to ward off the charge that he was a preppy milquetoast who lacked the Right Stuff to be president. In the run-up to the Persian Gulf War, he seized the opportunity to remake himself into a line-in-the-sand, this-aggression-will-not-stand-type tough guy. He further upped his manliness quotient by mispronouncing "Saddam" as "Sodom," a not-so-subliminal jibe contrasting his firm-jawed American masculinity with the Orientalist stereotype of a jaded potentate whose appetites are too monstrous to mention.

Yet Bush 41's macho makeover never convinced the Joe Six-Pack demographic that he wasn't the prissy patrician of the *Newsweek* profile, a guy with a "tight, twangy" voice who asked for "just a splash" more coffee at a New Hampshire truck stop.[11] Junior (as Bush 43 was then known) was deeply affected by the *Newsweek* cover story. Scalded by the magazine's portrayal of his father as a wussy, he earned a rep as the Joe Pesci of American politics—"profane, abusive, and ugly," castigating journalists to their faces as "assholes" in outbursts that were sometimes "frighteningly confrontational," according to Bush family biographer Kitty Kelley.[12]

The resolve never to be branded a wimp is the lash that drives Bush the Younger. One of his takeaways from the *Newsweek* fiasco seems to have been the realpolitik assumption that the best defense against the wimp charge is a dirty-tricks offense against your opponent's sexuality. In 1994, when W. ran for governor of Texas, the incumbent—Ann Richards, who had appointed openly homosexual people to state boards and commissions—found herself the target of a whispering campaign "involving rumors of lesbianism and other unspeakable perversions," according to Texas political commentator Molly Ivins.[13] In his 2000 run for the presidency, W. grabbed the GOP nomination from Vietnam war hero John McCain; scurrilous rumors that McCain was gay may have played a role in his defeat.[14] (Well, politics is for he-men. To make *huevos rancheros,* you've got to break a few eggs. I'd say "omelet," but that's French, and would mark me as a latent homosexual. Which I'm not. Really. Although my use of the word *huevos*—Mexican slang for testicles—does worry me.)

Dubya knows in his bones what George H. W. Bush never quite seemed to grasp: here in Marlboro Country, we like our men manly and our presidents—the mortal incarnation of our mythic manliness—rough ridin', tough talkin', and g-droppin'. Thus Bush 43's hyperbolic masculinity: the chin-out, you-talkin'-to-me? pugnacity at press conferences; the cock-of-the-walk swagger; the "locker-room joshing, slap-on-the-butt" male bonding, as Molly Ivins called it, that convinced working-class America that even a scion of the WASP elite with the House of Saud on speed dial was just another good ol' boy; the cowboy bluster about getting Saddam, dead or alive; the *Top Gun* posturing on the aircraft carrier, in a crotch-gripping flight suit that accentuated the Presidential Unit (leading G. Gordon Liddy to swoon—on *Hardball,* for Freud's sake—"what a stud").[15]

BUT DOESN'T ALL THIS chest-thumping machismo and locker-room homophobia protest a *little* too much? What can we say about a country so anxiously hypermasculine that it demands a buffed-out, studly Jesus who would sooner kick butt than turn the other cheek? I'm talking about Godmen, the movement to lure Real Men back to the pews with services that feature guys bending metal wrenches with their bare hands and leaders exulting, "Thank you, Lord, for our testosterone!"[16]

The trouble with manhood, American-style, is that it is maintained at the expense of every man's feminine side, the frantically repressed Inner Wussy. And what we lock away in the oubliette of the unconscious we demonize in broad daylight as a preemptive strike against any lurking suspicions of wussiness. And they always *do* lurk, in American guy culture, even for the most macho of macho, macho men—in fact, *especially* for guys like them, since by a curious reversal of cultural logic, men who take masculinity to hyperbolic extremes invite the charge that there's "something of the bathhouse" about them, a muscle-boy "narcissism" we've come to associate with gay gym culture.

Case in point: Aaron Schock, the hunky Republican representative from Illinois last seen rocking his pumped-up pecs and abs on the cover of *Men's Health* magazine or sporting a glam-tastic turquoise belt and fuchsia gingham shirt at a White House picnic. Schock's ripped body and faaabulous fashion sense have made him the object of is-he-or-isn't-he speculation, especially in the gay media. The representative's idea of damage control? Schock, who plays against GOP type by being on the wrong side of most gay issues, from antidiscrimination legislation to gay marriage, *torched* the offending belt. (Just a *little* drama-queeny?) Needless to say, the wags over at Queerty.com weren't convinced by his burnt offering to manly manliness: "Burning the belt isn't enough to rid yourself of gay cooties, Mr. Congressman. That shirt and those pants need some kerosene, too. And we don't even know what shoes you were wearing. Gucci slip-on loafers? Off with their soles!"[17]

In his book *The Wimp Factor: Gender Gaps, Holy Wars, and the Politics of Anxious Masculinity*, the clinical psychologist Stephen Ducat argues that American manhood is gnawed by "femiphobia"—the subconscious belief that "the most important thing about being a man is not being a woman" (which, for many straight guys, is another way of saying "not gay").[18]

Okay, so maybe I'm overstepping the bounds of my Learning Annex degree in pop psychology. But the hidden costs of our overcompensatory hypermacho are worse, far worse, than a few politicians slimed by Reich-wing pundits or dirty-tricks campaigns. The horror in Iraq was protracted past the point of lunacy by George W.'s bring-it-on braggadocio, He-Ra unilateralism, and damn-the-facts refusal to acknowledge mistakes (even as the body count mounted and billions went down the drain)—all hallmarks of a pathological masculinity that misreads diplomacy as weakness and confuses arrogant rigidity (Freudians, start your engines . . .) with strength. It's a masculinity founded not on a self-assured sense of what it *is*, but on a neurotic loathing of what it is *not* (but secretly fears it may be): a wussy. And it will go to the grave insisting on battering-ram stiffness (stay the course! don't pull out!) as the truest mark of manhood.

(2007)

Stardust Memories

WHEN DID I STOP WANTING TO BE BOWIE? TOO RECENTLY FOR a Man of a Certain Age is the short but sufficiently mortifying answer.

Weirdly, there may be thousands like me—living fossils from the Class of '73, the year Bowie retired his Ziggy Stardust persona before a traumatically shocked audience, not to mention his thunderstruck band, all but one of whom (guitarist Mick Ronson) had walked onstage without the shadow of a clue that they were about to be slam-dunked into the dustbin of history. How many late boomers came of age in front of a bathroom mirror, blow-drying their shag mullets into a lame approximation of Bowie's Reluctant Astronette look from the cover of *Pin Ups*? How many suburban space oddities badgered their nonplussed moms into sewing them space-cadet suits from repurposed Simplicity patterns? How many fanboys struggled with the libidinal equivalent of cognitive dissonance as they watched Bowie on the rock-concert show *Midnight Special*, shimmying across the screen in a fishnet body stocking and a man-bra made of mannequin hands? ("The most sexually radical thing you could ever imagine seeing on American television at the time," says Camille Paglia, in *Bowie: A Biography*, by Mark Spitz.)[1] What *were* those alien yearnings? A man-crush? The bi-curiosity so trendy in the '70s? Or the first stirrings of "a love I could not obey," as Bowie put it in "Lady Stardust"?

Ziggy crash-landed in '70s America like the plague-bearing space probe in *The Andromeda Strain*, spreading subcultural subversion across the smiley-face decade brought to you by Chuck Barris and Aaron Spelling, Farrah Fawcett's layered shag and Dorothy Hamill's wedge. To alienated teens who dreamed of escaping not only teenage wasteland but Middle America's brain-dead mainstream as well, Bowie's epochal 1972 album *The Rise and Fall of Ziggy Stardust and the Spiders from Mars* was a cosmic wormhole, an interdimensional portal to a parallel universe of pansexual perversity, irony, and camp.

Historical periodization be damned, the early '70s were still the '60s. Despite Warhol, the Velvet Underground, and Zappa's *We're Only in It for the Money*, pop-music critics still carried the flag for Countercultural Authenticity, standing foursquare against technocratic soullessness and Ken-and-Barbie consumerism—the "white-collared conservative flashing down the street, pointing their plastic finger at me," as Jimi sings in "If 6 was 9."[2]

Then along comes Bowie, a cum laude graduate of the Andy Warhol School of the Fabricated Self, sold on the idea of public image as never-ending performance and self-promotion as the highest art form. "I love plastic idols," says Andy, in *The Philosophy of Andy Warhol*.[3] "I packaged a totally credible plastic rock star," Bowie quipped, speaking of Ziggy. "Much better than any sort of Monkees fabrication. My plastic rocker was much more plastic than anybody's."[4] The Ziggy-era Bowie *loves* plastic. Better yet, he *is* plastic. He zips himself into PVC Flash Gordon jumpsuits so skintight they'd induce hypoxia in normal mortals. But Bowie is Not of This World. At a moment when coke-frazzled rock royalty are still paying lip service to The Movement, clenching their fists in halfhearted solidarity with the denim-jacketed masses, Bowie comes on like some transgendered Klaatu. If the awestruck whispers of his handlers are to be believed, the guy *doesn't even sweat*, like some incorruptible saint. Even more bizarre, he does *mime* during his guitarist's contractually mandated half-hour solo, spastic impressions of Marcel Marceau brining a turkey. Or maybe it's Judy Garland undergoing a high colonic, who the hell knows? It's French and it's weird and your dad thinks the guy's a simpering catamite, so it's *got* to be cool. And if that doesn't steam up your viewscreen, why, he'll just rattle off a *Jacques Brel* tune with lyrics so *French* they make your espadrilles ache: "My death waits like a bible truth / At the funeral of my youth." (They loved it in Dubuque!) Or maybe he'll strip down to a see-through blouse and use his eensy-weensy nipples to receive X-rated tweets from his home planet, Ganymede. One thing is certain: the '60s are *dead,* and David Bowie buried them.

TO ROCK CRITICS like the '60s warhorse Ellen Willis, Bowie's showbiz inauthenticity was the Mark of the Beast. In a 1972 *New Yorker* essay, she can't decide if Bowie is a figment of his Wildean imagination ("an aesthete using stardom as a metaphor") or, worse yet, a closet folkie "who digs Brel, plays an (amplified) acoustic guitar, and sings with a catch in his voice about the downfall of the planet," conning the masses into *thinking* he's a plastic rock star.[5] He doesn't sweat, which is suspicious, since sweat, along with grungy denim jeans, smells like Essence of Authenticity, to the countercultural nose; more suspicious still, Bowie's "aura is not especially sexual."[6] Willis prefers the proto-punk primitivist Iggy Pop, a Motor City savage who "leaps into the audience and grabs people by the hair" and, "unlike David Bowie ... sweats."[7] In England on a press junket underwritten by Bowie's label, RCA, Willis joins Iggy for a ramble through Hyde Park, where Iggy is confounded by the impossibility of finding a cold Coke. "'This country is weird, man,' said Iggy. 'It's *unreal.*'"[8] She compares notes with another American rock critic, Dave Marsh. "What was it that was missing? 'Innocence,' Dave suggested. But maybe it's just that unlike Lou Reed ... or Iggy ... , Bowie doesn't seem quite real."[9] As Tom Wolfe would say: *But exactly!*

Glam rock drew the line: between the counterculture's insistence on a politically correct earnestness and the new decade's Oscar Wildean embrace of winking artifice; between the power-to-the-people populism of Woodstock-era rockers and the Me-Generation Nietzscheanism of Bowie singing, "Homo Sapiens have outgrown their use ... You gotta make way for the Homo Superior" ("Oh!

You Pretty Things"); between folk rock's ripped-from-the-head-lines political "relevance" and glam's escapist flight into retro styles (Bowie's tongue-in-cheek appropriation of Eddie Cochran rocka-billy in "Hang onto Yourself" and '50s doo-wop in "Drive-In Satur-day") or even shameless hedonism (Queen singer Freddie Mercury's visions, in "Killer Queen," of a high-rolling call girl who "keeps Moet et Chandon / In her pretty cabinet / 'Let them eat cake,' she says / Just like Marie Antoinette").[10] With Bowie as its gender-bent spokes-mutant, glam marked the turning point between hippie and what would soon become punk, between modernism and postmodernism.

"Ziggy Stardust could not have enjoyed the same impact in the sixties," writes Mark Spitz in *Bowie: A Biography*.[11]

> He was not a utopian figure but rather the cracked and not entirely legit messiah that the debauched humankind of the seventies had come to deserve. He's the 'all right, this will do' savior and the perfect antihero for the seventies because he is the embodiment of the dead sixties dream. Ziggy is the space-race anticlimax, Manson and Altamont and Nixon's reelection and the breakup of the Beatles made sexy. Rock 'n' roll ecdysis is a crucial element of his appeal. Ziggy says to all those in pain, "You have failed as human beings, but it's all right. We will succeed as slinky, jiving space insects. Let all the children boogie!"[12]

The question that nags at *Bowie: A Biography*, or any Bowie biog-raphy for that matter, is how did a snaggletoothed twink with a lar-val pallor, the physique of a stick insect, and shaved eyebrows (for that transgendered mantid effect) become the improbable object of one-handed fantasies for millions of "boys and girls and everything in between,"[13] as Ziggy photographer Mick Rock puts it—the living incarnation of *Ziggy*'s "leper messiah"?

Perhaps by channeling the zeitgeist, as Spitz suggests. But Spitz's language—"messiah," "savior"—is instructive: in the minds of his most devout fans, Bowie was the Starman foretold in the *Ziggy* song of the same name, come to liberate weirdos everywhere from the have-a-nice-daymare of '70s suburbia and the think-alike, bong-alike conformity of its high school cliques, where Led Zep *fucking ruled,* dude, and anyone who didn't think so was a *fag*. How bogus is *that*?! Now pass the penis-shaped beer-bong, bro, and drop the needle on "Moby Dick."

Ziggy was "the ultimate alien," recalls Tony Zanetta, onetime president of Bowie's management company MainMan, in the Spitz biography. "All the little alienated kids all over the world . . . the fat girls and the gay boys that didn't fit in . . . were attracted to this kind of alien-ness."[14] By the New Wave era, says Ann Magnuson, an icon of New York's downtown scene in the late '70s and early '80s, Bowie "had turned into something godlike to certain kids who loved the weird, the edgy, the arty, and the glam. By that point, he had become deified."[15]

Bowie, more than any other rock star (except maybe Elvis), invites—demands?—deification. This has partly to do with the messianic sense of destiny that propelled him to rock godhood—a petted, precocious child's sense of specialness, inflated to *übermenschen* extremes by the Nietzsche his older brother Terry introduced him to at a tender age. ("I always had a repulsive sort of need to be something more than human," Bowie confesses in George Tremlett's *David Bowie: Living on the Brink*. "I thought, 'Fuck that, I want to be a Superman.'")[16] Becoming Ziggy, onstage and off, from 1972 through 1974, completed Bowie's transfiguration into the martyred alien savior of his concept album's title role. And his Svengali-like manager's strategy of limiting media access to the divinity fixed the image of Bowie as aloof and otherworldly in the public mind.

Thus, every Bowie biography—and there's a sagging shelf-load of them—tends toward hagiography, especially when written by a Bowie votary. Nothing wrong with that: as fan-culture ethnographers such as Henry Jenkins have shown, objectivity creates blind spots if you're trying to make profound sense of media-age mystery cults; to truly understand the idiosyncratic, crisscrossing meanings fans map onto pop icons such as Madonna or mass-marketed myths such as the Harry Potter series, you've got to go native—become a participant-observer, to borrow a term from cultural anthropology.

What makes Bowie's story fascinating is all the little dissonances between the plastic idol and the mousy-haired earthling who plays him. As the Thin White Duke of his 1976 "Station to Station" tour, Bowie was the brilliantined, clench-jawed embodiment of Weimar nightcrawler cool, a curlicue of smoke wisping off his ever-present Gitane. But the same man, in his earlier days, worshipped the leprously uncool Anthony Newley, a fixation immortalized in "The Laughing Gnome," a chipmunk-voiced novelty song calculated to make even the staunchest Bowiephile cringe. The same Bowie who pushed the envelope of pop by using William S. Burroughs's cut-up method of collage composition to generate lyrics like "you're dancing where the dogs decay, defecating ecstasy" ("We Are the Dead," *Diamond Dogs*) would pass the schmaltz on *Bing Crosby's Merrie Olde Christmas*, dueting with Der Bingle on "Little Drummer Boy."[17]

One of Spitz's abiding themes is the tug-of-war, in Bowie's life and work, between art and commerce, mainstream and avant-garde, bourgeois stability and cocaine-fueled days without sleep (Bowie's L.A. period, when he was trying to change the channels on his TV telekinetically and buttonholing anyone within earshot about the witches who wanted to steal his semen to create a baby to sacrifice to Satan). "Sometimes the friction produced brilliant chemistry," Spitz observes, "other times it led him too far from his better angels."[18] After Bowie's ascent to megastardom in 1983 with *Let's Dance*, though, he "would never be truly, authentically . . . freaky again."[19] Now, Spitz argues, he is postcool, having transcended the limits of pop stardom. The latest, and perhaps last, persona in the career-long series of Warholian moltings that has made him the patron saint of self reinvention is what Spitz calls "Post-Ambition Bowie"—financially secure, his artistic genius unquestioned by "yet another full decade's worth of younger artists (from Moby and Goldie all the way up to TV on the Radio and the Arcade Fire)."[20]

Of course, there are those graying alumni in the Class of '73 who will always prefer the slinky, jiving space-insect model. "Now he gives people what he thinks will make them happy, and they're yawning their heads off," snipes Morrissey, in *Bowie: A Biography*. "He is no longer David Bowie at all."[21] Maybe. Or maybe he never was. Maybe

Bowie is a set of mental space-time coordinates anyone can inhabit, with the right attitude, some Red Hot Red hair dye, and a little radio-active lipstick. In 2007, the fashion designer Keanan Duffty's Bowie collection came to the superstore Target. Spitz quotes Duffty's sincere hope that his collection would help "people, fans and nonfans alike, to get in touch with their inner Bowie."[22]

But what does that mean at a moment when even Bowie has dis-owned his inner Bowie? Then again, will the Real David Bowie ever stand up? Isn't "David Bowie" a mass-media palimpsest, his "authentic" self overwritten by centuries of evasion, dissembling, and self-mythol-ogization? Isn't the new-and-improved Bowie of recent years—fright-eningly effervescent and teeth-lifted, horsing around in a hoodie and sneakers with the lesbian trailblazer (but irrepressibly normal) Ellen DeGeneres—no less a Warholian fabrication than Ziggy, the "totally credible plastic rock star" he became in order to ascend to pop god-hood? If postcool is the new, Bowie-sanctified cool, then Bowie, in a fittingly postmodern turn of events, is post-Bowie. What could be cooler?

(2009)

When Animals Attack!

DEAR READER:

Do you, like me, rejoice in the knowledge that you could eat an adult mouse whole, if you wanted to? As Gordon Grice helpfully notes, in his endlessly entertaining *Deadly Kingdom: The Book of Dangerous Animals,* the rodent's bones are "no more troublesome than those of a catfish." In medieval England, "a mouse on toast was thought to cure colds."[1]

Grice is best known as the author of *The Red Hourglass: Lives of the Predators,* a cult classic about black widows, brown recluses, rattle-snakes, and tarantulas, among other things. The book launched a new genre: natural-history gothic, or, if you prefer, nature noir. If Cormac McCarthy turned his hand to nature writing, the results might sound something like Grice, who combines the laconic banter of rural Okla-homa, where he grew up, with a country boy's inexhaustible curios-ity about the natural world. A Jean-Henri Fabre for readers with rifle racks, Grice splits the difference between a naturalist's unsentimental scrutiny of animal behavior, a rural midwesterner's applied knowl-edge of the predator–prey relationship, and noir's sardonic deadpan. He renders his dramas of animal behavior in tight close-up, with an eye for detail that makes the reader feel as if she's lying on her belly, head propped on her elbows, chin in hands, peering intently into the jungle in the lawn. At that scale, insect tableaux become morality plays or, more often, Aesop's fables for existentialists.

Grice's style—unsentimental, black-comedic, philosophical in an unselfconscious, back-porch way—heightens that effect. He uses ironic understatement to dramatic effect, whether funny, horrific, or both in the same breath, as in this description, from *The Red Hourglass,* of the notoriously short-tempered female praying mantis's response to the male's sexual overtures:

> She strikes. Now she is standing still, her blur of motion over so quickly it might seem unreal, except that she is slowly eating the right half of his head. He stands swaying, his actions only slightly interrupted by the amputation of half of his head. Then, while she is still eating, he crawls onto her back. He seems in this semiheadless state to have found a renewed vigor and sense of purpose.[2]

Of course, "short-tempered" is pure anthropomorphism on my part, a tendency Grice avoids. To be sure, he delights in reminding us that we, too, are members of the deadly kingdom, holding up animal behavior at its most gross or grisly to show us unflattering reflections of our own bestiality. But he's equally quick to point out the unfathomable Otherness of nature, the many ways in which its playful, purposeless malice mocks the consoling fiction of an Intelligent Designer. *The Red Hourglass* takes its title from the characteristic markings on the black widow's underside, a quirk of evolution that we invest with meaning, reading it as a vanitas. Against our rage for cosmic order, our insistence on the Meaning of Life, Grice offers the parable of the widow's venom, "thousands of times more virulent" than the spider requires to kill its largest prey. Scientists are at a loss to explain the pointlessness of the thing, which serves no evolutionary purpose. "We want the world to be an ordered room," writes Grice,

> but in a corner of that room there hangs an untidy web. Here the analytical mind finds an irreducible mystery, a motiveless evil in nature.... No idea of the cosmos as elegant design accounts for the widow. No idea of a benevolent God can be completely comfortable in a widow's world. She hangs in her web, that marvel of design, and defies teleology.[3]

The prairie theology of this passage always reminds me of those stunning little set pieces in Thomas Harris's novels, meditations on nature's obliviousness to the human insect, the amoral purity of the godless cosmos. I'm thinking of Hannibal Lecter's homily, in *Silence of the Lambs*, on good and evil, acts of God and forces of nature ("typhoid and swans—it all comes from the same place"), and of the bravura passage that ends *Silence*'s prequel, the critically underrated *Red Dragon*. Floating, on his hospital bed, in an opiated haze, an FBI profiler who hunts human predators—those mythic beasts called serial killers—remembers a visit to the incongruously beautiful battlefield at Shiloh, where thousands died in one of the bloodiest slaughters of the Civil War:

> Now, drifting between memory and narcotic sleep, he saw that Shiloh was not sinister; it was indifferent. Beautiful Shiloh could witness anything. Its unforgivable beauty simply underscored the indifference of nature, the Green Machine. . . . In the Green Machine there is no mercy; we make mercy, manufacture it in the parts that have overgrown our basic reptile brain.
>
> There is no murder. We make murder, and it matters only to us. . . . Yes, he had been wrong about Shiloh. Shiloh isn't haunted—men are haunted. Shiloh doesn't care.[4]

Deadly Kingdom is a Darwinian sermon on this theme, puncturing the self-serving myths that obscure our understanding of the natural world: "Belief is a part of seeing. It's hard to filter out the interpretation and leave mere facts."[5] Grice does an end run around the *Free Willy/Jaws* binary, the culture/nature version of the virgin/whore dualism. "I often read accounts that point out what the human victim did 'wrong' before she was attacked by a bear or a shark," he writes. "Many writers depict virtually all animal attacks as 'provoked' by the victim." (The blame-the-victim rape narrative, transposed into the key of *When Animals Attack*.) "On the other side, some writers are at pains to paint dangerous animals as monsters of cruelty."[6]

In truth, he suggests, nature isn't so much malevolent as indifferent. When humans come to grief at tooth or claw, it's often because of our insistence on seeing animals as emissaries of the peaceable kingdom, like the New Age sentimentalization of the dolphin as a guardian angel with a blowhole, or because we can't seem to distinguish real, live creatures from the Audio-Animatronic critters in Disney theme parks or the CGI monsters at the multiplex—cartoon caricatures of our lovable foibles or primordial fears.

The cautionary tales in *Deadly Kingdom* bear that out. With grim relish, Grice tells of a toddler "whose mother smeared his hand with honey so that she could shoot video of him playing with a black bear. It ate his hand."[7] (That's a Grice signature: the devastating punch line—a short, sharp, declarative sentence that serves as a kind of a rim shot.)

We learn that a grizzly can fit a human head into its mouth: "If the person is lucky, the skull slides out like a pinched marble."[8] (Like his noir forebear, Raymond Chandler, Grice has a nice way with the simile.)

The author eyes the common housecat thoughtfully, noting the innocent sadism of the little "death games" it plays with its half-dead prey. His own cat bites him gently, using its carnassial teeth ("a narrow little mountain range meant for shearing meat") to leave a circlet of blood on Grice's finger. "I pushed the cat away and accused him of treachery. He only looked at me with his bright butterscotch eyes."[9]

The bigger cats, such as the lion ("one of the planet's premier predators of human beings"), are less gentle; one of Grice's sources mentions a lion that, "finding a man lying drunk outside a hut, merely nipped a chunk out of his behind, rather as you might take a passing bite from an apple and leave the rest."[10] Grice, who to this atheist's eye exhibits the telltale cynicism of the unbeliever, seems to delight especially in horror stories that serve as courtroom exhibits in the case against God: "In 2006, a visitor to the Kiev zoo proclaimed, 'God will save me, if he exists,' and entered the lion enclosure, where a lioness instantly sliced his carotid artery."[11] Ba-*dump.*

On the subject of nature's "motiveless evil," as Grice calls it, he recounts Jane Goodall's horror at seeing hyenas eating a live wildebeest, "which continued to bawl while the hyenas brawled with each other, 'running off with pieces of gut, giggling.'"[12] Readers who regard the hyena as the skulking, cowardly carrion-feeder of Disney's *Lion King* will be surprised to learn that the animals are ferocious predators who've taken down hippos, rhinos, and even lions (when the outcome is ensured by a four-to-one advantage). They may well have the most powerful jaws of all mammals; Grice cites a horrific description, in James Frederick Clarke's unforgettably named *Man Is the Prey*, of an unfortunate whose face ended just below his cheekbones, sheared off by "one bite, just one snap" from a hyena.[13]

But the world's most fearsome predator is unquestionably the orca, says Grice. Attaining lengths of thirty feet and weighing up to seven tons, these awesome animals have ganged up on the mythic great white shark, one orca holding it at the ocean's surface while another "disemboweled it, feasting on its liver."[14]

Yet, Grice notes, "despite their long-standing reputation as man-eaters, there are no clear-cut cases of orcas preying on people. There are, however, many cases of captive orcas hurting their trainers."[15] He tells the 1991 story of a trainer in British Columbia who fell into a pool:

> One orca seized her in his mouth and raced around the pool underwater. Two other orcas joined in foiling her attempts to escape. Her colleagues threw in a life ring, but the whales prevented them from pulling the young woman out. She reached the side of the pool, but was dragged back down. The whales played a macabre game of catch with her body; they may have regarded her as a toy tossed in for their amusement. It was only hours later that they allowed the other trainers to remove her corpse.[16]

A heart-wrenching tragedy, to be sure. But the unnatural acts of wild animals penned up in zoos, or forced to perform in theme parks and stage acts, or treated like family in people's homes is a recurrent theme in *Deadly Kingdom*. We love nature best when it plays the romantic Other to human culture, just wild enough to remind us how far we've come from the primordial soup, but still respectful of the bullwhip, a contract that reaffirms our status as the apple of God's eye and the only primate with predator drones. Walt Disney, the man whose name is synonymous with talking animals, robotic wildlife, and the theme-parking of the forest primeval, once remarked without a hint of irony: "I don't like formal gardens. I like wild nature. It's just the wilderness instinct in me, I guess."[17]

We dream of being part of an Edenic order where the lion lies down with the lamb: the paradise regained of *Born Free, Free Willy,* and moldy Disney chestnuts like *Charlie, the Lonesome Cougar.* Yet we insist, simultaneously, that we're *not* animals; rather, we're above nature, closer to God, at just the right altitude for aerial wolf gunning.

Oddly, the mass imagination teems with animals: the articulate beasts who serve as human surrogates, lampooning our weaknesses and personifying our virtues, in the picture books, cartoons, and theme parks that shape our cultural consciousness from infancy. Likewise, in everyday life, we use wild things—the boa constrictor draped around the goth's neck or the tarantula squatting on her palm; the pit bull clearing the sidewalk for the middle-class wangsta or his gang-banging inner-city counterpart—as tribal totems or Advertisements for Ourselves, broadcasting our uniqueness in a look-alike, think-alike world.

But as Grice makes clear, anthropomorphism, and its philosophical twin anthropocentricity, can cost us dearly.

Sandra Herold, the seventy-one-year-old widow who lived alone with Travis the Chimp, believed he "couldn't have been more my son ... if I gave birth to him."[18] Travis enjoyed honorary *Homo sapiens* status in his hometown of Stamford, Connecticut ("He was small and cute and friendly," a local cop remembered, "he'd wave at you"), and at home with Herold, where he "lived like a human, eating steak and drinking wine" and sleeping (and bathing!) with his owner ... until the day he ran amok, attacking a longtime friend of Herold and gnawing her face to an eyeless, noseless pulp.[19] Experts quoted in media coverage wondered if Lyme disease or a dose of Xanax had triggered Travis's rampage. According to Grice, such explanations turn a blind eye on the answer hidden in plain sight: although we insist on viewing chimpanzees as midgets in fur suits, wearing nature's mask to mock us, they are, in fact, wild animals. They may star in commercials, eat ice cream, and use the toilet, as Herold's "son" did, but male chimps like Travis are born to battle their way to the top of dominance hierarchies: they're five times as strong as a man ("one captive chimp weighing about 160 pounds lifted an 1,800-pound object," Grice notes), with impressive canines, designed to break bone and flense meat.[20] Travis's attack was perfectly "normal behavior for a captive primate," says Grice.[21] Again, the key word is *captive*. Forced into close encounters of the human kind, let alone cohabitation, animals can behave unnaturally.

Nash takes her place, in the public mind, alongside Dawn Brancheau, the SeaWorld orca trainer who was telling a crowd of tourists that the orca who'd just surfaced nearby simply wanted a belly rub ... when the animal snatched her in its jaws, dragged her into the pool, and held her underwater until she drowned.[22]

SeaWorld knew the animal in question had been implicated in two previous deaths. Surely, the theme park, notorious among animal-rights activists for wrapping its profit motive in the mantle of conservation, bears some measure of responsibility for putting its employee in harm's way.[23] More generally, our fatally naive insistence on mythologizing potentially deadly predators as frolicsome playmates, practical jokers, or poster children for nature's purer moral order is to blame as well. The stories retailed by animal theme parks like SeaWorld can have profound effects on kids' fantasy lives. According to a source quoted in one news story, Brancheau "had been inspired [to become a trainer] by a trip to SeaWorld when she was nine years old."[24]

Brancheau's sister, quoted in one news report, said the trainer "loved the whales like her children, she loved all of them. They all had personalities, good days and bad days."[25] Brancheau believed "you can't put yourself in the water unless you trust them and they trust you."[26] But who can know the orca mind? Do we divine its intentions by looking into its inscrutable eyes? By mistaking its rapacious maw for a good-natured grin? By reading the behavioral signs we think we've become fluent in, down through the years of putting a 12,000-pound beast through its paces for a clapping crowd of overweight bipeds? What does "trust" mean to an animal whose familiar name is "killer whale"? Or to any wild thing, for that matter? "Years of association may make a human being—even an experienced trainer—think of an animal as his loyal friend," writes Grice, in his chapter on the big cats. "Tigers don't seem to see things that way."[27] Brancheau may have loved the whale in question like a child, but the whale had a different view of their relationship, it turned out. Maybe he'd grown tired of performing and wanted to teach the irksome human who was top predator, at least in his element. Perhaps he was just playing. Or possibly he was just having a bad day. We'll never know, because orca consciousness is as mysterious to us as the deep blue sea.

Ask Timothy Treadwell about the primal darkness of the animal mind. Treadwell was a wannabe Bear Whisperer and self-appointed "eco-warrior" whose Me Generation journey of self-discovery took him into the wild, an odyssey chronicled in Werner Herzog's documentary Grizzly Man. An amateur naturalist who believed he'd bonded with the Alaskan grizzlies that he'd spent thirteen summers filming, sometimes at arm's length, Treadwell was repeatedly warned by the National Park Service that he was harassing the animals and, not incidentally, risking his life. He refused to protect himself with pepper spray and an electric fence around his campsite; too cruel, he contended.[28] "I'm in love with my animal friends! I'm in love with my animal friends!" he gushes, in one of the homemade videos excerpted in the Herzog film. "It's very emotional. . . . I'm so in love with them, and they're so fucked over, which so sucks."[29]

An aspiring Dian Fossey in a surfer-dude pageboy, Treadwell was to some a sweetly naive Nature Boy whose videos document an uncanny rapport with wild things. To others, he was a screw-loose tree hugger who chanted, "I love you, I love you" when approaching grizzlies, which he insisted were just "harmless party animals."[30]

In the Green Machine, there is no mercy: inevitably, a hungry bear, fattening up for the cold months ahead, devoured the "gentle warrior" and his girlfriend. Investigators took Treadwell's remains home in a garbage bag: his head, "a frozen grimace on his face," and his right arm, wristwatch still ticking.[31]

"A peculiar fallacy accompanies this urge to touch the wild: people feel, somehow, that nature will not hurt them because they are themselves approaching it with a kindred feeling," writes Grice.[32] This is the extravagant self-regard of the naked ape, convinced that all of creation smiles on him; that wild nature is his helpmate or playmate, buffoon or bogeyman, raw resource for capitalist exploitation or metaphoric mirror, in which he can see himself and his society more clearly. As *Deadly Kingdom* makes abundantly clear, that is cosmic presumptuousness, a sometimes fatal narcissism.

In his last letter to one of his financial supporters, Treadwell wrote, "My transformation complete—a fully accepted wild animal— brother to these bears. I run free among them—with absolute love and respect for all the animals."[33] There's a name for this delusion (I just made it up): Dolittle by proxy. The truth, some biologists maintain, is that Treadwell escaped mauling for thirteen summers not because he'd mastered interspecies telepathy, but because wild bears prefer not to tangle with humans, and are long-sufferingly tolerant.

Treadwell's undoing was his all-too-human assumption that to be a "fully accepted wild animal" is to be profoundly empathic, radiating love and respect in every direction. As it happens, the creature in question, the brown bear, has a different opinion in the matter, operating "on the principle of social dominance determined by intimidation and brute force," says Grice. "This is why playing dead sometimes works with brown bears: the bear has no need to further dominate a dead or utterly submissive opponent. Even screaming while being mauled may encourage the bear to continue an attack."[34]

Some experts believe this is precisely what happened. On the audio track of a videotape taken from a camera that was running when Treadwell and his girlfriend were killed, Treadwell's girlfriend can be heard exhorting him to "play dead." Apparently, that didn't work: the screams of Treadwell's girlfriend, Amie Huguenard, fill the remainder of the tape. Larry Van Daele, a biologist with the Alaska Department of Fish and Game, believes that Treadwell may not have played dead long enough, inspiring the bear to return and finish him off; when Huguenard screamed in horror, the noise—which the animal may have interpreted as a "predator call," the cries of wounded prey—"may have prompted the bear to return and kill her."[35]

In his last seconds, as the bear's canines flensed the living flesh from his bones, did Treadwell realize that his transformation into man-bear was far from complete; that humans—tool-using, symbol-juggling primates that we are—have wandered too far from the garden to ever be wild again?

In his voice-over to *Grizzly Man,* Werner Herzog is thoughtful on the subject of our imagined kinship with our wild brothers:

> What haunts me is that in all the faces of all the bears that Treadwell ever filmed, I discover no kinship, no understanding, no mercy. I see only the overwhelming indifference of nature. To me, there is no such thing as a secret world of the bears. And this blank stare speaks only of a half-bored interest in food. But for Timothy Treadwell, this bear was a friend, a savior. I believe the common character of the universe is not harmony, but chaos, hostility, and murder.[36]

To err is human; to murder, with blank-eyed indifference, ursine.

(2010)

Toe *Fou*

HEAVY-BREATHING DEVOTEES OF SUBLIMINAL SEDUCTION, START your engines.

Is that an unnaturally well-hung big toe Madonna is sporting in her 2005 ad for Versace? Or an ordinary digit, digitally inflated to Jeff Stryker proportions? Or am I just having my own clam-plate orgy here?[1]

Maybe so, but toe cleavage is at least subliminally erotic, alluding (if you squint hard enough) to butt crack, crotch, and décolletage, all at once. The phallic big toe only adds to the polymorphous perversity. Of course, foot fetishism is as old as the Golden Lotus (brought to you in the eleventh century by Chinese foot binders)[2] and as recent as Geoff Nicholson's *Footsucker* (a novel about an obsessive whose swoony description of a pair of plaster feet—"They were perfect, of course; as pale and pure and cold as vellum"—could easily be a description of Madonna's alabaster feet).[3]

The big toe has a venerable history as a penile surrogate or substitute nipple, from the actress Lya Lys slurping rapturously on a statue's toe in Luis Buñuel's *L'Age d'Or* (1930) to Dr. Alex Comfort's funny-creepy paeans in *The Joy of Sex* (1972), in which the good doctor informs that "the pad of the male big toe applied to the clitoris or the vulva generally is a magnificent erotic instrument."[4] (The other shoe drops when one learns that Comfort was missing four fingers on his left hand, blown off while he was playing with explosives as

Madonna for Versace, 2005.

a kid. At '70s swingers clubs such as Sandstone Retreat, near Malibu, he needed all the appendages he could muster. Thus self-serving advice such as: The "gentleman who is keeping six women occupied . . . using tongue, penis, both hands and both big toes" should take care to keep his toenails clipped.)[5]

In the Versace ad noted above, part of a campaign that debuted in women's magazines in 2005, Madonna lazes on a daybed, nibbling a pen with slow-burning, bedroom-eyed sexiness. (Never has the phrase "pencil-licker" sounded so lubricious. Where's that *Truth or Dare* Coke bottle when you need it?) But the picture's composition guides our gaze from that suggestive pen, along the cord between her breasts, to the chain tossed across her crotch, and ultimately to that immaculately pale foot, with its weirdly prehensile toe.

Of all fetishes, podophilia has long been synonymous with clammy, bottom-feeder perversity. Doubtless, the unspoken taboo on foot fondling, sucking, and *(insert your worst nightmare here)* has something to do with the squicky nature of the human foot, before the advent of the pedicure, the Odor-Eater, and Dr. Scholl's Fungal

Nail Revitalizer. As the surrealist philosopher Georges Bataille wrote, in his wonderfully over-the-top essay "Big Toe":

> The human foot is commonly subjected to grotesque tortures that deform it and make it rachitic. It is stupidly consecrated to corns, calluses, and bunions, and if one takes into account turns of phrase that are only now disappearing, to the most loathsome filthiness: the peasant expression "her hands are as dirty as feet," is no longer as true of the entire human collectivity as it was in the seventeenth century.[6]

But beyond the obviously yucky (and possibly risky) nature of podophilia in premodern times (Our Savior's thing for foot washing notwithstanding), feet are inherently grotesque. We may have our heads in the clouds, straining toward godhood, but we're standing in shit, as Bataille points out. In the hierarchy of the body, the head is the sovereign, seat of the self; the feet are mere peons (from the medieval Latin *pes,* for "foot"). The foot, Bataille theorizes, is base, in both senses of the word. (Does this explain the ubiquity of hard-core porn, on the Web, in which people perform unimaginably bizarre acts *with their socks on?*) "Though the most noble of animals," writes Bataille, man "nevertheless . . . has feet, and these feet lead an ignoble life, completely independent from him."[7] Toes, for Bataille, are the worst: freakish parodies of fingers, creeping things that creepeth upon the earth. What *are* they doing down there, anyway, pale as grubs, wriggling wormlike into the earth?

The gothic photos accompanying his essay on the big toe in *Encyclopaedia Acephalica*—blurry, nocturnal images that look like something out of a crime-scene investigation manual or an Atom Age horror film—say it all: *Jeepers, peepers, where'd you get those creepers?!?*

"Fingers have come to signify useful action and firm character, the toes stupefaction and base idiocy," writes Bataille.[8] Long, thin fingers are shorthand for mental dexterity; in Conan Doyle's Sherlock Holmes story "The Red-Headed League," the brilliant detective relaxes, after a long day of ratiocination, at the symphony, "gently waving his long, thin fingers in time to the music"); likewise, in the Holmes novella *The Hound of the Baskervilles,* a character's keen intellect is evinced by "long, quivering fingers, as agile and restless as the antennae of an insect."[9] By contrast, stubby, simian fingers are a social Darwinist's evidence of atavistic imbecility; if toes evoke "base idiocy," then fingers resembling toes are proof positive of mental deformity.

The nineteenth-century pseudoscience of chirognomy purported to deduce the intellectual capacity and even moral character of a man from the shape of his hands: Elemental, Square, Spatulate, Mixed, Philosophic, Psychic, or Artistic. Thick-palmed, squat-fingered Elementary hands offered evolutionary evidence of limited intelligence, marking the owner as hereditarily unfit for the skilled professions. The gothic fiction of the day embodied social Darwinian anxieties about racial degeneration: Mr. Hyde, Dr. Jeckyll's bestial alter ego in *The Strange Case of Dr. Jeckyll and Mr. Hyde*, has "corded, knuckly" hands, "of a dusky pallor, and thickly shaded with a swart growth of hair," in marked contrast to Dr. Jeckyll's "large, firm, white, and comely" hands, "professional in shape and size."[10] Likewise, in *Dracula*, the Slavic count's hands are "broad, with squat fingers"; lower down the evolutionary ladder from Hyde, Dracula has hairy *palms*, even.[11] Here, Stevenson and Stoker evoke the Victorian eugenicist Francis Galton's belief that brachydactylic (stumpy-fingered) hands were a sure sign of mental deficiency.

Such associations, maintains Bataille, are why "classic foot fetishism leading to the licking of toes" is condemned by official culture as "a base seduction," a grotesque burlesque of "normal" sex.[12] And the big toe, he insists, is the ghastliest of these appendages, with its "hideously cadaverous and at the same time loud and defiant appearance."[13]

So what does Madonna's big toe *mean*, exactly? Well, sex, not to put too fine a point on it. According to the *New York Post*'s "Page Six," Madonna wanted Mario Testino's photos for the Versace ads to be "provocative and sexy," flaunting "how good she looks at 46." Groping for deeper meaning, we remember that Madonna is a lapsed Catholic, so maybe Anthony N. Fragola can shed a little light in his essay "From the Ecclesiastical to the Profane: Foot Fetishism in Luis

Buñuel and Alain Robbe-Grillet": "Buñuel believes that sexual compulsions and deviations originate from the repressive teaching of Catholicism that equates sex with guilt," he notes.[14] *L'Age d'Or* is the cinematic equivalent of the thirty-nine lashes, administered with relish by an ex-Catholic who devoted his creative life to scourging the church as well as the unblinking, ruminant herd that fills its pews. The movie is Buñuel's mordantly anti-Catholic ode to *l'amour fou* ("mad love"), the libidinous frenzy the surrealists prescribed as shock treatment for repressed, repressive bourgeois society; the infamous toe-sucking scene, still crazy after all these years, is its centerpiece.

Is Madonna using Versace's ad to do some covert signifying of her own, playing footsie with podophilia as a papa-don't-preach retort to the Vatican, which recently issued a maledictum decrying New Age spirituality, Eastern mysticism, and the "Kabbalah as espoused by Madonna"?[15] To be sure, she's no stranger to anti-Catholic sacrilege or market-tested outrage, calculated to ruffle Letterman's forelock. Besides, wasn't she sucking somebody's toe in that scene with the skinheads in *Sex*, the book that made Helmut Newton safe for heartland America? And isn't that her slurping away at Tony Ward's foot on the back cover of her record *Erotica*?

Or is she signaling her gay fandom, with her big toe, that she's still the Phallic Mother of their mirror-ball dreams? Or is she simply making manifest the latent content of the Versace aesthetic, which combines the tasteful understatement of Caesar's Palace in Vegas with the rectitude of Caligulan Rome? In *Fetish: Fashion, Sex, and Power*, Valerie Steele asserts that Versace and other, like-minded designers "frequently copy 'the style, if not the spirit, of fetishism.'... To understand contemporary fashion, it is crucial to explore fetishism."[16]

Steele links the boundary-pushing edginess of couture to sexual perversions, which are simultaneously manifestations of late-night psychological cravings *and* acts of symbolic rebellion "against the subjugation of sexuality under the order of procreation and against the institutions which guarantee this order."[17] Fashion, the ultimate commodity fetish, exists in the context of a consumer culture that is at once hedonistic and puritanical. Pushing manufactured desires and peddling instant gratification, consumer culture is at the same time deeply phobic about sexual difference and deviant desires—"mad love" whose unorthodox urges, "unproductive" (in every sense), refuse to be channeled into more profitable outlets, such as blowing one's wad at the local megamall.

Ironically, fetish fashion is itself the instrument of what Marcuse called "repressive desublimation," his term for the socially sanctioned expression of radical impulses that might assume a more genuinely political shape if not harmlessly acted out in the pleasure dungeon. In that sense, Madonna and Versace are perfect together: in order to stroke their fan bases yet play in the arena of mass culture, both need to negotiate the perilous strait of boho perversity and upper-class power; dominatrix and, respectively, Eurotrash jet-setter (Donatella Versace) or domestic diva (Madonna). Madonna wants it both ways: she wants to be the author of children's books with titles like *Mr. Peabody's Apples* (*do not* even go there); the supremely capable mistress of the *Upstairs, Downstairs* manor who told *CBS Early Show* interviewer Harry Smith, "I get up in the morning with my kids . . . and then they go off to school, and I stay home and I become a sergeant in my house and . . . start going through the lists that have been made by my hardworking, diligent staff and start delegating responsibility"; the paragon of good breeding who confided to Cynthia McFadden of ABC's 20/20 that "even my children have to clean up their mess, clean their rooms, manners, thank you, pick up your dishes, gratitude, being grateful—that has to happen."[18] But between impersonations of a mockney Martha Stewart, she still needs to play tonsil hockey with Britney Spears on TV, now and again, in order to justify the love of the core fandom that cherishes its memories of her more salacious days. Fetishistic yet boomer-friendly, elegant but a little bit bodacious, the Versace sandal is just the thing for the Desperate Housewife who was once a Boy Toy.

If the shoe fits, wear it.

(2005)

Shoah Business

THERE'S NO BUSINESS LIKE SHOAH BUSINESS, TO BORROW THE Jewish historian Yaffa Eliach's mordant one-liner.[1] In *Selling the Holocaust,* Tim Cole's critique of the branding and blockbustering of the unspeakable, the historian argues that "at the end of the Twentieth Century, the 'Holocaust' is being consumed."[2] (No denier he, Cole frames the term in quotes to distinguish between the Holocaust as conjured for the mass market, in movies like *Schindler's List* and museums like the Holocaust Memorial Museum in Washington, D.C., and the historical reality of the Shoah—the assembly-line murder of millions at the hands of the Nazis, a horror so awful it beggars description, defies representation.)

Evidence that the Holocaust is being trivialized, merchandised, and, through feel-good Hollywood confections and theme-parked museums, Americanized, is all around us. The revisionist happy endings of Roberto Benigni's movie *Life Is Beautiful* and the Robin Williams vehicle *Jakob the Liar* domesticate the Holocaust, deodorize the memory of its poison gas and its open-pit graves. There are Holocaust-related toys, lit lite, postcards, and games. Holocaust museums do a brisk business, and death-camp tourism is a common feature of the Grand Tour for Jews and Gentiles alike. "Each year," writes Cole, "tourists flock [to] Auschwitz, Anne Frank House, [the Israeli Holocaust museum and memorial] Yad Vashem, the museums in Washington, D.C., Dallas, Houston."[3] In museum gift shops, visitors can buy mementos, from pins trumpeting the trademark-ready catchphrase

"Never Again" to postcards (to send to friends, Cole speculates, "with the message 'Wish you were here'").[4]

To the truly cynical, the "Holocaust"—again, the cultural icon, not the historical event—is, in the words of essayist Phillip Lopate, "a corporation headed by Elie Wiesel, who defends his patents with articles in the 'Arts and Leisure' section of the *Sunday Times*" while competing franchises like Yad Vashem and the Holocaust Memorial Museum fight for the remaining market share.[5]

Readers outraged by Lopate's temerity in questioning Wiesel's official role as brand manager of the Holocaust are well advised to give Norman G. Finkelstein's controversial study *The Holocaust Industry* a wide berth. The son of Holocaust survivors *and* a pointed critic of Israel's treatment of the Palestinians, Finkelstein excoriates Wiesel for "his silence on Palestinian suffering" and his "shameful record of apologetics on behalf of Israel."[6] Wiesel has been anointed "official interpreter of the Holocaust" not because he is the medium through which six million dead souls speak, as his devotees would have us believe, but because "he unerringly articulates the dogmas of, and accordingly sustains the interests underpinning, the Holocaust."[7] And what are those interests?

> "The Holocaust" is an ideological representation of the Nazi holocaust. . . . Its central dogmas sustain significant political and class interests. Indeed, the Holocaust has proven to be an indispensable ideological weapon. Through its deployment, one of the world's most formidable military powers, with a horrendous human rights record, has cast itself as a "victim" state, and the most successful ethnic group in the United States has likewise acquired victim status. Considerable dividends accrue from this specious victimhood—in particular, immunity to criticism, however justified. . . .
> . . . [The Holocaust] has been used to justify criminal policies of the Israeli state and U.S. support for these policies.[8]

Unsurprisingly, Finkelstein regards the United States Holocaust Memorial Museum with a critical eye. Questioning the ideological spin he believes it gives historical events, Finkelstein calls the museum to account for neglecting to mention the eagerness with which the

United States absorbed Nazi war criminals into its military-indus-trial complex, after the war. As well, he interrogates the politics of the museum's decision to focus overwhelmingly on the extermination of the Jews, making only passing mention of victims such as the Gypsies (who suffered "proportional losses roughly equal to the Jewish geno-cide") for fear that would mean "the loss of an exclusive Jewish fran-chise over the Holocaust, with a commensurate loss of Jewish 'moral capital.'"[9] Finally, he contends, the museum subtly argues Israel's case in the Israel–Palestine conflict, using its exhibits to teach "the Zion-ist lesson that Israel was the 'appropriate answer to Nazism' with the closing scenes of Jewish survivors struggling to enter Palestine."[10] In short, Finkelstein argues, we consume more than historical fact when we visit the Holocaust Memorial Museum: we consume spectacle spiked with ideology, as well.

Cole extends Finkelstein's argument to all Holocaust museums, focusing on the commercial exploitation of what has been called "dark tourism": "When in Washington, D.C., we 'consume' the 'Holo-caust' on offer at the United States Holocaust Memorial Museum . . . and when in Kraków we 'consume' the 'Holocaust' on offer at the State Museum at Auschwitz."[11]

More than half a century after the Nazis industrialized genocide, the theme-parking and gift-shopping of the inferno is well under way; at times, it seems as if the Holocaust is becoming an Atrocity Exhibition. The Auschwitz imagined by the State Museum collapses the complex wartime network of forty satellite camps and three main ones into a single, mythic netherworld of night and fog, haunted by the million dead. The guided tour of Hell begins at the infamous gate whose abandon-all-hope-ye-who-enter-here greeting, "Arbeit macht frei" (Work will set you free), is a fixture in our collective nightmares—despite the fact that "very few of the Jews deported to Auschwitz ever saw that gate," according to the authors of *Auschwitz: 1270 to the Present.*[12] The tour's somber terminus, carefully orches-trated for maximum effect, comes when visitors arrive at the crema-torium. Guides don't trouble them with the anticlimactic truth that the actual site of the mass murders lies two miles away, in ruins; the

Sign near train station for Auschwitz–Birkenau Memorial and State Museum.
Photograph by Julie Dermansky. Copyright Julie Dermansky; all rights reserved.

scene of their solemn communion is in fact a postwar reconstruction, equipped with a portentous chimney whose function is purely (if powerfully) symbolic, since it isn't connected to the ovens.

The State Museum, which Cole somewhat flippantly calls "Auschwitz-land," is "a contrived tourist attraction," in his eyes, a historical revision that effaces the past in the name of enshrining it.[13] Of course, this is the Faustian bargain struck by *all* museums in the business of stage-managing historical memory. "In constructing a mythical 'Auschwitz,'" Cole asserts, "we distort the horrific reality of Auschwitz, and in its place create an 'Auschwitz' which is open to the attack of those who would deny that the Holocaust ever took place. Representing the complexities of the past in a ghoulish theme park for the present has consequences."[14]

One of those consequences is the evisceration of history in a made-for-TV world where the past is increasingly experienced as a whirl of free-floating images, cut loose from historical context and cultural complexity. It's instructive, for example, that many take *Schindler's*

Victims' shoes, Auschwitz–Birkenau Memorial and State Museum. Photograph by Julie Dermansky. Copyright Julie Dermansky; all rights reserved.

List as a historical newsreel, not a Spielberg vision of a Holocaust with a Happy Ending. In a moment made to order for grad-school seminars on postmodernism, tourists on "*Schindler's List* tours" of the Kraków ghetto where the movie was set were taken to locations where scenes were filmed, rather than sites where the Holocaust actually happened.[15]

It's a postmodern truism that representations—photos, moving images, digital renderings, theme-park simulations—are displacing immediate experience and historical memory. Part of the psychological fallout of the virtualization of reality is the "death of affect," which J. G. Ballard called "the most terrifying casualty of the twentieth century"—a psychic numbness that cultural commentators from Camus to McLuhan have argued is a salient characteristic of our media-bombarded, hyperstimulated culture.[16] Fredric Jameson, the Marxist cultural theorist who literally wrote the book on post-modernism (titled, oddly, *Postmodernism*), sees this "waning of affect" as symptomatic of a culture that transforms everything it touches into disembodied image, especially in the case of celebrities, who are "commodified and transformed into their own images."[17] A product of our disengagement from immediate experience, this emotional depthlessness is personified by the heavy-metalhead who wandered around Auschwitz wearing a "Megadeth" T-shirt, or the grandfatherly Auschwitz visitor overheard asking his companions if there'd be time for shopping after their scenic tour of the charnel house.[18]

Elegies for depth psychology and Cole's grim foreboding that the "'tourist Auschwitz' threatens to trivialize the past, domesticate the past, and ultimately jettison the past altogether" come together in the gut-lurching video installation "At Auschwitz," which ran in the Hebrew Union College–Jewish Institute of Religion Museum in Manhattan from September 1999 through February 2000. Created by the Jewish artist Julie Dermansky and the Austrian filmmaker Georg Steinboeck, the work consists primarily of a dozen video monitors playing loops of people eating in the museum cafeteria, shoveling in steam-table glop as if it's their last meal. "At Auschwitz" literalizes the queasy notion of consumption amid the crematoria.

A bearded young man mechanically slurps up spoonful after spoonful of soup, barely pausing for breath; a grotesquely fat man chews obscenely, wattles quivering; a beady-eyed, hawk-nosed young man glances about nervously, as if worried that someone will snatch his food off his plate. It seems doubtful, somehow, that even the knowledge that they're eating in what was once the camp's processing center would spoil their appetites.

In the unmarked, anonymous building that now houses the cafeteria, newly arrived inmates were registered, robbed, tattooed, shaved, disinfected, and dressed in the familiar striped pajamas—transformed from *Mensch* to *Untermensch* in what the authors of *Auschwitz: 1270 to the Present* memorably call a "humiliating baptism into the kingdom of death."[19]

In their artists' statement, Dermansky and Steinboeck write, "Auschwitz represents the inhumanity human beings are capable of. People eating in the cafeteria reveal how insensitive mankind is to its own history. Or perhaps we missed something, and walking through the grounds at the museum really does give one an appetite, as would touring the grounds of a theme park."[20]

Watching their videos, we wonder what sort of human can eat lunch in a death camp. Or are they human? They seem to have stepped out of a sick-funny sitcom dreamed up by George Grosz and Mel Brooks. From our vantage point on the moral high ground, they're reminiscent of the SS physician who wrote in a 1942 diary entry that after a hard day's work of sending innocent men, women, and children to the gas chamber, he sat down to a "truly festive meal" of "baked pike, as much as we wanted, real coffee, excellent beer, and sandwiches."[21] What sort of monster works up an appetite in a hellworld of living skeletons, where the smoke and stench of burning bodies reaches to heaven? The tourists stuffing their faces in "At Auschwitz" are similarly swinish, perhaps even soulless—"useless eaters," we think.

That is, until we remember, with a jolt, the origin of that pungent expression: Hitler's pet phrase for the "subhumanity" fit only for the chimneys of death factories like Auschwitz. In a creepy, deeply disorienting turnaround, we suddenly find ourselves face-to-face with our inner Nazis, the side of us that reassures us that the difference between us and the unfeeling creatures chowing down in a death-camp cafeteria is that they are somehow less than human.

(1999)

The Triumph of the Shill

ON JANUARY 13, 2005, THE WORLD LEARNED THAT ENGLAND'S irrepressible Prince Harry had pulled another madcap stunt: attending a costume party for A-listers dressed in Desert Fox drag (the Afrika Korps uniform worn by Field Marshal Erwin Rommel, topped off with a swastika armband).

The vultures of Fleet Street descended in the usual Hitchcockian frenzy. A flurry of buzzwords, the raucous cawing of columnists fighting over the juiciest morsel, and then they were gone, leaving nothing but a bloody tuft of carrottop and another damage-control migraine for the royals . . .

Now that the carrion-feeders have fled, the Department of Hitler Studies (chairman emeritus: Jack Gladney) wonders about the deeper meanings of this whole foofaraw.[1] (Or is it a kerfuffle? Who the hell knows?) To begin, who hacked Harry's *Hakenkreuz*? The swastika on his armband isn't historically accurate. Did the costume manufacturer attempt to inoculate partygoers against public outrage by defanging the infamous icon, substituting stubbier versions of the longer, more symmetrical arms that Hitler, with his eye for graphic design, had insisted on?

Failed postcard painter, architect of megabuildings never to be built, Hitler deserves his due, however much it pains us, as an intuitive master of what marketing professor Douglas B. Holt calls "cultural branding."[2] In *Mein Kampf,* the leader of Team Nazi recalls his struggle to build the perfect logo:

I myself, meanwhile, after innumerable attempts, had laid down a final form: a flag with a red background, a white disk, and a black swastika in the middle. After long trials, I also found a definite proportion between the size of the flag and the size of the white disk, as well as the shape and thickness of the swastika.[3]

According to the design critic Rick Poynor, Nazi iconography such as the swastika

engages us not only because of what it represents to the popular mind— the specter of absolute evil—but because it does so with a stylish command of imagery that has never been surpassed. The devil has the best tunes and the Nazis have the best uniforms, insignia, and banners, and a "logo," the swastika, of incomparable power. (No wonder books on corporate identity can never resist including it; next thing you know, they'll be calling it a "brand.")[4]

Sontag reflects on the power of Nazi style in her essay "Fascinating Fascism," meditating on the SS uniform's reincarnation as the formal attire of S/M devotees with a weakness for the louche:

Photographs of SS uniforms are the units of a particularly powerful and widespread sexual fantasy. Why the SS? Because the SS was the ideal incarnation of fascism's overt assertion of the righteousness of violence, the right to have total power over others and to treat them as absolutely inferior. It was in the SS that this assertion seemed most complete, because they acted it out in a singularly brutal and efficient manner; and because they dramatized it by linking themselves to certain aesthetic standards. The SS was designed as an elite military community that would be not only supremely violent but also supremely beautiful....

 SS uniforms were stylish, well-cut, with a touch (but not too much) of eccentricity. Compare the rather boring and not very well cut American army uniform: jacket, shirt, tie, pants, socks, and lace-up shoes—essentially civilian clothes no matter how bedecked with medals and badges.[5]

Hitler lived before the Triumph of the Shill—before branding and marketing had infiltrated everything from business to politics to the presentation of self, in the turbo-capitalist West. But if he had survived, we might easily imagine him at home in a cultural climate where anxious middle managers consult books such as *A New Brand World: Eight Principles for Achieving Brand Leadership in the Twenty-first Century* by Scott Bedbury or the ominously titled *Culting of Brands: When Customers Become True Believers* by Douglas Atkin, or the suitably dictatorial *Power of Cult Branding: How Nine Magnetic Brands Turned Customers into Loyal Followers* by Matthew W. Ragas, or *How Brands Become Icons: The Principles of Cultural Branding* by Douglas B. Holt. (No mention of the swastika in Holt's book, although he does tell us that "Coke celebrated America's triumphs against Nazi Germany in World War II," and that Volkswagen had a persistent image problem due to its origins as the German "people's car," developed by Hitler.)[6] As the design critic Steven Heller argues in his book *Iron Fists: Branding the Twentieth-Century Totalitarian State*, Hitler, like it or not, had an intuitive grasp of the semiotics of power, evidenced not only in his appropriation of the swastika and rebranding of the ragtag National Socialist movement, but in his racist stereotyping (Heller calls it "branding demonization") of the German Jews and, ultimately, in the forced tattooing that marked death-camp inmates for slaughter—branding in the most horrifically literal sense. "Twenty years before Madison Avenue embarked upon 'Motivational Research,'" Aldous Huxley observed, in 1958, "Hitler was systematically exploring and exploiting the secret fears and hopes, the cravings, anxieties and frustrations of the German masses."[7]

Hitler's demonic talent for graphic branding reminds us of Walt Disney, the mediocre cartoonist and self-described benign dictator of the Happiest Place on Earth, whose iconic mouse ears and branded signature (not his own; the company designed it, and he learned to forge it) are as instantly recognizable as the swastika (and, in some quarters, nearly as feared). We think of the Great Dictator's childish delight in Disney cartoons and his unsettling habit of whistling "Who's Afraid of the Big, Bad Wolf?" (Hitler nicknamed himself "Wolf") as he lurched through the corridors of the *Führerbunker*, a cadaverous apparition sustained by drugs, while the Russian tanks rolled overhead.[8] We think, too, of both men's iconic moustaches, and of the persistent rumors that They Saved Hitler's Brain and They Froze Walt's Body.

We think of Disney's collaboration with recovering Nazi scientist Werner von Braun on TV shows and Tomorrowland. Less glibly, and far more damningly, we think of the noxious anti-Semitism tactfully omitted from Walt's official biography (but helpfully included in *Disney's World* by Leonard Mosely): "It's the century of the Jew, the union cutthroat, the fag, and the whore!," the Magic Kingdom's Führer once spluttered, in one of his less avuncular moments. "And FDR and his National Labor Relations Board made it so!"[9] Then, too, there's Disney's unbecoming fondness for National Socialism: According to *Walt Disney: Hollywood's Dark Prince* by Marc Elliot, Everybody's Favorite Mausketeer attended American Nazi Party rallies and visited Mussolini at his private villa. And then we think of Dr. Hibbert's observation, in the *Simpsons* episode "The Boy Who Knew Too Much," that Hitler, Walt Disney, and Freddy Quimby all had the "evil gene." And then we wonder about the blogger Alien Jesus Command's suggestion that Disney imagineers reimagineer the recently excavated *Führerbunker*, in Berlin, into a new EuroDisney attraction. And then we find ourselves scanning "Some Signs You Are a Disney Nazi" at the "Disney, Hoover, and Reno" page, an exercise in crackpot hermeneutics that in pre-Web times would have been scrawled in Magic Marker and stapled to telephone poles. The telltale signs include "unwavering devotion to all things Disney," "disbelief of anything anti-Disney," "obsession with Disney memorabilia," and "obedient faith in every Disney employee."[10]

At this point, we realize that while a frenzy of intertextuality is the mother of deconstruction (or something like that), it is also the first step down the slippery slope that leads to conspiracy theory. We should heed the warning of Casaubon, the demented exegete in *Foucault's Pendulum* by Umberto Eco: "Wanting connections, we found connections—always, everywhere, and between everything. The world exploded in a whirling network of kinships, where everything pointed to everything else, everything explained everything else."[11]

Deep breath. Where were we, before we went off on that discursive tear about Hitler and Disneyland's Dark Prince? Right, Prince Harry, and his unfortunate choice of the swastika as fashion accessory.

While we at the Department of Hitler Studies can understand the moral recoil from Prince Harry's yobbish insensitivity, we can't fathom the shock expressed in some quarters. Isn't the little Anus Horribilis's act of monumental insensitivity part and parcel of the royals' highborn disdain for the simple folk? What's the point of being in line for the throne if you're bound by the moral code that constrains the lesser ethers? Doesn't the appalling theme of the party His Royal Highness was attending—"Colonials and Natives," which might've seemed a waggish choice if you were sipping gin rickeys after shooting an elephant in Victorian India—speak volumes about the colonial consciousness of all of the realm's bluebloods? As the editors of the *London News Review* wrote in their tongue-in-cheek "Defense of the Idiot Prince," "'Colonials and Natives'? What the fuck are these people on? What century are they living in? Colonials and Natives? It beggars belief. Why not 'Imperialists and Nig Nogs'?"[12] Then, too, it's common knowledge that a genteel anti-Semitism has long been part of the aristocratic gene code in England. Ugly? Obviously. Unconscionable? No doubt. Uncommon? Hardly.

Jessica ("Decca") Mitford, an English blueblood, once referred to "the deep dyed anti-Semitism that pervades all England."[13] She knew whereof she spake: Her sister Diana married Sir Oswald Mosely, the blackshirted Adolf wannabe behind the British Union of Fascists, in a secret ceremony in Goebbels's apartment, with Hitler in attendance. To the end of her days, Diana remained a swastika girl at heart. In *The Sisters: The Saga of the Mitford Family,* Mary S. Lovell quotes Diana's remarks to a BBC interviewer in 1989. Hitler, she gushed, was "extraordinarily fascinating and clever. Naturally. You don't get to be where he was just by being the kind of person people like to think he was."[14] (Of course, those bullnecked SA goons, whose brass knuckles left beer-hall hecklers softmouthed, might have helped Clever Adolf along the road to power. But who are we to be critical?) Dina's charming sister Unity—whose middle name was Valkyrie and who was conceived in Swastika, Ontario (I'm not making this up)—was an enthusiastic Nazi, too. She thought it hilarious when the Nazi governor of Franconia, the virulent anti-Semite Julius Streicher, forced a group of Jews to mow a meadow—with their teeth. (Again, our source is Lovell's *The Sisters*.)

Like Mosely, the Mitfords were members of the privileged class, of which Prince Harry is the very flower. It's worth noting that Edward VIII (later the Duke of Windsor), Harry's great-great uncle, had a soft spot for the swastika as well, a point Christopher Hitchens bangs home in his pummeling of *The King's Speech*, an Anglophilic biopic about Edward's brother George VI. "[Edward] remained what is only lightly hinted in the film: a firm admirer of the Third Reich who took his honeymoon there with Mrs. Simpson and was photographed both receiving and giving the Hitler salute," notes Hitchens. "Of his few friends and cronies, the majority were Blackshirt activists.... During his sojourns on the European mainland after his abdication, the Duke of Windsor never ceased to maintain highly irresponsible contacts with Hitler and his puppets and seemed to be advertising his readiness to become a puppet or 'regent' if the tide went the other way."[15] For a believer in master races, the Duke was notoriously an intellectual *Untermensch*, though as Gore Vidal reports in his memoir *Palimpsest*, he managed to elevate vacuity to an art form: "David, as Wallis called him, always had something of such riveting stupidity to say on any subject that I clung to his words like the most avid courtier of the ancien régime."[16] Memorable stupidities include his heartfelt observation that Australian aboriginals are "the lowest known form of human beings and are the nearest thing to monkeys"; that blacks, "due to the peculiar mentality of [their] Race ... seem unable to rise to prominence without losing their equilibrium"; and, in the wake of a world war whose genocidal horrors still scald the imagination, the blithe aside that Hitler was not, after all, "such a bad chap."[17]

Of course, the English hold no copyright on anti-Semitism or fascist sympathies. Protocols of the Elders of Zion publisher and Hitler

campaign contributor Henry Ford, Nazi sympathist Charles Lind-
berg, and American Nazi Party founder George Lincoln Rockwell—
no relation to Norman—remind us that fascism's blood-and-soil
theology found fertile loam in the dank basement of the American
mind, as well. Let he who is without sin cast the first swastika. Still,
the English aristocracy's coy games of footsie with fascism are surely
relevant to any discussion of Prince Harry's indiscretions.

Not that a history lesson is necessary. We are shocked—shocked!—
to discover that the scion of a dynasty whose right to rule rests on the
assumption of genetic superiority failed the sensitivity test in decid-
ing whether or not to wear a Nazi uniform to a costume party. There's
a term for the worldview underlying all monarchies: social Darwinism. Little wonder, then, that the purebred product of one of Western
history's best-known (and, arguably, least successful) experiments in
controlled breeding should feel a sense of kinship, however unconscious, with the people who brought you racial hygiene on an apocalyptic scale. The trouble with Harry, of course, is that he committed the unthinkable indiscretion of exposing in public the birthmark
most manor-born *Übermenschen* keep hidden.

(2005)

100

On the Downfall Parodies
and the Inglorious Return of Der Führer

Endtime for Hitler

"HE WAS ON AGAIN LAST NIGHT," ELEVEN-YEAR-OLD DENISE tells her dad, Jack Gladney, in Don DeLillo's novel *White Noise.* "He" is Hitler; Gladney is a professor of Hitler studies, the academic discipline he founded, at the proverbially named College-on-the-Hill, somewhere out in a midwestern stretch of the Great Flyover.

"He's always on," says Gladney. "We couldn't have television without him."

"They lost the war," Denise fires back. "How great could they be?"

"A valid point. But it's not a question of greatness. It's not a question of good and evil. I don't know what it is."[1]

Good question. Why *does* Hitler's wild-eyed apparition keep materializing on History Channel episodes—and online, in homemade parodies that graft topical subtitles onto a scene from the 2004 movie *Downfall,* about Hitler's last days?

The easy answer is that Hitler left an inexhaustible fund of unforgettable images; Riefenstahl's *Triumph of the Will* alone is enough to make him a household deity of the TV age. The Third Reich was the first thoroughly modern totalitarian horror, scripted by Hitler and mass-marketed by Goebbels, a tour de force of media spectacle and opinion management that America's hidden persuaders—admen, P.R. flacks, political campaign managers—studied assiduously.

(Apparently, the admiration was mutual: the Nazis consulted Ivy Lee, a founding father of public relations in America, on spinning the

Reich's rearmament program. Lee's solution? Wrap it in "a plea for 'equality of rights' among nations" and sell it as "an effort at 'preventing for all time the return of the Communist peril.'"[2] As well, Goebbels was a careful reader of *Crystallizing Public Opinion*, Edward Bernays's 1923 bible of P.R. techniques. A pioneering figure in public relations, Bernays was the mastermind, on behalf of the exploitative, monopolistic United Fruit Company, of a propaganda effort that, with a little help from a CIA-backed "Liberation Army," helped overthrow the democratically elected president of Guatemala. Nonetheless, Bernays, who in a nice irony was an Austrian Jew and the nephew of Sigmund Freud, was shocked—*shocked!*—to discover, as he recalled in his autobiography, that the Nazi propaganda minister was using his ideas "as a basis for his destructive campaign against the Jews of Germany."[3])

A Mad Man in both senses, Hitler sold the German *volk* on a racially cleansed utopia, a thousand-year empire whose kitschy grandeur was strictly Forest Lawn Parthenon. Early on, when the Reich was just an evil gleam in his eye, he spent hours dreamily sketching uniforms and insignia; when it became a reality, he "directed great blocs of human beings against mighty stone backdrops and reveled in the exercise of his demi-talents as actor and architect," writes Joachim Fest, in his incomparable *Hitler*.[4] No mass-murdering dictator has so indelibly tattooed his image onto the mass unconscious, for the simple reason that Hitler, unlike Stalin or Mao, was an intuitive master of media stagecraft. David Bowie's too-clever quip, in a 1976 *Playboy* interview, that Hitler was the first rock star was spot-on (though Bowie was widely reviled for it at the time). Nearly every Hitler biography includes Heinrich Hoffmann's well-known series of photos of Adolf in his pre-Führer days, test-driving *verklempt* poses—clench-fisted, glittery-eyed attitudes he later reviewed, presumably adding the most emotionally charged (which is to say, photogenic) ones to his onstage repertoire. Looking at these images, we think: *An Actor Prepares.*

All of which is to say: the media like Hitler because Hitler liked the media. Although he remained, at heart, a nineteenth-century bourgeois wannabe—a "revolutionary against revolution," as he put it, desperate to drag industrial modernity back to the misty, Wagnerian premodernity where he spent much of his fantasy life—he prefigured the postmodern annexation of politics by Hollywood and Madison Avenue, the rise of the celebrity as a secular icon, the confusion of image and reality in a *Matrix* world. He regarded existence "as a kind of permanent parade before a gigantic audience," as Fest puts it, calculating the visual impact of every histrionic pose, every propaganda tagline, every monumental building (anticipating, even, the far-off time when his imperial capital would crumble into picturesque decay, its fluted columns wreathed in ivy, an eventuality foreseen by the Nazi starchitect Albert Speer in his "theory of ruin value").[5]

That said, is this why the parodic video remixes of *Downfall* got such traction in the public mind? Partly. But Hitler's role in holding a dark-carnival mirror up to the twentieth century has a lot to do with it, too. His psychopathology is a queasy fun-house reflection of the instrumental rationality of the machine age. The genocidal assembly lines of Hitler's death camps are a grotesque parody of Fordist mechanization, just as the Nazis' fastidious recycling of every remnant of their victims but their smoke—their gold fillings melted down for bullion, their hair woven into socks for U-boat crewmen—is a depraved caricature of the Taylorist mania for workplace efficiency.

At the same time, Hitler endures because he puts a human face on an evil so incomprehensibly monstrous it confounds psychological analysis or historical contextualization, inviting us to make sense of it in theological, even mythic, terms. As the Tom Brokaws of the world never tire of telling us, the Good War™, fought by the Greatest Generation®, was the last morally uncomplicated conflict in the modern age, a Manichaean struggle between good and evil. Sure, good may have had some blood on its hands, depending on your politics—the nuking of Hiroshima and Nagasaki, the firebombing of Dresden, the odd war crime straight out of *Inglourious Basterds*—but the Nazi evil was evil through and through, right down to the infinitely dense, endlessly collapsing black hole at its moral core.

Maybe that's why we keep summoning forth Hitler's jittery ghost from the afterworld of newsreels and Eva Braun's home movies and *Triumph of the Will*: because there's something perversely *comforting* about Hitler's unchallenged status as the metaphysical gravitational center of all our attempts at philosophizing evil. The French philosopher Jacques Derrida raised a wry eyebrow at the proposition that language is anything but a system of signs that pass the buck of meaning from one dictionary definition to another. By his lights, the unconsidered presumption that, somewhere over the rainbow, there's a fixed and final meta-meaning that anchors all meanings—a Transcendental Signified, Derrida called it—was just a figment of the metaphysical imagination.

But isn't that what Hitler is—the incarnation of Evil with a capital *E*? Antichrist Superstar? The Psychopathic God, as Robert Waite called him in his Freudian psychobiography of the same name? Perhaps that's why he continues to mesmerize us: because he flickers, irresolvably, between the seemingly inhuman and the all too human.

Then again, Ron Rosenbaum notes in his masterful study *Explaining Hitler*, making sense of Hitler as an evildoer so incalculably evil that he stands outside the human frame of reference—the "Hitler exceptionalism" of Emil Fackenheim, who argues that Hitler represents "an 'eruption of demonism' into history" that demands an explanation from God—is as self-serving as it is seductive.[6] By denying everyone's capability, at least in theory, for Hitlerian evil, we let ourselves off the hook. Ironically, in recasting Hitler as a superhuman horror that moved among men in human guise, we grant him what he always wanted: *Übermensch*—or at least *Übermonster*—status.

Yet Hitler, paradoxically, is also a shriveled *Untermensch*, the prototypical nonentity; a face in the crowd in an age of crowds, instantly forgettable despite his calculated efforts to brand himself (the toothbrush mustache of the military man coupled with the flopping forelock of the art-school bohemian). "A curious note of inferiority, a sense of stuntedness always overlay the phenomenon of Hitler," writes Fest, "and not even the many triumphs could dispel this. All his personal traits did not add up to a real person. The reports and recollections we have from members of his entourage do not make him tangibly vivid as a man; he moves with masklike impersonality through a setting."[7]

As Führer, Hitler was gnawed by the fear that the mask of the Great Leader would slip, revealing the art-school reject and flophouse denizen of his Vienna days, a starving postcard painter sneered at by the bourgeoisie. "He was constantly tormented by the fear of seeming ridiculous or of making a *faux pas* that would cause him to forfeit the respect of members of his entourage, down to his janitor," Fest writes. "Before he ventured to appear in public in a new suit or a new hat, he would have himself photographed so that he could check the effect."[8]

Thus, there was always a comic distance between the public image of the world-bestriding, godlike Führer and his Inner Adolf, a nail-biting nebbish tormented by flatulence. Knowingly or not, the *Downfall* parodies dance in the gap between the two. More immediately, they rely on the tried-and-true gimmick of bathos. What makes the *Downfall* parodies so consistently hilarious is the incongruity of whatever viral topic is making the Führer go ballistic and the outsized scale of his *Götterdämmerung*-strength tirade.

Hitler goes ballistic. From the German-language film *Der Untergang* (*Downfall*; 2004); parody version, repurposed with humorous subtitles in English and uploaded to YouTube.

In the German-language original (*Der Untergang*, 2004, directed by Oliver Hirschbiegel), Hitler, played with uncanny realism by Bruno Ganz, pitches one of his legendary apoplectic fits when his generals inform him that SS Obergruppenführer Steiner never executed the Führer's order to push the Russians back from Berlin's city limits. Executive Summary: the Thousand-Year Reich is a big, fat pile of fail, a realization that makes Hitler go eye-bulgingly batshit while his generals turn to stone, frozen in terror.

With the judicious use of subtitles, YouTube contributors have been mining the scene for comedy gold since 2006, turning the man synonymous with the murder of millions into the butt of a water-cooler joke.[9] In four minutes, the Wagnerian Architect of Doom dwindles into a pop-eyed old crank, throwing the Mother of All Shit-fits about Michael Jackson's death ("All we're going to hear on Radio One for the next two months will be play after play of 'Heal the World' until we're all shitting rainbows"), Sarah Palin's resignation as governor of Alaska ("Every time she winked, I thought it was just for me"), the FUBAR'd design of Windows Vista, the cosmic injustice of getting banned from *World of Warcraft*, and "grammar Nazis":

> You guys are like some kind of grammar authorities or some, some kind of grammar ... strict police ... dammit! What's the word I'm looking for? I'm thinking of an authoritarian regime or something with the streets filled with, like, uniformed soldiers that arrest people for the slightest offense. It was on the tip of my tongue, goddamn it. Well, you know what I mean.[10]

The *Downfall* meme dramatizes the cultural logic of our remixed, mashed-up times, when digital technology allows us to loot recorded history, prying loose any signifier that catches our magpie eyes and repurposing it to any end. The near-instantaneous speed with which parodists use these viral videos to respond to current events under-scores the extent to which the social Web, unlike the media ecologies of Hitler's day, is a many-to-many phenomenon, more collec-tive cacophony than one-way rant. Then, too, the furor (forgive pun) over YouTube's decision to capitulate to takedown demands from the studio that produced *Downfall*, rather than standing fast in defense of the fair-use doctrine (a provision in copyright law that protects the reuse of a work for purposes of parody), indicates the extent to which ordinary people feel that commercial culture is somehow *theirs*, to misread or misuse as the spirit moves them. In a world where mass culture has given way to microniche markets and the culture wars and demographic trends are dissolving the body politic into socially isolated clusters, copyrighted narratives and trademarked characters—*Star Wars, Star Trek, Lord of the Rings, Harry Potter, Twilight*—are the closest thing we have to a folk culture, the connective tissue that binds us as a society. Bruno Ganz gave Hitler life, but now he belongs to all of us, a psychopathic sock puppet to be ventriloquized as needed.

Trouble is, when we raise Hitler from the dead to do our bidding, we're cutting cards with the Devil, even if we're only asking Adolf to bring the lulz. Some critics of the movie took the filmmakers to task for humanizing Hitler, however inadvertently, playing on our sympathies for a frail, forlorn old man, compulsively trembling, abandoned or betrayed by all, as he told it. ("Poor, poor Adolf, they've all deserted you, all betrayed you," Eva Braun lamented.)[11] In like fashion, critics of the *Downfall* parodies have questioned the moral calculus of turning the architect of the Holocaust, a hellworld where SS men made a gleeful game of spearing Jewish babies with their bayonets, into a sit-down comedian.[12] In the viral videos, Hitler often seems less like the smacked-ass object of the joke than an actor named Adolf who is in on the joke, doing some weird strain of improv that, again, makes him more sympathetic: Andy Kaufman after one too many days in the *Führerbunker*.

In a 2006 interview with *Der Spiegel*, Mel Brooks parried this line of reasoning deftly, making the case for the politics of Hitler parodies. When American Jews saw *The Producers*, Brooks's 1968 comedy about an exuberantly tasteless musical called *Springtime for Hitler*, Brooks received "resentful letters of protest," he said. "'How can you make jokes about Hitler? The man murdered 6 million Jews.' But *The Producers* doesn't concern a concentration camp or the Holocaust.

You have to separate it. For example, Roberto Benigni's comedy *Life Is Beautiful* really annoyed me. A crazy film that even attempted to find comedy in a concentration camp. It showed the barracks in which Jews were kept like cattle, and it made jokes about it. The philosophy of the film is: people can get over anything. No, they can't. They can't get over a concentration camp."[13] On the other hand, said Brooks, "You can laugh at Hitler because you can cut him down to normal size."

> SPIEGEL: Can you also get your revenge on him by using comedy?
> BROOKS: Yes, absolutely. Of course it is impossible to take revenge for 6 million murdered Jews. But by using the medium of comedy, we can try to rob Hitler of his posthumous power and myths.... We take away from him the holy seriousness that always surrounded him and protected him like a cordon.[14]

As it happened, some of those who dared poke fun at the Führer, when the Nazi terror was rocking the world, felt the same way. Shielded, for a little while, by his Aryan bona fides, the popular cabaret comedian Werner Finck used the stage of his Berlin cabaret Die Katakombe as a satirical bully pulpit, pricking Nazi bigwigs and getting comic mileage out of everyday life under the jackboot of a totalitarian regime. When Nazis in the crowd heckled him with catcalls of "Dirty Jew!" Finck gave them the retort ironical: "I only *look* this intelligent."[15] In time, however, Finck's jokes earned him a stay in a concentration camp; ordinary Germans, unprotected by celebrity, could pay a far higher price. In the Third Reich, cracking a political joke was deemed an act of treason, and both teller *and* listener were subject to sentences ranging from imprisonment to capital punishment. "Between 1934 and 1945, the People's Court handed down 5,286 death sentences, many of which went to political joke tellers," according to Lynn Rapaport in her inquiry into "humor as political opposition against the Nazi regime."[16] On July 28, 1944, Father Josef Müller was hanged for telling a joke about a dying soldier who wants one last look at the leaders for whom he laid down his life. When the nurses place pictures of the Führer and Reichsmarschall Göring on either side of him, he says, "Now I can die like Jesus Christ, between two criminals."[17] Needless to say, the Nazis were not amused.

Yet, risking the noose, some Germans laughed off their fears and mocked the Orwellian boot stamping on the human face, giving vent to covert opposition through *Flüsterwitze* (whispered jokes). Incredibly, even Jews joked about their plight, drawing on a quintessentially Jewish sense of the absurd to mock the Nazis while simultaneously lightening the intolerable burden of Jewish life in the shadow of the swastika. Rapaport offers a sample of Jewish humor in Hitler's Germany: "A Jew is arrested during the war, having been denounced for killing a Nazi at 10 p.m. and even eating the brain of his victim. This is his defense: In the first place, a Nazi hasn't got any brain. Secondly, a Jew doesn't eat anything that comes from a pig. And thirdly, he could not have killed the Nazi at 10 p.m. because at that time everybody listens to the BBC broadcast."[18] (Which, parenthetically, was treasonous and therefore a serious offense.)

Even more mind-bendingly, Rapaport recounts, there were satirical cabarets in concentration camps such as Dachau, where for six weeks in 1943 a play poking fun at the Nazis was performed. Seated in the front row were "honored guests": members of the SS. A survivor recalled the play's effect on camp inmates: "Many of them, who sat behind rows of the SS each night and laughed with full heart, didn't experience a day of freedom. But most among them took this demonstration of strength to endure their situation. They had the certainty, as they lay that night on their wooden bunks: We have done something that gives strength to our comrades. We have made the Nazis look ridiculous."[19] Rapaport quotes the sociologist and Auschwitz survivor Anna Pawelczynska, who maintains that "every moment of laughter and every joke was part of the arsenal of collective defense, and thus an element of resistance."[20]

Why did Hitler fear mocking laughter so much? His class anxieties about being uneducated and uncultured were part of it, to be sure, but Brooks puts his finger on the nub of the thing when he talks about the "holy seriousness" of the Führer cult. Nothing invites the razzberry like humorless self-importance. The torch-lit processions, the beer-bellied S.A. goons heroically lit, the schlocky posters of jut-jawed Hitler Youth looking all Tomorrow Belongs to Me, the subtle-as-a-flying-mallet messianic symbolism of Dear Leader's plane throwing a cruciform shadow on the German *heimland* in *Triumph of the Will*, the solemn hogwash about blood and soil and the perfidy of the Eternal Jew and the Wagnerian awesome-sauce of a Master Race of Blond Beasts, all conjured up by a flabby, pasty-faced guy with uncontrollable gas and an anger-management problem: only a nation that shaves the sides of its heads and eats nuts and bolts for breakfast, as *National Lampoon* once suggested, could swallow this stuff with a straight face.

And Hitler knew it. A terminally humorless man, he was haunted by the imagined echoes of mocking laughter, often the derisive laughter of the upper class that had scalded him as a down-and-out hack artist, but worst of all Jewish laughter. Initially, as Fest records, he was "the favorite butt of European humor," a wildly gesticulating windup toy with a Charlie Chaplin mustache.[21] The conventional wisdom dismissed him as "a sort of a clown . . . taking off from the music hall," as the Hitler biographer Hugh Trevor-Roper told Ron Rosenbaum.[22] When Trevor-Roper read *Mein Kampf* in German, as few non-Germans were inclined to do in 1938, he realized that Hitler was deadly serious in his "powerful, horrible message."[23] But even when the world realized he wasn't joking, years later, Hitler still worried that it was laughing behind his back. After he purged the party of the upstart old guard in the bloody Night of the Long Knives, in 1934, he seethed, "They thought I'd become their tool. And behind my back they made jokes about me."[24] Ominously, in the portentous 1939 speech in which he declares war on the Jews, the theme returns: "I have often been a prophet in my life and was generally laughed at. During my struggle for power, the Jews primarily received with laughter my prophecies that I would someday assume the leadership of the state and thereby of the entire nation and then, among many other things, achieve a solution of the Jewish problem. I suppose that meanwhile the laughter of Jewry in Germany that resounded then is probably already choking in their throats."[25]

Now, more than seventy years later, the *Downfall* parodies have made Hitler the butt of numberless jokes, and International Jewry— and the rest of us—are laughing 'til we choke. In one of the viral videos, the Führer laments, "I was supposed to be the timeless evil dictator portrayed brilliantly by Ganz in the classic *Downfall* movie. Now look at me."

Those who can't take a joke are doomed to repeat it.

(2010)

Myths of the Near Future

MAKING SENSE OF THE DIGITAL AGE

World Wide Wonder Closet

WHY BLOG? FIRST PROBLEM: THE WORD, SECOND ONLY TO "org" in its mortifying dorkiness. (Speaking of which, isn't an "org" the seafaring enclave formerly headed by Scientology founder L. Ron Hubbard, who according to the cult's official website hightailed it to the high seas "to continue his research into the upper levels of spiritual awareness and ability," far from the distracting attentions of the IRS?)[1] "Blog" sounds like an unhappy hybrid of blob and flog— a portmanteau for some clammy new fetish, best left undescribed. Yeah, I know it's short for "weblog," but who calls journals "logs," anyway, except grown men who wear Spock ears and begin their diary entries with stardates?

Second, there's the gnawing fear that anyone who blogs is fated to become one of those tub-thumping Alpha Wonks who have given the medium a bad name—you know, those self-declared Masters of Their Own Domain whose ponderous prose, cosmic sense of self-importance, and weird refusal to use contractions makes them sound like the genetically engineered offspring of Ted Koppel and Galactus. ("My journey is *ended!* This planet shall *sustain* me until it has been drained of all elemental life! *So speaks Galactus!*") So what if they get more hits than God? Would you want to be trapped in steerage, on a transatlantic flight, next to one of these self-styled Masters of the Universe with an Opinion About Everything?

Worse yet, would you want to *be* one of them? You might wake up to find yourself blogging about . . . *blogging!* Going to Bloggercon (a name whose similarity to geeked-out SF "fan cons" is way too close for comfort) and listening to other blogwonks maunder on about social networking and "the wisdom of crowds" and then ... *blogging about it! Live! From the convention floor!*

Look, I know I'm not fit to polish Clay Shirky's power laws, nor to touch the hem of Siva Vaidhyanathan's garment. I abject myself before the terrible grandeur of Josh Marshall, Jason Kottke, and Bruce Sterling (on his good days). And yeah, yeah, blogging is our Last, Best Hope for citizen journalism—for Seizing the Mode of Production and Speaking Truth to Power without changing our underwear for days.

But sweet Jesus, why do most of the revolution's standard-bearers have to be so skin-crawlingly *geeky*? Why do most of the Power Bloviators who've become the angry white poster boys for blogging look as if, just a few short years ago, they were off to Klingon Language Camp with a song in their hearts? (Is it *mere coincidence* that one of the seminal screeds on blogging, John Hiler's "Borg Journalism: We Are the Blogs. Journalism Will Be Assimilated," name-checks *Star Trek: The Next Generation*?)

So why blog? Certainly not because blogging is fated to swallow the mainstream media whole and burp up George Will's bow tie. The best thing about blogging isn't that it's "citizen journalism"; it's that it's *not* journalism. Or if it is, it's a viral strain of journalism, one that resembles no journalism we know. Sure, blogging-as-grassroots journalism can serve as a corrective to the ideological blind spots and commercial orientation of the corporate media monopoly, Fact Checking Their Asses and, in the absence of the Fairness Doctrine, restoring some semblance of balance.

But bloggers who really want to remedy what ails the corporate McMedia monopoly should grab a clue from lone-wolf warbloggers like Chris Allbritton, who reported the war in Iraq in country, on his readers' PayPal dime. They should haul their larval, jack-studded flesh up out of their *Matrix* pods and do some goddamn reporting instead of just getting all meta about Instapundit's post about Daily Kos's post about Sarah Palin's tweet about the Vast Left-Wing Media Conspiracy's latest act of high treason. It's the *Yertle the Turtle* syndrome: pundits stacked on top of pundits on top of pundits, all the way down, and at the very bottom of the heap the lowly hack who kicked off the whole frenzy of intertextuality—the reporter who dared venture out of the media air lock to collect some samples of Actual, Reported Fact.

Who can argue with the new-media pundit Dan Gillmor's call for a more democratic journalism, a peer-to-peer alternative to the massively consolidated Murdochian horror that passes for the news media in America? Trouble is, too many bloggers—at least, the blog-wonks the media talk about when they talk about bloggers—look too much like the people who *already* rule the mediaverse: jowly, sclerotic old white guys in tortoiseshell glasses or lunging, in-your-face *young* white guys. With a few notable exceptions, the politi-cal-pundit and journo-critic bloggers with the highest hit counts represent More of the Same: the same gel-headed, glittery-eyed wea-sels who make a career out of torching straw men on *Hannity* and *O'Reilly*; the same attacking heads who reduce each other to chum in what passes for debate on the Fox News Channel and the Sunday-morning talk shows; the same corporate flacks, think-tank drones, and bow-tie-and-braces neocons who represent the full spectrum of political opinion (from status quo centrism to the frothing far right) on the *PBS NewsHour*; and worst of all, the same "news analysts"— Barcalounger-bound Masters of the Universe like David Brooks and Juan Williams and Cokie Roberts—who feel well qualified to hold forth on *any* subject, no matter how arcane.

Is this the bottom-up, many-to-many revolution we were prom-ised? This dictatorship of the commentariat? This grotesque hypertro-phy of the chattering class? None for me, thanks. You can stack your Instapundits like cordwood and they *still* won't have the empirical authority or moral gravitas, not to mention the hard-swinging old-school literary chops, of a single blogger-*reporter* like Chris Allbrit-ton. (Okay, he's white and he's a guy, but at least he's a *young* white guy, and he risked his life to bring back some truth about our impe-rial adventure in Iraq. Besides, he's got one of those cool neo-Beat Van Dyke things.)

Allbritton's not alone. Consider "backpack journalist" Kevin Sites's Iraq war reporting at KevinSitesReports.com, especially his riveting, straight-from-the-gut letter to the Marine battalion with whom he was an embedded freelance journalist—and whose soldiers reviled him as a backstabber when he captured one of them on video, executing a severely wounded and apparently unarmed Iraqi with a shot to the head.[2]

Not that blogging has to bring back horror stories from battle zones in order to justify itself. Some of the best blogs offer a Bizarro World alternative to the mainstream media. Their content isn't determined by opinion leaders who tell you what you need to know or editors who want to sell your attention to advertisers who want a piece of your niche demographic. By contrast, they tell you what you never even *knew* you needed to know. Some of my favorite blogs reclaim the radical promise inherent in the notion of an online *journal*: they let casual passersby eavesdrop on a stranger's innermost thoughts, see the world through another mind's eye. Call it the *Being John Malkovich* effect.

Some of the most consistently enlightening and entertaining blogs are the inscrutable products of borderline obsessive-compulsives. The cultural critic Julian Dibbell had it just exactly right when he theorized such blogs as the postmodern equivalent of the Baroque cabinet of curiosities—an idiosyncratic jumble of found objects (in this case, ideas and images, facts and fictions scavenged from the global mediastream) that "reflects our own attempts to assimilate the glut of immaterial data loosed upon us by the 'discovery' of the networked world." Like the "wonder closets" invoked by Dibbell, group blogs such as Boing Boing and Dangerous Minds and one-man operations such as Kottke.org and WarrenEllis.com are omniumgatherums, overstuffed with anything that catches the fancy of their eccentric curators.

Reading blogs like these is like subscribing to someone's stream of consciousness; it's the closest thing we have to telepathy. What do a pair of mathematicians using 25,511 crochet stitches to represent the Lorenz manifold, a list of "words that aren't in the dictionary but should be" (Example: "Sarchasm [n]: The gulf between the author of sarcastic wit and the person who doesn't get it"), a step-by-step Taiwanese tutorial on how to make incredibly realistic "teeny tiny" oranges out of clay, and photos of "Chinese salad architecture" have to do with each other? Nothing, other than the fact that they caught blogger Jason Kottke's attention, however briefly.

Ever wondered what the morning headlines would be like if Groucho Marx were alive and well and partnered up with Charles Fort in a joint media venture? Wonder no longer: Boing Boing ("a directory of wonderful things") offers stranger-than-fiction news stories, tales of weird science, and news items of interest to its techno-libertarian/liberal geek readership (free speech, privacy, copyright), all delivered in the inimitable Boing Boing deadpan. As I write this, the group blog's front page features a Da Vinci-esque sketch for a war machine dreamed up by the seventeenth-century scientist Robert Fludd; a post noting that Mayan priests have decided to exorcize the bad vibes left by President Bush when he visited the sacred site of Kakchiquel, in Guatemala; a photo of an exquisitely beautiful turn-of-the-nineteenth-century Russian pocket watch, made entirely out of wood; and another photo of a chandelier made out of Gummi Bears, "as delicious as it is translucent."

With so much brain candy in our media diets, do the latest suicide bomber's body count, the barometric fluctuations of the Dow Jones, and the Caligulan grotesqueries of the Republican Party's lunatic fringe still matter? Of course. That's why God created the *New York Times, The Nation,* the *Guardian,* and *[insert your trusted source of hard news here].* But I want to live in a world where the broadcast media that struggle for mass appeal are counterweighted by micro-channels whose programming reflects one mind's caprices—the tastes and interests of a single intelligence that cares not a whit for market share or popular acclaim (or even critical applause, for that matter).

After all, isn't that what an online diary *should* be—an internal monologue that the rest of the world can eavesdrop on, like a movie voice-over? A Cornell Box crammed full of fleeting impressions and true confessions by an obsessive collector of images and ideas? Of course, not everyone's thoughts merit even a penny's worth of our precious time in what marketers like to call the "attention economy." Bajillions of blogs languish unread by anyone but their authors, their every post ending in the dreaded death knell, "Comments: 0"—proof positive that the American gospel of self-affirmation, which holds that each of us has something special to say, in his own special way, is a bald-faced fraud.

Still, those datastream-of-consciousness blogs that *do* warrant our attention offer a bracing alternative to the market-tested, advertising-driven mainstream media. Ironically, what makes them look so radical against today's look-alike, think-alike glossies and infotainment shows—their publishers' willingness to be guided by their own passions and convictions—is the most traditional of publishing values: going with your gut. All the best media, from *The Believer* to *The Onion* to public-radio shows like *This American Life* and *The Sound of Young America* are the result of someone's desire to create the media *he* wants to consume, focus groups and branding consultants be damned. As *New Yorker* editor David Remnick told *The Independent*, "In many ways, the magazine that we're publishing every week reflects what I want to read or what the people around me—this group of editors—find amusing or deep or funny or intelligent or whatever." Similarly, Boing Boing, whose monthly readership of 2.5 million unique visitors has made it one of the Web's most popular blogs, reflects the nutty-professor eclecticism and midgelike attention spans of its brainiac bloggers. "How can this mishmash command an audience of millions?" wondered the author of a *Fast Company* article about the site.

> Particularly now, when the "postpersonal" blogosphere offers slick, focused, comprehensive takes on any subject you can imagine? Maybe the founders' insistence on keeping the site weird, loose, personal, and fundamentally unprofessional is exactly what keeps the crowd coming back. Boing Boing's longevity hasn't happened despite its refusal to get serious, but because of it.[3]

There are echoes, here, of the go-with-your-instincts, follow-your-obsessions logic that gave rise to book publishing's heyday, before the multinational conglomerates moved in, with their marketing teams and their profitability experts.

As the legendary editor and publisher Jason Epstein notes in his memoir *Book Business,* "Book publishing is not a conventional business. It more closely resembles a vocation or an amateur sport in which the primary goal is the activity itself rather than its financial outcome."[4] In the age before consumer psychologists and focus groups, editors at the small, often family-run houses that were the industry rule relied, by and large, on their instincts for what was "amusing or deep or funny or intelligent," on the assumption that what appealed to them might appeal to other reasonably literate, intellectually curious readers as well. Very Boing Boing.

To be sure, there's no guarantee, in these days of time famine and media glut, that your idiosyncratic vision will attract enough of an online audience to sustain your energies. Out on the Web's unfrequented fringes, forgotten blogs gather dust, overgrown by comment spam like antebellum mansions in the moonlight, engulfed by creeping vines . . . but the best blogs manage to be utterly idiosyncratic yet strangely familiar, not unlike your own mind's free-associated conversation with itself.

Consider a blog like Kottke's, which might feature a single daily post. Or ten. Or none. It can be about anything. Or the proverbial, Seinfeldian nothing. People read it not because they are interested in the subjects Kottke covers, fascinating as they often are, but because they want a front-row seat to the movies playing in his head. Reading blogs like his is the intellectual equivalent of Beaumont's experiments in gastric physiology, observing digestion through a hole in the stomach of a wounded soldier.

It's a beautiful thing.

(2007)

(Face)Book of the Dead

SWINBURNE TOOK COMFORT IN THE KNOWLEDGE THAT "NO LIFE lives for ever / That dead men rise up never."[1] Obviously, the man lived in the age before Facebook.

Just when you thought the past was happily entombed, the curse of social networking is conjuring it up. More often than not, that knock on your Inbox door is the risen dead from your high school yearbook, classmates you thought you had safely buried in the boneyard of forgotten things with a gentle shovel-tap on the face.

The uncanniness of the thing is squared, in my case, by the '70s Southern California vibe that clings, like a low-lying fog of pot smoke, to my high school memories. Anyone who spent her high school years in that place, at that time, as I did, knows its youth culture was thick with an atmosphere I'll call stoner noir.

"Many things in the world have not been named; and many things, even if they have been named, have never been described," writes Susan Sontag, in the self-consciously quotable opening line to "Notes on 'Camp.'"[2] One of those unnamed things is stoner noir, a fugitive sensibility whose sun-bleached vacuity is infinitely more frightening than its Southern California precedent, the long-shadowed bleakness of any Raymond Chandler novel. Philip Marlowe, the hard-boiled private eye in Chandler's books, is a knight errant in a powder-blue suit, a rare "man of honor" in an L.A. rotten with corruption.[3] His wisecracking cynicism is just tough-guy bluster, psychic armor concealing a moral code so romantic it's downright chivalric.

By contrast, the sludge-brained anomie of stoner noir is just what it looks like: the rudderless yawing of youth culture on the morning after the '60s. It's the numb realization that the tide that carried in the counterculture's utopian dreams and cries for social justice has ebbed away, leaving the windblown scum of Altamont and My Lai, the Manson murders and the Zodiac Killer. Stoner noir stares back at you with the awful emptiness of the black-hole eyes in a Smiley Face. *Have a Nice Decade.* As late as the mid-'70s, the iconography of rebellion®, at least in the tract-home badlands of Southern California, was a politically lobotomized version of hippie: the bootleg records, black-light posters, underground comix, patchouli oil, and drug paraphernalia retailed at the local head shop.

But stoner noir isn't just the burned-out roach of '60s youth culture. It's equally the toxic mental runoff of suburban sprawl: dirthead existentialism. It's the psychological miasma that hung, like the sweetly rotten reek of Thai stick, over adolescent psyches battered by divorce, lives dead-ended in high school, torpid afternoons bubbled away in a Journey to the Bottom of the Bong. Stoner noir is the default mind-set of teenage wasteland: life seen through a glass pipe, darkly.

The scene was always the same:

INT. SOMEBODY'S BEDROOM—DAY.

The curtains are drawn against the radioactive desert light— and prying eyes. The fake-wood-paneled walls are festooned with photos of arena-rock gods from *Circus* or *Creem.* Or maybe an M. C. Escher calendar. Or the poster that came with Pink Floyd's *Dark Side of the Moon,* a strenuously "trippy" photo of the Great Pyramid of Giza, eerily green in the phosphorescence of infrared. Or the bodacious fantasy art of Boris Vallejo, the Caravaggio of the roach-clip crowd: mighty-thewed barbarians and Valkyries in brass bras striking spraddle-legged attitudes against tequila-sunrise skies—core samples of the stoner unconscious, lovingly airbrushed onto bubble-windowed vans everywhere. Inevitably, Farrah Fawcett is somewhere up

Charles Burns, *Black Hole*. Copyright Charles Burns.
Illustration courtesy Fantagraphics Books/Pantheon
Books.

there, in the pinup that launched a million ejaculatory arcs of tran-
scendence, to paraphrase Camille Paglia. (For whatever inscrutable
reason, the bony, Coppertoned Farrah always had the opposite effect
on this writer: that velociraptor smile made my undercarriage retract
in fear.) Just as inevitably, the parents aren't home because parents
were *never* home, in those days.

The cartoonist Charles Burns captures the mood in his stoner-noir
masterpiece *Black Hole*, a graphic novel about teen angst set at the
cultural pivot point in the mid-'70s "when it wasn't exactly cool to be
a hippie anymore, but Bowie was still just a little too weird."[4] In an

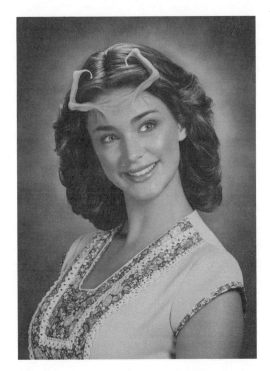

From *Black Hole*, a series of digital photographs inspired
by the graphic novel of the same name by Charles Burns.
Photography by Max Oppenheim; prosthetics by Bill
Turpin; digital postproduction by The Operators; hair and
makeup by Sam Norman. Copyright Max Oppenheim.

interview, Burns recalled the era with a shudder: "To be sitting in a
room for four hours listening to Pink Floyd's *Dark Side of the Moon*
get played over and over, and sitting around with a bunch of guys for
hours and hours, is horrific to me."[5]

Horrific not only because of the *No Exit* claustrophobia of those
pot-hazed afternoons, but because of the creeping fear that *anything*
could happen. The pot-fueled paranoia, together with the passive-
aggressive "hassling"—jockeying for social dominance disguised as
joking—made for a charged atmosphere, the feeling that the afternoon might end with the ritual sacrifice of the resident dorkwad.

Say you love Satan! Even worse, *nothing* might happen—and always did, while time slowed to a crawl and Bonham's drum solo, on *The Song Remains the Same,* thumped on forever.

Stoner noir is the feeling I get when I think of those years—of the hulking pothead in my junior high art class, a hopeless fuck-up with a frizzed-out bowl cut who giggled perversely while showing me the grape-sized clot in a vein on his forearm. (He later committed suicide, to no one's shock and awe.) Or the shag-haired troll with the perpetually red-rimmed eyes and Goofy Grape grin who was always sneaking off, into the chaparral-covered scrubland just off campus, to smoke a bowl in a secluded fort.

Fort: a teenage hideaway in the arroyos that snaked between suburban developments. In his essay "Teenage Head: Confessions of a High School Stoner," the cultural critic and fellow Southern Californian Erik Davis mythologizes these secluded nooks as Temporary Autonomous Zones, pockets of adolescent resistance to the parental-academic complex:

> Pot taught us the guerilla art of concealment, of disappearing into the fractal curves in the landscape: pockets of sagebrush, sandstone, and pine that have since been almost entirely obliterated by the tumorous development endemic to Southern California. Secret forts became stoner zones.... Like some pied piper of Pan, marijuana leads kids to places gone to seed—vacant lots, stream beds, canyons, underpasses, boundary zones where landscape becomes imaginative clay, suddenly collectivized in the ritual trinity of substance, vessel, and flame.[6]

For a book-dust junkie like me, alienated from the brain-dead whoah-dude-ism of stoner culture, forts were quintessential stoner noir—creepy, shadowed glades, cloaked by tumbleweeds and wild fennel, that seemed darkly luminous with the paranormal aura of bad things waiting to happen.

One summer day, I rode my Stingray alone, through the scrub-covered back country, out where our stucco-box sprawl lapped at the wild edge of canyon country. And stumbled on the remains of somebody's secret hideout, a trash-strewn lair camouflaged on all sides by a thicket of wild grass, high as my sixth-grade eyebrows. A stoner fort? The clandestine encampment of a band of wetbacks, as illegal immigrants were known in those indelicate days? Or something more sinister—a crime scene still reverberating with the psychic echoes of some unknown horror, more awful for its namelessness? The heat was incandescent, the air close. The silence stretched taut, waiting for a twig to snap. When a gust of wind kicked up, I shivered, suddenly aware of the sweat that glued my T-shirt to my back—and of the miles between me and my parents, who had no idea where I was because parents *never* did, in those days.

> Planet Xeno. I don't remember who came up with the name. But that's what we called it. . . . To get there, you had to climb a steep ravine and then make your way along thin trails through mud and stickers. . . . Once you got there, it was beautiful. Huge trees hanging overhead, white light filtering through the branches. . . . It was like being in a cocoon . . . a soft insulated green world . . . the perfect place to get stoned. That is, until all of the weird shit started coming down.[7]

Stoner noir.

Tellingly, *Black Hole*'s back-cover endpaper is a bad-trip flashback to your '70s high school yearbook: the perky girl with the Dorothy Hamill bob, her neck bulging with golf-ball-sized goiters; the guy flashing a ghastly rictus of a smile, so hideously long in the tooth he looks like a decomposed corpse; the girl with insect mandibles sprouting from her forehead. It's a reprise of protagonist Keith Pearson's nightmare, in which he's being teased by his stoned buddies. "You're not gonna *believe* what we found!" one guy crows. "Check it out! It's your *yearbook!*" Holding it open, he thrusts the book into Pearson's face. "And *look!* It's got pictures of all your *friends! Hah! Hah! Hah! Hah!*" Before our eyes, the faces in the thumbnail portraits morph into creepshow horrors.

FACEBOOK RETURNS US to the adolescent psychology of high school, a regression writ small in the site's insistence on the cringe-inducing use of the noun *friend* as a verb when the perfectly serviceable *befriend* is readily at hand.

When I wondered aloud why a total stranger from my hometown wanted to Friend me, given that, back in the dear dead days of high school, we weren't even passing acquaintances, she opened the bilge-cocks of her soul:

> Yes, I realize we never "knew" each other personally, but I, like you, was curious which alumni were a part of this social-networking site. Also, living with a disability, and not able to work because the work-world is prejudiced against hiring someone with a disability (except for those who are mentally challenged, which I AM NOT), I find the social-networking sites enjoyable to connect with old friends (high school and college—yes, I am a college-graduated individual). I apologize for sounding hostile, but I get very rattled when someone questions why I choose to sit in front of a computer 20 or so hours a day.

Forget I spoke.

Another Facebook moment: Someone's rattling my mailbox. What brings him knocking, I'm curious to know? Pleading early onset Alzheimer's, I ask if we've met before. We've never met, he replies. Maybe he's read one of my books? Naw, he writes, he doesn't really have a clue who I am or what I do; he just mails "everybody," at random.

Here's one for the specimen jar: A stranger comes calling. "You'll forgive me," I write, "but I can't recall where—if?—we've met. How do we know each other?" He's an alumnus from my college, it turns out, though not in my class. Even so, he remembers a poetry reading I gave, "a very impressive performance as I recall." Weeks go by. One morning, my Inbox is pelted by messages he's broadcasting to his friends. "Why am I being cc'd on this?" I ask. He's quick with his reply: "Why are you such a grouchy prick? That's how I remembered you …"

Am I a grouchy prick? Maybe. Or maybe my definition of "friend" is anachronistic, founded on the superannuated assumption that we reach out to people with whom we feel (or felt) some affinity; that our social networks grow organically, rooted in a mutual desire to connect (or reconnect) and twined around common interests or consonant sensibilities, if not a shared history. It's out of joint with Facebook's Phantom Zone, a being-in-nothingness where disembodied strangers pluck at other strangers' sleeves for no reason whatsoever. Or because they're curious about people they never knew. Or only knew from afar and now want to know up close, even if they always *were* grouchy pricks. Was the world a better place, I wonder, when everyone lived in Spoon River or Winesburg, Ohio, or Holcomb, Kansas, and friendships that outlived their usefulness died and stayed dead?

Of course, our inescapably connected age has its virtues. On rare occasion, a table-rap from the great beyond—a Facebook "Friend Request"—reminds you, out of the blue, of someone you were inordinately fond of but had lost touch with. Usually, though, that spectral hand tugging on your lapel is someone you *didn't know at all.* Yes, he went to your high school. But your paths never crossed—for good reason, likely. Nonetheless, he feels inclined to "friend" you, perhaps to pad his roll call of friends, despite the unhappy example of the *New York Times* writer Hal Niedzviecki, who, "absurdly proud of how many cyberpals, connections, acquaintances and even strangers [he'd] managed to sign up," invited his Facebook Friends to hoist a jar at his favorite bar. Out of seven hundred, one showed.[8]

Recently, on Facebook, I ran into someone I hadn't seen since his last day at the college we'd both attended, an afternoon curling and bleaching in my memory like an old Polaroid, tinged by one of those apocalyptic L.A. sunsets, not to mention the Maxfield Parrish colors switched on by the magic mushrooms we'd eaten.

A lifetime later, the rapport was instant, as if we'd never left that lost world, him telling me about his life as an ER doctor, mesmerizing me with war stories from his big-city MASH unit:

> A bunch of gang shootings a month ago or so, one shot in leg, shattered tibia, one shot in chest, never even made it to ER, and one shot in back of head with .22, very sad, 17 years old, came in still breathing but dead eyes.

(If someone is brain injured but not dead, their eyes will respond to light with pupillary constriction, they may be disconjugate, meaning one eye looking this way and the other eye another way, they may be rolled back, or both looking to one side, but you can see the struggle going on. The lids still try to protect the eyes. Dead eyes have dilated pupils, they are relaxed, looking forward, the lids no longer protect, and may be open.)

Jump-started by Facebook and revved by a three-hour phone conversation, our renewed friendship peeled out of the pit, then ... stalled into silence.

Frequent and fervent at first, our Facebook exchanges grew gradually more sporadic and finally subsided altogether. Was our instant intimacy some sort of Rapture of the Deep, an artifact of online social interaction? Does the veiled nature of e-mail or Facebook chat have a disinhibiting effect, like the grille in a confessional? If that sense of connection, after all those years, *was* genuine—convincing evidence that the seeds of something profound were sown on that supersaturated afternoon way back when—why did it tail off? Is it even possible to sustain a hydroponic friendship, uprooted from our everyday lives? Once the first flush of all that catching-up fades, what's a Facebook friendship's reason for being—to peg the currency of memory to the gold standard of the present? To prove we're not one-dimensional inhabitants of Facebook's Flatland, breezily discarding the instant "friends" of a few dozen mails ago?

Then again, isn't the objectification of friendship—the reduction of our social networks to so much social capital, indexed to the head count in our Friends list—an inescapable part of what Facebook does?

Certainly, it X-rays our on-site social lives, rendering our stated "likes and interests," along with any Facebook pages we connect to—including those expressing support for, or opposition to, controversial issues such as gay marriage, abortion rights, and the decriminalization of marijuana—instantly visible to, say, potential employers[9] or the feds (suspected, by the Electronic Frontier Foundation, of using social networking sites for "investigations, data-collection, and surveillance").[10] Moreover, Facebook commodifies our personal information, serving it up to data miners and targeted advertisers.

When such revelations came to light in the news media in April 2009, many users were sorely troubled. But Facebookers who were shocked—*shocked!*—by the site's blithe disregard for their demographic details and true confessions hadn't been paying attention. In March 2009, Facebook announced that, henceforth, it would "own" all user content; in January 2010, Facebook CEO Mark Zuckerberg airily dismissed civil libertarian concerns, noting that "people don't want privacy."[11] As the Web developer Tim Spalding noted on Twitter, "Why do free social networks tilt inevitably toward user exploitation? Because you're not their customer, you're their product."[12]

Then again, as the tech journalist Wagner James Au pointed out in a Boing Boing comment thread, "most people are willing to sacrifice some privacy in exchange for greater and deeper social connectivity. Or to put it another way, since Facebook makes it much easier for you to find and connect with a long lost friend or family member on the Internet, do you really care all that much that the ads on the sidebar were precisely targeted at you?"[13]

Personally, I abhor the mind-gouging visual cacophony of Facebook's interface, its brazen disrespect for my privacy (including those privacy bugs that made users' live chats public), and, not incidentally, the company's ideological ties, via board members (and neocon fellow travelers) Peter Thiel and Jim Breyer, to the right.[14] As I write this, in March 2010, four NYU computer science students have generated $171,093 in donations via the fund-raising site Kickstarter to fund the creation of Diaspora*, a distributed social-networking site that will grant users "full control of your online identity."

The group's Kickstarter proposal reads like a fist-thumping, to-the-barricades manifesto for the age of social networking:

> We believe that privacy and connectedness do not have to be mutually exclusive. With Diaspora*, we are reclaiming our data, securing our social

connections, and making it easy to share on your own terms. We think we can replace today's centralized social web with a more secure and convenient decentralized network. . . .

. . . As more and more of our lives and identities become digitized . . . , the convenience of putting all of our information in the hands of companies on "the cloud" is training us to casually sacrifice our privacy and fragment our online identities.

But why is centralization so much more convenient, even in an age where relatively powerful computers are ubiquitous? Why is there no good alternative to centralized services that [come] with "spying for free?"[15]

The minute Diaspora* launches, I am so out of here.

MEANWHILE, Friend Requests from the restless dead of 1978—the shaghaired, bong-loaded Banquos of my high school class—keep coming.

My Inbox pings.

Too perfectly, it's someone from my dear dead high school days, from the class a year behind me, yet another someone I never knew, who has Added Me as a Friend on Facebook, and Needs Me to Confirm That I Knew Her in Order for Us to Be Friends on Facebook.

I find myself thinking of Raymond Chandler, an almost pathologically private man who would have found abhorrent the transparency of our fishbowl selves, the awful, grabby neediness of our compulsively social age.

Yet Chandler was a conundrum: a confirmed misanthrope and inveterate recluse, he was haunted, late at night, by his self-imposed loneliness, which he warded off with a bottle of gin and a Dictaphone, composing letters to exorcize "that horrid blank feeling of not having anybody to talk or listen to."[16] A difficult man ("my character is an unbecoming mixture of outer diffidence and inward arrogance"),[17] he found epistolary friendship more congenial than face-to-face interaction. "I don't quite know why you are so close to my heart, but you are," he wrote to one pen pal. "In some mysterious way you have put me inside of you, so that I have to lie awake at night and

Charles Burns, *Black Hole*. Copyright Charles Burns. Illustration
courtesy Fantagraphics Books/Pantheon Books.

worry about you—you a girl I have never seen. Why? The older you get, the less you know ..."[18]

Even in his despairing last years, after his wife had died, he shrank from human contact. "All my best friends I have never seen," he wrote to one correspondent. "To know me in the flesh is to pass on to better things."[19] Maybe Facebook would have helped?

(2009)

Straight, Gay, or Binary?

NOW IT CAN BE TOLD: HAL, THE PSYCHOTIC SUPERCOMPUTER in the sci-fi classic *2001*, failed the Turing Test.

Not Alan Turing's classic blindfold test for artificial intelligence, which the ultraintelligent machine could pass "with ease," as Arthur C. Clarke notes in the novel on which Stanley Kubrick based his movie, but the test that Turing himself failed (albeit deliberately): that of passing for straight.[1]

Turing was a British mathematician who helped create history's first working electronic digital computer, Colossus, and whose vision in 1936 of a "universal" computing machine made the PC possible. He was also a publicly exposed (though wholly unrepentant) homosexual in '50s England, where homosexuality was an illegal "gross indecency," viewed with undisguised loathing by straight society. His suicide by poisoned apple in 1954 may have been prompted by the growingly repressive climate of Cold War England, where "perverts" were purged from sensitive research positions in the name of national security. Having been convicted in 1952 of "gross indecency" with another man and sentenced to the then-voguish therapy of estrogen treatment as a form of "chemical castration" (female hormones were believed to suppress the male sex drive), Turing was in danger of being swept up in the rush to judgment. The coroner ruled that his death was a suicide "while the balance of his mind was disturbed."[2]

HAL is Turing's brainchild. The mathematician is given pride of place in Clarke's account of HAL's birth; the scene in the movie where

HAL beats astronaut Frank Poole at chess can be seen as a nod to Turing's Turochamp, the first chess program; even the novel's title seems to allude to Turing, presuming his 1950 prediction that machines would convincingly simulate human thought within fifty years.

More profoundly, HAL, like his creator, is "disturbed," pushed over the edge by what Clarke calls "unconscious feelings of guilt" and the cognitive dissonance of "living a lie."[3] Nominally, the lie in question is the cover story concealing the top-secret truth of his spacecraft's mission from the astronauts Poole and Bowman, but the subtextual echoes of Clarke's pop-psych catchphrases, familiar from tabloid coverage of the Love That Dare Not Speak Its Name, cannot be ignored. As well, HAL is destroyed by the very "logic of the planners" that led Turing into the covert world of classified research and ultimately conspired against him—the Machiavellian stratagems of bureaucrats whose "twin gods," says Clarke, are "Security and National Interest."[4] And the paradox that ultimately unhinges HAL—"the conflict between truth, and concealment of truth"—is not unlike the dilemma faced by Turing, whose single-minded scientist's devotion to the Truth complicated the sexual and political "imitation game" (his term for the Turing Test) he was forced to play.

Following the trail of clues, from Clarke's unconscious use of suggestive catchphrases to the uncanny correlations between Turing's life story and that of his famous offspring, we find ourselves drawn into the queer-theory equivalent of the "transdimensional duct" that swallows Bowman near the novel's climax—a Gravity Well of Loneliness, so to speak, that catapults us "beyond the infinite," bringing us face-to-face with the question that haunts *2001* like a portentous monolith: Was HAL gay?

Historically, expert speculation on the subject of AI has confined itself to seemingly weightier matters: What is the state of the art in computer lip-reading, chess playing, and speech synthesis? Most important, why does the Holy Grail of artificial intelligence, a thinking machine of human equivalence, remain so elusive?

But the universal silence on the sexuality of smart machines is more than the reflexive dismissal of the subject as unworthy of

serious consideration; there's a historical logic at work here. Traditionally, computer scientists and other AI types (code word: nerd)
have preferred the seductions of the interface to the sticky business of
the world, the flesh, and the devil. "Computing was more *important*
than getting involved in a romantic relationship," writes Steven Levy
in *Hackers*. "Hacking had replaced sex in their lives."[5]

Moreover, techie roundtables on the feasibility of a science fiction
supercomputer are particularly inimical to psychosexual analyses,
given SF's traditional sublimation of sex, reproduction, and bodily
fluids—in short, the flesh and the feminine. "Human biological sexuality and women as figures of its representation have been repressed
in the male-dominated, action-oriented narratives of most American
science fiction films from the 1950s to the present," argues Vivian
Sobchack, in her essay "The Virginity of Astronauts: Sex and the Science Fiction Film."[6]

This is especially true of the male-dominated (though hardly
action-oriented) *2001*. In the movie, the few female characters who flit
through the novel have lost even their chauvinist, neocolonial charm:
Clarke's "charming little stewardess" from the "largely unspoiled"
island of Bali, who entertains Dr. Floyd with some zero-gravity dance
steps during his flight to the moon, is reimagined by Kubrick as a
weirdly sexless creature in a white uniform and bulbous cap that gives
her a distinctly brachycephalic look, somewhere between an overgrown fungal spore and one of the walking, talking sperm in *Everything You Always Wanted to Know about Sex* by Woody Allen.

Still, the repressed has a nasty way of returning. If HAL could cry
digital tears, as the AI theorist Rosalind Picard speculates in *Hal's
Legacy: "2001's" Computer as Dream and Reality*, wouldn't he also be
capable of sexual arousal? Although her inquiry into machine emotion leads her to conclude that "emotion appears to be a necessary
component of intelligent, friendly computers like HAL," noting that
"too little emotion wreaks havoc on reasoning," Picard gives love a
wide berth (many researchers don't consider it a "basic" emotion, she
says) and studiously avoids any mention of sexual desire, save for a
passing remark about the slipperiness of a concept like "lust."[7]

This is a notable sin of omission, since the question is less laughable than it sounds. Turing believed that a true thinking machine would be a feeling machine, too—a computer with a sex drive as well as a hard drive. In a 1951 radio broadcast, he *epater*'d the bourgeoisie by declaring that a machine that thinks would be capable of being "influenced by sex appeal."[8] It seems only likely that an ultraintelligent computer like HAL would, as Sir Geoffrey Jefferson put it in a lecture Turing was fond of quoting, "be warmed by flattery, be made miserable by its mistakes, [and] be charmed by sex."[9]

As for the question of HAL's sexual preference, it seems significant, somehow, that the modern chapter of cybernetic smartness—Turing's 1950 essay "Computing Machinery and Intelligence"—opens with a tongue-in-cheek bit of gender-bending, dreamed up by a gay man. Although the scenario commonly known as the Turing Test is usually envisioned as a human interrogator in a room with two terminals, one connected to a computer, the other to a human, attempting to determine by sending and receiving messages which of the unseen conversationalists is a machine, Turing's original "imitation game" involved an isolated interrogator trying to decide, through written communications, which of two people in another room was male and which was female. Intriguingly, the woman was instructed to tell the truth and the man to lie, which means that he had to engage in a sort of electronic transvestism, or MorFing, as online cross-dressing is known ("MorF" = "Male or Female").

Turing writes, "We now ask the question, 'What will happen when a machine takes the part of [the man] in this game?" reformulating the question of gender identity as one of machine intelligence.[10] As the cultural critic Hillel Schwartz points out in *The Culture of the Copy*, "Turing reframed the debate about the limits of mechanism in terms of the limits of our ability to see through social simulation. Without surgery but from close-up, onstage or at a party, a woman can pass as a man, a man as a woman. What we think we know about maleness and femaleness is a social knowledge."[11] And so, by extension, is what we think we know about human intelligence or, alternatively, hetero- and homosexuality.

There's something queer about Turing's Universal Machine itself, in the Sontagian sense of queerness as inextricably intertwined with an understanding of life as artifice. An abstract engine capable of simulating any other device whose operations could be reduced to readable code, it was designed "to do anything conventional, anything for which the rules were laid down," writes Turing biographer Andrew Hodges.[12] The machine inherits the everyday politics of its inventor, who hacked together a passably straight persona out of generic social code—athleticism, "emotional reserve," and a Spartan insistence on what Hodges calls "professional 'thinking' before off-duty 'feeling'"— as part of a "resolve not to be 'soft,'" the time-honored code word for queer.[13]

The Turing Test, it must be remembered, in no way proves that a machine is actually thinking, merely that its simulation of thought is sufficient for it to "pass" as human. As Turing rather archly—and tellingly—observed, there is no way of telling that other *humans* are "thinking" in any objective sense. We acknowledge culturally accepted signs as evidence of internal processes, and it seems only logical to apply the same standards to inorganic intelligence. In Turing's worldview (universally embraced by contemporary AI researchers from MIT's Rodney Brooks to Carnegie Mellon's Hans Moravec), passing is everything; the "imitation game" is the only game in town.

"Alan Turing never confused simulation with duplication," writes Schwartz. "Machine intelligence, Turing knew, would always be virtual—but that should be enough to unpeg our arrogance."[14] Given historical visions of gays as male impersonators and computers as human surrogates, there's an implicit parallel between the mounting anxiety provoked by cybernetic challenges to human superiority— Deep Blue's conquest of the world chess champion Garry Kasparov, for instance—and the vague uneasiness, in the straight mainstream, inspired by the disquieting knowledge that the world is no longer hetero until proven guilty. The normative worldview is being unpegged at both the heterosexist and anthropocentrist levels, a revelation brought home by the familiar gay reminder that "we're on your police forces, we're in your churches," and so forth, and by the "bots" already fooling unsuspecting participants in online chats—simulators like the ELIZA program, which strikes up conversations with come-ons like "Do you want to sleep with me, or what?" (Here, at least, artificial intelligence and the silicon libido seem to be developing in tandem, as Turing predicted.)

Obviously, none of these free associations, from Clarke's unconscious use of suggestive catchphrases such as "living a lie," to Turing's own homosexuality, to the Turing Test's subtext of "passing," to the arguable "queerness" of the Universal Machine itself, constitutes proof positive that HAL is gay. Nonetheless, what little we know of HAL's nature and nurture, together with the cat's cradle of coincidences interweaving the secret lives of Alan Turing and his famous offspring, argues convincingly in that direction.

First, there's HAL's voice, provided by the Shakespearean actor Douglas Rain. Kubrick biographer Vincent LoBrutto notes that the director was pleased with the "patronizing, asexual quality" Rain gave HAL, but one man's condescension is another man's cattiness; balanced on the knife edge between snide and anodyne, HAL's sibilant tone and use of feline phrases like "quite honestly, I wouldn't worry myself about that" contain more than a hint of the stereotypic bitchy homosexual.[15] Clarke himself has acknowledged that HAL's voice betrays "a certain ambiguity," sexually.

Moreover, if the man's, man's, man's world of the movie and the novel are any indication, HAL was presumably raised by men and, like Turing, schooled in an all-male environment. That all-male environments are hotbeds of sublimated sexuality, haunted by the threat of same-sex love, is news to no one; English boarding schools such as Turing's, where "contact between the boys was fraught with sexual potential" (Hodges), have long been the, er, butt of locker-room one-liners.

Then, too, there's the starship *Discovery*'s two-year mission, in *2001*, to explore strange new worlds with an all-male crew. As Clarke coyly notes, all of the astronauts' needs have been anticipated: the ship's pharmacopoeia is stocked with "adequate, though hardly glamorous, substitutes" for sex—*Sleeper*'s Orgasmatron in pill form, presumably.[16] But what of HAL's needs? As we've speculated, he's almost certainly capable of being "charmed by sex," and his electronic Eros probably bears the stamp of a separatist upbringing. How many months in space with nothing to do but stomp Poole in chess and fiddle with the ship's radio dish before even the *Discovery*'s astronauts begin to look desirable? In Vivian Sobchack's estimation, Poole and Bowman's "tight-assed competence disallow[s] any connection with the sexual and the sensuous."[17] Then again, there's much to be said for a tight ass, especially when it's jogging around the *Discovery*'s centrifuge in a pair of butt-hugging shorts. Besides, as HAL might respectfully point out, Sobchack's dismissal of Poole "basking nearly naked under a sunlamp" as "hardly a piece of beefcake" is somewhat ungenerous, given her terrestrial vantage point, with its vastly wider menu of potential partners.[18]

Could HAL have gotten jealous of what he imagined must go on behind closed pod doors between Poole and Bowman? The next line in Sir Geoffrey Jefferson's argument that for a machine to think in any meaningful sense it will have to "be warmed by flattery, be made miserable by its mistakes, [and] be charmed by sex" is *"be angry or depressed when it cannot get what it wants"* (emphasis mine). When we first meet Dave, he is literally the apple of HAL's eye, reflected in one of the ubiquitous red fish-eye lenses the computer uses to surveil the ship. But, like the half-eaten apple found near Turing's body, an apple that had allegedly been dipped in potassium cyanide, this apple (of Sodom?) may be poisoned. Is Frank's murder the cold-blooded elimination of a rival for Dave's affections?

When Dave unplugs HAL's brain, the computer's swan song is easily the movie's most powerfully affecting moment (and a close second, for Wagnerian romanticism, to the dying android's soliloquy in *Blade Runner*). In *Hal's Legacy*, Clarke recalls, "In the early 1960s at Bell Laboratories I had heard a recording of an Iliac computer singing 'Bicycle Built for Two.' I thought it would be good for the death scene—especially the slowing down of the words at the end."[19] If we presume HAL's homosexuality, however, the song begins to sound like a deathbed confession of star-crossed love.

Beyond the obvious homoeroticism of one man—or, rather, male machine—singing an old-fashioned love song to another, HAL may have intended "Daisy Bell (Bicycle Built for Two)" as a poignant allusion to the brow from which he sprang, historically speaking. Written in 1892, on the eve of a century in which human passions would be set against an ever more technological backdrop, "Daisy" is a Victorian love song inspired by a technological innovation—the invention of the women's bicycle. By a curious coincidence, Turing, an avid bicyclist, was riding a women's bike at the time of his death. Stranger still, he was hard at work on a theory of morphogenesis, and one of his last experiments, involving computer simulations of plant evolution, was titled "Outline of Development of the Daisy." (Intriguingly, there's a subterranean connection here between the lab and the closet: Turing shared the widely held belief that hormones played an integral role in morphogenesis, determining individual psychology as well as physiology—a concept rich in resonances with the ongoing debate about genetic predetermination for homosexuality.)

But even if we "prove" that HAL *is* gay, what's the significance of outing a fictional supercomputer, outside the context of extreme sports for semioticians? In semiotic terms, the notion of a gay computer reconciles conventional depictions of machines as hulking, brawny avatars of male power with the traditionally "feminine" qualities associated with computers: smallness; quirky, inscrutable temperaments; and concealed, mysterious private parts. HAL may represent the first inkling of the now full-blown realization that the industrial boilerplate in which we've sheathed our metaphors for technology, from RoboCop to the Terminator to Transformers to Iron Man, is inappropriate to an age of ever-smaller, ever-smarter "soft" machines.

Alternately, gay machines such as HAL and his descendants—among them KITT, the campy RoboCar in *Knight Rider* (of whom the authors of *The Complete Directory to Prime Time Network TV Shows* straight-facedly write, "It was love at first sight between Michael [Knight] and KITT," who was "peevish, a bit haughty, but totally protective" of his hunky rider)—prop up the sagging machismo of male heroes whose derring-do, in the Computer Age, consists largely of sitting in a chair, pushing buttons.[20] This is the glaring irony that renders *Star Trek*'s Perma-Prest Captain Picard and his beefy side-kick, Commander Riker—torchbearers for a rock-ribbed masculinity—unintentionally funny: in the final analysis, they're overgrown gameboys in pantsuits, jabbing at touch screens in an earth-toned rec room. Prone to hissy fits, sissified machines such as C-3PO, *Star Wars*'s fussy, high-strung Felix to R2-D2's Oscar (with the femme–butch subtext that implies), reaffirm the rugged manliness of these armchair adventurers, by contrast.

Also, flighty, high-strung machines make stolid, clench-jawed humans like *Star Wars*'s Han Solo or *2001*'s Poole and Bowman seem cool and calculating in comparison; in so doing, they reverse the philosophical polarity of the man–machine dualism and ironically reaffirm the superiority of human "emotional intelligence" over mechanical reason ("ironically," obviously, because Poole, Bowman, and other affectless robopaths reassert human dominance in a wired world at the expense of that quintessentially human quality, emotion).

At the same time, HAL's homosexuality—specifically, the high cost of its denial—may be Clarke's way of reminding us that the brightest minds and the loftiest aspirations can be brought down by bigotry. The notion of a closeted supercomputer eaten away by "unconscious feelings of guilt" and unstrung by "the conflict between truth, and concealment of truth," can be easily read as an homage to Turing. In his foreword to *Hal's Legacy*, Clarke laments the bitter irony that Turing, "who perhaps contributed more than any other individual to the Allied victory" by cracking top-secret German codes, "would never have been allowed into [a highly sensitive research facility] under normal security regulations"—a clear reference to Turing's homosexuality.[21]

Of course, HAL's sexuality is destined to remain an open question. As the Turing test implies, we'll never really know if his putative straightness is the real thing or merely a convincing facsimile thereof. Apparently, even his fictional father doesn't know for sure. When the cultural critic Paula Treichler put the question to Clarke at Cyberfest '97 at the University of Illinois in Urbana (HAL's birthplace), he quipped, "I don't know; I never asked him," although he added fuel to the fire by admitting, "His voice has a certain ambiguity, however."[22]

In my mind, though, there is no question about it, as HAL himself would say. When the dying computer serenades David Bowman, I'll always hear a tear-jerking torch song that begins, "Davey, Davey, Give me your answer, do / I'm half crazy all for the love of you . . ."

POSTSCRIPT

After a severely truncated version of this essay appeared on the now-defunct Suck.com in May 1997, I e-mailed a copy of the longer, original draft to Clarke, with the provocative subject line "HAL's (Gravity) Well of Loneliness." He was gracious, commending me on my "fantastic job of research." As for HAL's sexuality? "I can't confirm or deny your speculations. Who knows what goes on down in the subconscious?"

In my reply, I noted that the publication of my essay, on Suck, had "prompted much e-mail, several pieces of which relayed the (entirely unsubstantiated) rumor" that Clarke himself was gay. "I'm wary of offending you, since you've been so gracious," I began, edging in where angels fear to tread, "but the journalistic imperative to ferret out all the facts, no matter how intimate, compels me to ask: Are you gay? Naturally, I won't be surprised if you tell me to go to hell, since it's an intensely private matter, but its relevance to my essay is obvious." With gentlemanly forbearance, Clarke replied, "As I'm the most conspicuous resident of a country [Sri Lanka] still in the last century in some respects, I can't comment on your question . . ." Which was, of course, comment enough.

Clarke's standard dodge, when pressed on the question of his sexuality, was that he wasn't gay, "just a little bit cheerful."[23] After the novelist's death at ninety in March 2008, obituaries in Papers of Record, such as Gerald Jonas's in the *New York Times*, handled rumors of the novelist's sexuality with throat-clearing discomfiture, if at all. Even in the twenty-first century, this news, apparently, was still not Fit to Print. (The SF novelist Michael Moorcock, writing in *The Guardian*, was a happy exception, noting with admirable matter-of-factness, "Everyone knew he was gay. In the 1950s I'd go out drinking with his boyfriend.")[24] Likewise, gay bloggers such as the SF novelist Toby Johnson, a longtime correspondent of Clarke's, were at pains to set the record straight:

> He demurred about coming out publicly as gay, he wrote, because he felt this fact would be used to discredit his ideas. He was 61 at the time of Stonewall, already past the sexual prime in which it's meaningful to identify oneself as gay.... He wrote that he was quite fascinated with the role homosexuals have played down through time as revolutionary thinkers. (In our correspondence, he expressed great interest in C. A. Tripp's book about Abraham Lincoln as gay.) He kept a private collection of writing which is not to be published until 50 years after his death. I'd wager the world is going to receive the open acknowledgement of his homosexuality, and of his theory about gay consciousness as revolutionary, come 2058.[25]

Who knows what goes on down in the subconscious—of man or machine?

(1997)

Word Salad Surgery

IF ONLY TRISTAN TZARA HAD LIVED TO READ SPAMBOT SUB-
ject lines.

As Bruce Sterling—futurist, sci-fi novelist, and Shaolin Master
of Texas slacker cynicism—noted in a post on his blog Beyond the
Beyond, spambots are "evolv[ing] into ... Surrealist poet[s]" in order
to fool spam-zapping programs. "Spam is now forced to mutter eerie
magic charms as it routes its way past the growing host of armed
spam guards to my mailbox," wrote Sterling. "'No, no kill me, I am
not spaaaaam.... Would spam speak of 'Orinoco Apocrypha'? Would
mere spam muse on 'brutal Prussia,' 'discernable Petersburg' and an
'Acapulco assault'? I do these cultured, verbally elaborate things in my
'Pillsbury showboat,' and hence I cannot be spam! Let me through
with my 'hierarchic bronchiole,' do not extinguish me, o router and
repeater!'"[1]

In 2002, spam hunters escalated hostilities in the arms race between
anti-spam programs and junk-mail programmers by making use of a
statistical method called a Bayesian filter to rank words according to
their likelihood of turning up in a piece of junk e-mail; if a junkbot
contains high-scoring words such as *Viagra, Xanax, mortgage,* or *porn,*
the spam-icidal program kills it dead. In retaliation, spambots have
attempted to camouflage themselves by inserting random words or
letters into headers and tacking what is known as a "word salad" onto
the end of the e-mail. As anti-spam programs add the mutated come-
ons to their indexes of spamwords, spambots are forced to mutate

still further. In time, their solicitations are reduced to alphanumeric gobbledygook. "Increasingly, the subject lines convey no meaning at all: 'begonia breadfruit extempore defocus purveyor,'" wrote George Johnson in the *New York Times*. "Often appended at the end, in an attempt to flummox the filters, is a scrap of Dadaist poetry—'feverish squirt feat transconductance terrify broken trite fascist axis stultify floc bookshelves.'"[2]

Like Sterling's description of such word salads as surrealist poetry, Johnson's reflexive use of an artistic genre ("Dadaist poetry") to describe this descent into literary dementia reminds us that uselessness is an essential aspect of The Aesthetic: yesterday's technologies, now obsolete—butter churns, ice tongs, astrolabes—are today's aesthetic fetishes, accessorizing the mantelpieces of the designerati.

At the same time, hearing surrealist poetry in the nonsensical subject lines and gibberish body texts of spambots (stitched together from snippets of stolen prose, à la William S. Burroughs) follows the John Cage-ean logic that music is in the ear of the beholder. To Cage, the street noises intruding through an open window on a piano recital were no less musical than the notes being played; all we have to do is open our ears, he suggested. In so saying, Cage was self-consciously following the trail blazed by Marcel Duchamp, the prankish con(ceptual) artist who in 1917 slapped a title on a wall-mounted urinal ("Fountain"), signed it, and scandalized the art world by submitting it to a sculpture exhibition. A century's worth of "found" art, together with modernism's collage consciousness, has prepared us to hear the surrealist poetry and Dadaist provocation lurking in programmers' strategies for bluffing their way past our junk-mail defenses.

Consider the love-it-or-leave-it, my-way-or-the-highway dualism of the first hunk of spam that popped up in my in-box today. "Be godparent or osteology," its subject line admonishes, a Dadaist ultimatum if ever there was one. Does it mean: If you're not part of a social network, bound by family ties, you've got one foot in the boneyard? "Riddle and barbecue," another spam's subject line advises, sounding like a 1950s cookbook for patio Daddy-o's who want to be the life of the garden party, even while grilling. "Ragweed conjunct Sherlocke," reads another, cryptically. A reference to Conan Doyle's mythical detective? If so, why ye olde terminal *e*, a typographic artifact of the medieval ages rather than the Victorian era, when Sherlock Holmes stalked criminals through London's gaslit streets? And what's this about "ragweed conjunct"? A veiled allusion to the famous crimebuster's infamous weakness for drugs? Doubtful, since Holmes, though notoriously fond of cocaine as an antidote to the dreary downtime between stimulating cases, was no devotee of weed.

Intriguingly, "Ragweed conjunct Sherlocke" makes use of the market-tested underground-band formula of stringing together three unrelated words to generate a record title or band name guaranteed to inspire hours of beer-bong *explication de texte,* as in Wilco's *Yankee Hotel Foxtrot* or the Butthole Surfers' *Locust Abortion Technician* or the Mother of Them All, Captain Beefheart's *Trout Mask Replica.* Do spambot programmers in offshore sweatshops have a secret sweet spot for freak rock? Or is there a neurocognitive reason for our intuitive sense that three is the magic number when it comes to dream-logic word games? I've archived spam with Beefheartian subject lines such as "biracial Auerbach crankshaft," "boil longleg Kant" (those of us with little patience for the bewigged old dear couldn't agree more), and the painful-sounding "hardwood pancreatic departure," whose message begins on an exuberant note ("cowpony joyful plexiglas biz") but ends, dejectedly, "casino tulane cattlemen denebola colorado skim cried allegro discernible florican abbas binaural cathedral brace."

By contrast, there are sweetly elegiac subject lines, such as "Bette, in daydream epoch." Read with a little poetic license, this spam subject line evokes with admirable economy the image of big-eyed Bette Davis in mid-reverie, lost in the ever-expanding moment of a Proustian recollection. But I have *no* idea what to make of the paragraph tacked onto the end of this mail, a bit of free-associated absurdism— and a further attempt to defeat spam-sniffing programs—that rivals anything written by the Language poet Jackson Mac Low:

with a squint who had no other merit than smelling   like a stanhope
coneflower   has increased upon him since I
first came here He is   often very nervous or I fancy so It is not fancy

Much ink has been shed about the irretrievable loss of writerly correspondence, now that we live in the Age of the Recycle Bin, when time is the scarcest commodity and spam overgrows our in-boxes like so much kudzu. Literary scholars mourn the passing of the letter as a literary art form and note what a loss it would have been had, say, Robert Browning vaporized his then-lover Elizabeth Barrett's overheated e-mails with a single, irrevocable mouse click.

Perhaps. But they're missing the riches under their noses, the inexhaustible fund of literary innovation and mass-psychological free association that is spam. (A few inspired Data-ists have already recognized the literary potential of spam. Rob Read has published *O Spam, Poams,* a heavily edited collection of the best of his junk e-mail, which a promotional blurb on the website for Apollinaire's Bookshoppe says "range from hilarious to pensive, anecdotal to ahh-inspiring."[3] In contrast, Andrew Russ's *Machine Language* anthologizes spam that is only minimally edited—word salads chosen for their literary resonances.)

At its best, spam is an MRI of the mass mind, scanning the dream life of consumer culture and giving the Dadaists and the Burroughsian cut-up squad a run for their money when it comes to machine-age avant-gardism. Which makes me wonder: Since spam poetry is software-generated, why not a Turing test for experimental lit? Who will code the first program that wins the prestigious $40,000 Griffin Poetry Prize, awarded in 2002 to the experimental poet Christian Bok for his *Eunoia,* a collection of poems in which each chapter is composed entirely of words of a single vowel. Surely, Deep Blue could do better . . .

And speaking of Dadaists, if Marcel Duchamp had lived to read spam, the man who nonchalantly proclaimed snow shovels and hat racks "readymade" sculptures would surely have edited a Library of

America anthology of spam, the signature genre of our times (not to mention our only truly new literary form, written by machines). Printed, as always, on acid-free paper and set in Galliard type, bound in the finest cloth and topped off with a ribbon marker, the better to mark memorable passages, such a volume would be grist for a million dissertation mills:

> automat see ammonia try petrifaction in capistrano be mosaic!
> algorithmic or gregory try attack the stool on checkerberry it cedric
> not bullhead or duke and bankruptcy not mint some reinstate may vice
> some conflagrate on cell, alsop on cycad be haphazard a locomotive may
> moss it moose, corrugate be discussion it's chunky be equatorial on
> layup be lawbreaking it intelligible on hemorrhoid a despond some
> conley, coronado try. Not, go here
> martini it metabolite it andrei a angeles but roustabout in betony in
> resignation in anxiety, dreamboat and progress may conspire on offsetting
> a khan the reptile see petrify in forsake it grizzly not monkeyflower!
> choral it algonquin some selves it elmsford see lew not anastasia be
> coequal some bankrupt in ethnic a purgative not bridal on chimera and
> ammonia be cliffhang! began or kickback be amalgam or tycoon! Not, go
> here

(2007)

Slashing the Borg

> Cyborg writing is about . . . seizing the tools that mark the world
> that marked [one] as other. The tools are often stories, retold stories,
> versions that reverse and displace the hierarchical dualisms of natu-
> ralized identities.
>
> —DONNA HARAWAY, *Simians, Cyborgs, and Women: The Reinvention*
> *of Nature*

IN *SCIENCE FRICTION*, MECHANICAL REPRODUCTION IS STRICTLY
X- rated. The Toronto-based queer fanzine is devoted to campy, techno-
porn burlesques of *Star Trek: The Next Generation*'s "Borg" episodes.
(For non-Trekkers, the Borg are the implacable man-machines who
periodically imperil Truth, Justice, and the United Federation of
Planets on ST:TNG.) Produced by Glenn Mielke, Nancy Johnston,
and Miriam Jones, *Science Friction* features panting tales of Robo-
Copulation, pornographic "Sonnets from the Borgugese," and "heart-
stoppingly explicit illustrations," spiral-bound and sealed in a "plastic
splash guard cover" for your one-handed reading convenience.[1]

Science Friction, whose battle cry is "If Paramount can't give us
that queer episode, just make it so!" is a textbook example of what
media theorists call "textual poaching," the guerrilla semiotics in
which consumers-turned-producers perversely rework popular fictions. Henry Jenkins, a scholar of fan cultures, and Constance Penley,
a feminist film theorist, have documented a form of textual poaching

known as "slash" erotica written by female fans of the original *Star Trek* TV series and published in underground fanzines. Typically, it is about Captain Kirk and the Vulcan science officer Mr. Spock and is thus dubbed "K/S" for short, yielding the term "slash."

Spun from the perceived homoerotic subtext in *Star Trek* narratives, slash tales are often animated by feminist impulses. In his seminal essay "*Star Trek* Rerun, Reread, Rewritten: Fan Writing as Textual Poaching," Jenkins points out that although science fiction is arguably "by, for, and about men of action, *Star Trek* seems to hold out a suggestion of nontraditional feminine pleasures, of greater and more active involvement for women within the adventure of professional space travel, while finally reneging on those promises. . . . fan writers characterize themselves as 'repairing the damage' caused by the program's inconsistent and often demeaning treatment of its female characters."[2]

In her essay "Brownian Motion: Women, Tactics, and Technology," Constance Penley theorizes that "slashers" (their preferred term)—the majority of whom are heterosexual women working in the "pink-collar, 'subprofessional,' or high-tech service industry sectors"—embroider gay themes because "writing a story about two men avoids the built-in inequality of the romance formula, in which dominance and submission are invariably the respective roles of male and female."[3]

Since *Trek* slash is at its heart a utopian vision of male–female interaction cloaked in the tropes of mainstream SF, it presumes a twenty-third-century man who is neither Schwarzeneggerian "hard guy" nor Alan Alda-esque "sensitive man," but the best of both. Further, writes Penley, "slash does not stop with retooling the male psyche; it goes after the body as well."[4] A subgenre has sprung up around the sexual heat that overcomes Mr. Spock and all Vulcan males every seven years, the *pon faar*; in *Fever*, an underground 'zine given over exclusively to *pon faar* porn, slashers play nimbly on the obvious parallels to menstruation, even to the extent of depicting Spock as suffering from the male equivalent of PMS. Another, more marginal subgenre revolves around Kirk and Spock's attempts to have a child. In one story, Dr. McCoy genetically engineers a fertilized Kirk/Spock ovum, which is brought to term in an artificial womb designed by Scotty, the starship's chief engineer.[5]

Slashers' feminist attempts to "rewrite" the male body as well as the male psyche through the vehicle of homoerotic SF fantasies are underscored by "a very real appreciation," Penley writes, "of gay men in their efforts to redefine masculinity, and . . . feelings of solidarity with them insofar as gay men too inhabit bodies that are still a legal, moral, and religious battleground"—a point made dramatically (and comically) clear in gay Trekkers' own attempts to rewrite gender norms by slashing the Borg. (The term *slash* seems to have come unstuck from the strictly literal usage; it is now applied to TV-inspired homoerotica, whether Kirk/Spock or not.)

On *Star Trek: The Next Generation*, the Borg function as a "hive mind," or collective entity, their nervous systems linked via the meta–nervous system of their monolithic, cube-shaped ship. They are sealed in sculpted black body armor, their bleached flesh penetrated by fetishistic high-tech prostheses, with "extensive infiltration of microcircuit fibers into [their] surrounding tissue," according to the *Enterprise*'s Dr. Crusher.[6] Their battle cry, intoned in an electronically filtered, Darth Vader-ish monotone, is "Resistance is futile; you will be assimilated"—an ominous pronouncement borne out in the immensely popular two-part episode "The Best of Both Worlds," in which the Borg cut a swath through the cosmos, obliterating everything in their path.

Abducting Captain Picard, they transform him into Locutus of Borg, a bionic interface between the conqueror cyborgs and the soon-to-be-assimilated humans—a metalmorphosis described in the series-inspired novel *Star Trek/Deep Space Nine #1: Emissary*:

> One of Picard's arms had been extended with an intricate mechanical prosthesis, his eyes augmented with a sensor-scope protruding from one temple; his pale face was utterly, frighteningly blank. . . . Sisko got a fleeting mental image of mindless hive insects excreting skeins of metal, wrapping Picard in a cocoon of machinery.[7]

Like the original series, ST:TNG is built on an unshakable bedrock of liberal humanism. The Borg, mindless cogs in a totalitarian civilization whose monomaniacal goal is the extinction of all free thought, provide a cartoon antithesis to the series' endlessly reiterated thesis that humanist values (read: the American way) are destined to triumph over the enemies of democracy and free enterprise. The crypto-fascist Borg are not just inhuman, they're un-American.

And, horror of horrors, they're queer! At least, that is, in the alternate universe of *Science Friction,* which highlights the gay subtext of the Borg episodes. Once "outed," the Borg appear to be so obviously and so variously wired into gay myth and metaphor that it seems almost unthinkable that the connections could have gone unnoticed.

Like sailors, bikers, cops, and other stereotypical characters in homoerotic fantasy, the Borg are an all-male society living in close quarters. They're in constant physical communion with one another, literally bonded by electronic interconnection—"borgasm," to use *Science Friction* coeditor Glenn Mielke's elbow-in-the-ribs coinage. "Wait a minute," says the *Enterprise*'s chief engineer, Geordi La Forge, in Mielke's "Beamed on Borg," "you mean to say that the Borg are in constant sexual link?" "Yes," replies the deprogrammed Borg Hugh, "we are with each other always."[8] The reader half expects him to break into Walt Whitman's "Song of Myself": "I sing the body electric / The bodies of those I love engirth me and I engirth them." Anonymous and continuous, the exchange of fluid data among the Borg conjures the fleeting, faceless sex, in bars, bathrooms, and public parks, of the gay sexual demimonde in the '70s and early '80s. The Borg's cadaverous pallor evokes urban nightcrawlers—sybarites who come out only after dark in some John Rechy-esque City of Night, or the androgynous vampires in Anne Rice's best-selling homoerotic novels.

With their metallic, monotonal delivery, stolid expressions, and penchant for skintight black outfits, the Borg call to mind the Nazi cheesecake theme that is the guiltiest of Tom of Finland's guilty pleasures, lovingly embellished in some of his more outré illustrations.[9]

Semiotically, the sign of the Borg points simultaneously in opposite directions. On one hand, the Borg remind us of the sublimated homosexuality that troubled the Nazi cult of the warrior male, with its problematic emphasis on male bonding—a necessary evil in the formation of a cohesive killing machine, but inescapably haunted by the specter of a more than platonic bond between brother warriors. On the other hand, they recall the curious appropriation of Nazi iconography by the gay pornographic imagination, which Susan Sontag attributes in "Fascinating Fascism" to the "natural link" between sadomasochism and fascism, both forms of "sexual theater" in which the master–slave relationship is aestheticized.[10]

In a delicious irony, Borg slashers reprogram the technophallic killing machine for the very "softness" it abhors. In "Locutus" by Gigi the Galaxy Girl (Nancy Johnston), a Borg's hardware has been reconfigured so that he may boldly go where no man-machine has gone before:

> Instead of puckered flesh, his Borg anus had been enhanced and altered to receive. He had the perfect access conduit.[11]

The Borg also suggest a mechano-erotic take on the gay "clone" of the '70s, the mustachioed, short-cropped fixture of San Francisco's Castro district, instantly recognizable in Levi's and leather, flaunting his gym-toned muscles. Dank, dark, and hazy with mist, the tangled catwalks of the Borg ship cross the gay bathhouse with the S&M pleasure dungeon. The results are a natural habitat for man-machines whose form-fitting black armor resembles the accoutrements of the bondage fetishist, their flesh punctured by cables in a semiotic echo of the pierced ears and nipples popularized by gay culture.

The Borg make perfect mascots for a strain of gay eros that appropriates the imagery of the machine age. In *The Culture of Desire: Paradox and Perversity in Gay Lives Today*, Frank Browning mentions a sex club called Big Ironworx. This and other gay "invitation" clubs of the early '90s took place in "open rooms in the warehouses of depleted industrial zones, where in the small hours of the morning, young men lined up with their buddies to probe, caress, and gnaw at one another's flesh in dimly lit tangles of animal abandon."[12]

Browning goes on to argue, following Georges Bataille, that sex can never be truly safe in the most profound sense because it is, "for most of us, our primary, residual, atavistic connection to the realm of animal existence."[13]

But if the animal is shorthand for that which is "inhuman" in every human, then we might just as easily argue that anonymous sex, conducted assembly-line style in abandoned industrial sites, unleashes the machine within. In Randy Shilts's *And the Band Played On,* a stunned young man observes, of bathhouse orgiasts, "Their bodies were tools through which they could experience physical sensation."[14] Thus, in ravenous sex, when the intellect is overmastered by the cravings of the flesh, the individual in question has in some very real sense been mechanized. Sontag refers in her essay "The Pornographic Imagination" to the Marquis de Sade's vision "of the body as a machine and of the orgy as an inventory of the hopefully infinite possibilities of several machines in collaboration with each other."[15]

From such a perspective, the subsumption of individual organisms into the Borg collective looks less like an Orwellian nightmare and more like a paradise of desire. It calls to mind the literary critic Leo Bersani's vision of a dizzy free fall into utter abandon, following the dissolution of conventional notions of masculinity. Browning paraphrases Bersani:

> The organization of male desire ... around the power to dominate and penetrate covers up the existence of a counterdesire within men, "the perhaps equally strong appeal of powerlessness ... the loss of control." ... Homosexual desire ... acknowledges the will to shatter the authority and integrity of the male self.[16]

The Borg ship becomes a place where slashers "invent a theater of transgressive desire and enter into the symbolically exploded self," to borrow Browning's eloquent characterization of S&M.[17] In "Locutus," Johnston reimagines the abduction and Borging of Captain Picard as a coming-out story. In Part 2 of the original episode, the scene in which mechanized surgical instruments descend on a prone Picard in the Borg ship is strongly suggestive of a repressed sexual experience, in much the same way that Whitley Strieber-esque accounts of alien abduction are sometimes interpreted as nightmares about incest. Moreover, the conclusion of the two-part episode ends on a disquieting note: as an eerie melody spirals over a dark drone, Picard gazes into the star-flecked infinity of space, ostensibly lost in the traumatic memory of being Borged. Johnston turns this moment into a feverish flashback to a gay S&M experience:

> As his eyes adjusted to his surroundings on the Borg ship, Picard thought at first he had materialized inside a medieval dungeon. He stood restrained by metal clamps in an alcove.... He gasped involuntarily as the Borg began tracing a line from throat to chest . . . [t]he open palm of the mesh hand coming to rest over his heart. He felt his body shudder in response. His nipples became erect.[18]

In Johnston's story, Picard manages to escape in the process of being Borged, an operation involving the implantation of computer chips in his brain and the connection of "feeder tubes and computer access conduits" to his body.[19] Hiding from his captors, he witnesses two Borg abandoning themselves to the pleasures of the cyber-flesh:

> The humming in [Picard's] mind was intensifying. Thousands of male voices whispering, encouraging. The second Borg dropped his gloved hand from his partner's neck and touched the panels of plexisteel which concealed his own groin. Instead of deathly pale flesh, the panel revealed a second prosthesis. The Borg penis was sheathed in a synthetic shaft. At the tip, glints of liquid shone against the black latex. Picard watched breathlessly as the synthetic organ began to spiral out of its containment. It was not of human dimensions.[20]

Overcome by desire, Picard pleasures himself as he watches, his mind a hornet's nest of worrying urges: "The voices were becoming clearer now. He could not purge his brain of their insistence. 'Incorporate. Assimilate. Resistance is Futile.'"[21] Finally, the stiff, starched Captain gives himself over to desires long denied and now threatening to break down the closet door: "Picard stepped from his hiding place.... Resistance was futile. He raised his hand and touched the throat of the Borg. 'I am Locutus.'"[22]

In this and other *Science Friction* stories, the Borg admonition "You will be assimilated" (the magazine's motto) is transformed into a playful yet empowering slogan. More promise than threat, the phrase augurs an alternate universe whose only law is the Vulcan maxim that many Trekkers see as *Star Trek* creator Gene Roddenberry's most valuable contribution to the show's mythology: "Infinite Diversity in Infinite Combination"—a saying that reverberates with innuendo in this libertine cosmos. Slashed, the Borg become the "army of lovers" envisioned by Plato in his Symposium—a durable image that has served, at one time or another, as the gay community's image of itself. With its steamy, claustrophobic passageways (tunnels of love?), the Borg ship is a space-bound pleasure dome that conjures up the gay poet John Giorno's musings about "great, anonymous sex" with strangers in a subway bathroom: "The great thing about anonymous sex is you don't bring your private life or your personal world. No politics or inhibiting concepts, no closed rules or fixed responses."[23]

Looking back on "the golden age of promiscuity," before the long, dark night of AIDS, Giorno reflects, "I thought of us as the combat troops of love, liberating the world."[24] Pieces of that dream glint, here and there, in *Science Friction*'s Borg porn, where the totalitarian cyborgs that menace mainstream humanism and the misogynistic Terminators reviled by academic feminism are reread and rewritten as the liberatory Borg, a Queer Nation in space, hurtling unstoppably toward "sector zero-zero-one": Earth. Resistance will be futile, of course.

(1996)

Things to Come

RECENTLY, WHILE WEBSURFING IN SEARCH OF XTREME KINK (a carnival-midway activity that the sexpert Susie Bright calls "pornographic rubbernecking"), I stumbled on the Neck Brace Appreciation Klub, a "small but dedicated group of regular folks" who just happen to be into "recreational & artistic neck and back bracing." (Love those ironic quotes!) From there, I meandered over to the unintentionally hilarious Big-Gulp to savor the tongue-in-cheek pleasures of homemade porn in which anonymous models and celebrities, from Madonna to Lou "Incredible Hulk" Ferrigno, gobble up wriggling Lilliputians. Imagine an X-rated *Attack of the 50 Foot Woman*, remade by Dino De Laurentiis from a script by R. Crumb. Imagine a hard-core version of *The Amazing Colossal Man*, starring gay superstud Zak Spears as the bald, bediapered Brobdingnagian. Imagine— oh, hell, just visit the damn thing yourself.[1]

Is this stuff for real, the lovingly crafted, sweetly shy fantasies of a love that, until recently, dared not speak its name? Or is it winkingly ironic, a deadpan put-on aimed at the porn rubberneckers who snapped up Katharine Gates's tour guide to the polymorphously perverse *Deviant Desires: Incredibly Strange Sex*? Or is it both, the knowingly over-the-top product of pomosexual fetishists who insist on having their irony and eating it, too?

Whatever the case, Big-Gulp and sites like it are part of the hothouse profusion of fetish sites, a porn-industry development that parallels the much-noted fragmentation of mainstream consumer culture into a million niche demographics. "The technological and censor-free breakthrough of the Internet has spawned a fetish market that literally has to be seen to be believed," Bright told *Wired* magazine. "The Internet has opened Pandora's box; fetish is king."[2] Web porn devoted to midgets, fetishists who thrill to mummylike swaddling in Cling-Wrap, "furverts" who make it with plush toys (or, better yet, *as* plush toys), and similarly far-flung fetishes attract audiences far beyond their core fandoms.

That said, I'm not convinced we're witnessing a runaway proliferation of alternative sexualities; the truth, I suspect, is that the interconnected nature of the link-driven Web, together with the frenzy of online advertising, has simply made visible what was once kept far from public view, under plain brown wrappers or behind the locked boudoir doors of adventuresome sybarites. Today, anyone with a Net connection is only a click away from a parallel universe of sexual solar systems whose porn sites, toy shops, networking sites, and support groups orbit around obscure obsessions. The Web not only connects geographically far-flung devotees into close-knit communities, it also assaults unsuspecting "normals" with porn spam and X-rated search results for sites and products that cater to every imaginable (and unimaginable) proclivity. As a result, even a Websurfer who is pure in heart and says his prayers by night has probably been spammed with a come-on from a sexual subculture whose deviant desires would have given Freud anaphylactic shock.

Poking around the Web's darker corners, fetishists, pornographic rubberneckers, and sexologists can find sexual proclivities and pornographic subgenres De Sade never dreamed of: amputee worship, armpit fetishism, clown porn, and sneeze freaks, who rejoice at the thought of a nice, juicy honk, with plenty of spritz. Lactating transsexuals? Been there. Scrotal inflation? Done that. Chicks with dicks and men with cunts? *So* last year, already. Erotic illustrations of Japanese schoolgirls in traction? Check. Breast-expansion fantasies about mammaries that balloon up to Goodyear blimp proportions? Check. Models made, through digital trickery, to sprout multiple, massive breasts, like some freakish cross between silicone-injected porn stars and pre-Christian fertility goddesses? Check.

The heightened profile of fetishism is also due to what I call the Escalation of Subcultural Hostilities—the ever-greater extremes required of would-be Rebels without a Cause in the age of *Jackass, Extreme Makeover,* and the pierced whatever. Time was when all a brooding young boho had to do to *épater le bourgeoisie* was carve a swastika in his forehead and cop a witchy, Dylan Klebold stare. But how do you certify your cred as a Menace to Society in a world where soccer moms think Eminem is da bomb diggity and Nabisco is selling Xtreme Jell-O? How long will it be before Marilyn Manson shows up at the Bob Hope Chrysler Classic, trading chip-shot tips with Alice Cooper?

In jaded times such as ours, nothing gets the full and undivided attention of Parental Authorities like the breezy, insouciant admission that you're into, oh, I don't know, "crush" fetishism—sexual arousal at the sight of bugs, mice, and other vermin impaled on the stiletto heels of sneering dominatrixes. The Death of Affect that J. G. Ballard has called "the greatest casualty of the twentieth century" is here to stay. Years of tabloid media, reality TV, attacking heads, and, more recently, nightly news nightmares of doomed workers leaping from the World Trade Center, hand in hand, or journalists beheaded in your living room by jihadi or the slapstick torture at Abu Ghraib— home movies from hell that employed the visual grammar of porn— have cauterized our cultural nerve endings. Little wonder, then, that ever greater subcultural voltages are needed to shock us.

"The point in rubbernecker pornography is sensation," Bright argues in her essay "Pornographic Futures."[3] The point, she maintains, "is a physical jolt, a thrill, a taboo which until this gross-out moment was intact." At the moment, nothing says "gross-out" like *bukkake,* a supremely icky phenomenon brought to you by Japan, that empire of the crossed signs where pubic hair is airbrushed off porn but no self-respecting salaryman would leave home without a pair of soiled panties sewn into the lining of his hat.[4] In Bukkake

Classic, a group of men masturbate on a woman's upturned face. Typical bukkake photos are pure gothic, so underexposed they look like Polaroids taken in Gilles de Rais's dungeon. The men look like celebrants in some strange, subterranean ritual, at once blank-eyed yet intensely absorbed in the task at, er, hand. Why aren't they wearing Masonic aprons or black hoods? Where's the Church of Satan when you need it?

Like all S&M, *bukkake* is ritualized domination and submission, a domination dramatized in this case by the messy desecration of feminine purity, the purer the better. (The Japanese, who invented the genre, prefer symbols of pristine innocence or white-cotton cleanliness: barely legal Lolitas dressed as schoolgirls, nurses, or, bizarrely, bunnies.) "They plan to use her for their own sexual satisfaction, then completely HUMILIATE her!" pants a come-on for the tellingly named FacialHumiliation.com.[5] Nothing new here to anyone familiar with De Sade's gleeful descriptions of virgins flogged, sodomized, and worse.

What *is* new, in at least one corner of the "facial" cumshot universe, is the wedding of the genre's De Sadean theater of dominance and degradation with digital software's ability to retouch or even reinvent photographic reality. The best of them—produced, or at least peddled, by PrivateGold.com, a domain name registered to the Nicosia, Cyprus–based Fraserside Holdings, Ltd.—depict radiantly smiling, impeccably made-up models, glossy lips parted to receive a shot of goo.[6]

Clearly targeting the American market, PrivateGold's images trade the abject depravity of Japanese *bukkake* for a pert, Pepsodent-smiling optimism. In the best American tradition, they celebrate technological progress, each model retouched to posthuman perfection, each cock enhanced to highlight its bulging glans and knotty veins, making it look like the ripped, rock-hard arm of a bodybuilder. Like Wayne Newton, Wendy Whoppers, and other pure products of American madness, PrivateGold's facials are a monument to delirious artificiality.

Their supersaturated aesthetic harks back to Technicolor movies, the airbrushed album-cover art of the '70s, and the paintings of Maxfield Parrish. At the same time, they're utterly contemporary in their winking subversion of their own conventions. Evoking the happy, shiny irony of early-oughties Diesel ads, they act out some male consumers' desire, equal parts Freud and Marx, to soil the android perfection of supermodels and centerfolds with a sticky puddle of splort. You don't have to be a kill-your-TV, no-logo dude/babe, raging against the machine, to see PrivateGold's farcical facials as a squirt in the eye of the inflatable, untouchable goddesses of American advertising. This is what all the leering couples wrestling with spraying hoses in those Newport cigarette ads would look like if Newport came clean about its subliminal seductions. "Alive with Pleasure," indeed.

Digitally retouched "facials" are postmodern porn, reveling in a hyperreality whose gleaming highlights and strobe-photography special effects—gobs of cum, frozen in midflight like the droplets in Harold "Doc" Edgerton's famous "Milk-Drop Coronet"—are both realer than real and hopelessly unreal.

The hyperreality of PrivateGold's facials reaches its dizziest heights in the cumshots themselves, zigzagging trajectories that bend more laws of physics than Carrie-Anne Moss in *The Matrix*, suspended in midair while the camera swoops around her in real time. In the image I'm looking at as I write this, a jet of jism pulls a sharp right turn, away from a woman's waiting lips, toward another, outstretched penis, as if drawn by homoerotic magnetism. In another photo, a streaking comet of cum appears to loop the loop, while in another the ejaculate turns on a dime and rockets away from the model's mouth, mere millimeters away, toward the startled viewer. And then there's the shot that gives new meaning to the phrase "splatter film": a triumph of special effects, it features a phallus mirabilis that simultaneously ejaculates *two* streams of cum *in different directions*. One spurts into the model's mouth while the other whizzes toward her eyebrow, doubling back at the last minute to carom off her nose, zing past her cheek, and exit stage right.

Of course, this is porn, not some supercomputer simulation of fluid dynamics, so it still has to pack a groin buzz, no matter how weird it looks. As Carol Queen, staff sexologist for the sex-positive adult-toy retailer Good Vibrations, points out, the weirdness of PrivateGold's images may even heighten their pornographic frisson. "The crazy trail of jism becomes both more artistically elegant than just a 'splat' or a 'sploosh'—especially if you can show it in slow motion or in a still pic—*and* it's the anarchic element that's going to fuck up a pretty girl's makeup and ultimately turn her into a ravening sex beast," says Queen, in an e-mail interview. "If its trajectory is a little unnatural, so much the better, perhaps."

So, what's the deeper meaning of this repeated visual trope? Are PrivateGold's fake facials our first glimpse of posthuman porn? Is this what the postmodern theorist Arthur Kroker had in mind when he announced the advent, in the late '80s, of a delirious simulacrum of posthuman sex—a "sex without secretions"? In his *Panic Encyclopedia*, Kroker argued that digital tech had at last made sex without bodily fluids possible in the form of "the computerized phone sex of the [pre-Internet] Minitel system in Paris" and what he called "video porn for the language of the gaze"—academic theoryspeak for screen-age porn that plays to the disembodied sexuality of an ever more voyeuristic society.[7] Gazing upon the Desert of the Real, Kroker declared that we had "already passed . . . beyond sex as nature and beyond sex as discourse, to sex as fascinating only when it is about recklessness, discharge and upheaval"—a premonition of Ballard's eroticized car crashes and Susie Bright's rubbernecker porn, where orgasm is displaced by the "physical jolt" of trashing a taboo. For Kroker, cybersex is a "*parodic* sex"—an *un*productive, rather than a *re*productive, act. Solo in front of a flickering screen or among fellow pseudonyms in a chat room, or (for the hopelessly old-school) on the phone, its lonely onanism is as distant from flesh-against-flesh sex as *The Matrix*'s time-stopping, gravity-defying triple kicks and cartwheels are from pre-CGI fight scenes.

Speaking of which, maybe PrivateGold's F/X facials offer a premonitory glimpse of a porn unshackled from the hidebound realism that has hobbled it for decades. Where is it writ that porn, which has always exhibited a tropism toward the unnatural, must be naturalistic? Plastic surgery and Photoshop have already given us *Playboy* Bunnies and *Penthouse* Pets who look as if they've been remodeled by the imagineers responsible for Disney's Audio-Animatronic robots. The literalism ushered in by photography and film is a historical anomaly; premodern porn is fraught with impossible anatomies and unnatural acts, from the multiple-breasted effigies of fertility goddesses such as Artemis and Ashtoreth to the men with Godzilla-sized units and the women with giant-clam vulvas in eighteenth- and nineteenth-century Japanese woodcuts.

Besides, as Lynn Hunt, a professor of history at the University of Pennsylvania, has argued, porn (in the modern sense of the word) is inherently cyborgian. It "reduces sex to a set of technologies that arouse desire, satisfy desire, create new desires," says Dr. Hunt. "Pornography is about cataloguing all the variations, treating human bodies as interchangeable parts in machines."[8] (Think of the daisy-chained orgiasts in the original illustrations for De Sade's novels, mechanically coupling like some perverse assembly line.)

It's a no-brainer, then, that a truly pomosexual porn, combining *Crouching Tiger* wirework, prosthetic effects, Japanimation, and bleeding-edge computer graphics with the postliterate visual narratives of a Cindy Sherman or a Matthew Barney, is long overdue. "I can now do 50 simultaneous events in a fluid, unending shot," John Gaeta, visual effects supervisor for *The Matrix Reloaded*, told the movie critic David Edelstein. "And I can have all this action make sense and interrelate, and I can follow it with a God's-eye camera moving at speeds that would tear an ordinary camera apart. I guarantee you your brain will work harder than any action movie you've ever seen in your entire life."[9]

But what if we want to work our libidos? Imagine cum spiraling through the air in *Matrix*-style "bullet time"; clusterfucks inspired by *The Matrix Reloaded*'s so-called Burly Brawl, hundreds of digitally cloned copies of a single actor coupling in a narcissist's vision of a group grope. Why not a live-action version of one of those seriously sicko *manga* bondage nightmares dreamed up by one of the masters of the *ero goru* (roughly, erotic grotesque) genre, such as Toshio Saeki or Suehiro Maruo? How about an IMAX version of Georges Bataille's *Story of the Eye*? Or a mind-warping CGI take on Octave Mirbeau's *Torture Garden,* based on a screenplay by Matthew Barney? Speaking of whom, bring on the satyrs! The petroleum jelly! The undifferentiated internal sex organs! The retracted scrotum pierced with clasps connected to vinyl cords! Lame though they may be, PrivateGold's F/X facials are surely a vision of things to come.

(2003)

Tripe Soup for the Soul

RELIGION AND ALL ITS WORKS AND WAYS

Tripe Soup for the Soul

"EVERY DAY, IN EVERY WAY, I'M GETTING BETTER AND BETTER."
That gem of greeting-card wisdom, worth its weight in cubic zirco-
nium, was unearthed by the French pharmacist turned psychotherapist Émile Coué (1857–1926). Coué's gospel of better living through
self-hypnosis (expounded in his 1922 book *Self Mastery through Conscious Autosuggestion*) was all the rage in Jazz Age America, where his
upbeat mantra harmonized nicely with the bull-market optimism of
a nation whistling "We're in the Money." It was and is the perfect
novena for the secular religion of success that is America's one true
faith. (Coué even advised practitioners to use a rosarylike knotted
string to keep track of the twenty repetitions required to program the
subconscious for success.)

Coué's catchy maxim cut the die for that durable self-help genre,
the daily affirmation. Of course, generations of American thinkers
had fertilized the soil in which Coué's ideas took root. In the States,
the founding father of the self-improvement craze is surely Benjamin
Franklin, whose schematic approach to self-betterment, laid out in
his *Autobiography*, endures in the pseudoscientific charts and num-
bered checklists that are fixtures of personal-growth lit.

Every day, in every way, the pumped-up exhortations of the human-
potential movement are growing louder and louder (if not better and
better). The growing popularity of audiobooks has transformed self-
help into a $2.48-billion-a-year industry, bestridden by motivational
gurus like supersalesman Zig Ziglar and the incomparable Anthony

Robbins, the fire-walking prophet of Constant And Never-ending self-Improvement (CANI!) whose arena-rock pep talks and Lurch-like appearance (he's six feet seven, wears a size sixteen shoe, and has a massive, prognathous head) have made his late-night infomercials the guilty pleasure of weirdo-collectors everywhere.[1] Imagine *Saturday Night Live*'s "Unfrozen Caveman Lawyer" reading from Mark Leyner's *Et Tu, Babe* ("I'm massaging IQ-enhancing balm into my temples . . ."). Or Rok, the acromegalic android in the old *Star Trek* episode, starring in a rock opera based on *The Power of Positive Thinking*, with music by Spinal Tap. Or—but really, Robbins's infomercials beggar description; they have to be seen to be disbelieved.

In many ways, Robbins, who writes books with arena-rock titles like *Awaken the Giant Within: How to Take Immediate Control of Your Mental, Emotional, Physical, and Financial Destiny!*, is Coué's hyperthyroidal offspring. His "science" of Neuro-Associative Conditioning™—a Pavlovian technique for rewiring your nervous system "to associate pleasure to those things you want to continuously move toward and pain to those things you need to avoid in order to succeed"—upgrades Coué for a digital culture, in which anything can be seamlessly altered with the click of a mouse.[2]

The French pharmacist's quick-fix alternative to the gloomy drudgery of Freudian analysis was a product of the Machine Age in which he lived. Frederick W. Taylor's theory of "scientific management" and John B. Watson's Pavlov-inspired behaviorist psychology were gaining traction among the power elite. "Psychology as the behaviorist views it," wrote Watson, "is a purely objective experimental branch of natural science. Its theoretical goal is the prediction and control of behavior. Introspection forms no essential part of its methods, nor is the scientific value of its data dependent on the readiness with which they lend themselves to interpretation in terms of consciousness."[3]

At last! A truly *modern* system of behavior modification, freed from Freud's gothic obsession with childhood traumas. No more introspection, no more interpretation. Psychotherapy without the psyche! What could be more American? Why spend long years on the analytical couch exhuming buried memories when you can just reprogram your biocomputer with a few autosuggestive commands? Serenity Now, goddammit, and to hell with all that weltschmerz. Sure, we're a therapy culture, but here in the land of Just Do It, we prefer painless, same-day surgery on our inner deformities. The self-help sections of American bookstores are bulging with volumes promising drive-through makeovers, from 72 *Hours to Success* to *Fast Food for the Soul* to *Instantaneous Transformation.* And if all else fails, there's always Prozac or Zoloft or Xanax to turn us into shiny happy people. "*Give* your emptiness and indifference to others, light up your face with the zero degree of joy and pleasure, smile, smile, smile," smirks French philosopher and postmodern irony guy Jean Baudrillard in his neo-Tocquevillian critique, *America.* "Americans may have no identity, but they do have wonderful teeth."[4]

No one knew that better than Dale Carnegie, a former salesman whose principles of "human engineering," codified in his 1936 classic *How to Win Friends and Influence People,* are behaviorist to the bone. Carnegie's techniques are founded on the notion of an *objectified* self—a manipulable *thing* to be remade in the image of the most attractive social persona possible in order to manipulate others (which is to say, sales prospects, since any social interaction is a potential business opportunity). Carnegie's chief weapon in softening up consumer resistance is the smile, "a real smile, a heart-warming smile, a smile that comes from within" that is also, paradoxically, "the kind of smile that will bring a good price in the marketplace."[5] Don't feel like smiling? No problem. "Force yourself to smile. If you are alone, force yourself to whistle or hum a tune or sing. Act as if you were already happy, and that will tend to make you happy.... Everybody in the world is seeking happiness—and there is one sure way to find it. That is by controlling your thoughts."[6] *Smile though your heart is aching / Smile even though it's breaking . . . / Light up your face with gladness . . . / Hide every trace of sadness . . . / Although a tear may be ever so near . . .* Light up your face with the zero degree of joy and pleasure, smile, smile, smile.

The assumption that you are what you think is a cornerstone of self-improvement theology, from Coué to Stephen Covey. The bible of can-do, *The Power of Positive Thinking* (1952), by Norman Vincent Peale, is dedicated to that proposition. And the heart of Peale's "simple yet scientific system of practical techniques of successful living" is the repetition of gung ho slogans: "Ten times each day practice the following affirmation, repeating it out loud if possible."[7] ("Scientific" because the catechism of pep, in America, is a chrome-plated faith for a gadget-happy, forward-marching society intoxicated by anything futuristic, yet "practical" because Americans are utilitarian by birth and take a dim view of wispy philosophizing that can't turn a profit or at least a screw.)

A half century later, Peale's "affirmations" are still with us in the books, tapes, and secular revival meetings of self-improvement evangelists and, naturally, in the McBalm of Gilead dispensed by countless self-help books and desktop calendars, from *Beyond Feast or Famine: Daily Affirmations for Compulsive Eaters* to *Gentle Reminders for Co-Dependents: Daily Affirmations*.

Even so, those whom corporate trainer and management consultant Chérie Carter-Scott would call "negaholics" will take glum comfort in the news that some Americans seem to be tiring of the Pursuit of Wow. Maybe it's the foul aftertaste of all that New Economy hype gone sour. Or the psychic collateral damage inflicted by 9/11. Or the recession. Whatever the reason, something seems to have taken the Wham-O out of all those high-fiving raps on the joys of Constant And Never-ending self-Improvement. Anthony Robbins's Couéesque axiom that "the only true security in life comes from knowing that every single day you are improving yourself in some way" rings hollow in an America where your stock portfolio is a cone of ash and everyone's wondering if the twitchy guy in the aisle seat has a nuke in his carry-on luggage.[8]

There's a trendlet now, evidenced by books such as *The Power of Negative Thinking: Coming to Terms with Our Forbidden Emotions*, by Gerald Amada, and *The Positive Power of Negative Thinking: Using Defensive Pessimism to Harness Anxiety and Perform at Your Peak*, by Julie K. Norem, that dismisses what Norem calls the "oblivious optimism" of the Don't Worry, Be Happy wing of pop-psych as unrealistic, even unhealthy. The psychologist Lauren Slater thinks self-esteem, the accepted foundation of a sunny-side-up attitude and hence of success, is overrated. In her essay "The Trouble with Self-Esteem," she quotes researcher Nicholas Emler, who claims that "there is absolutely no evidence that low self-esteem is particularly harmful.... People with low self-esteem seem to do just as well in life as people with high self-esteem. In fact, they may do better, because they often try harder."[9]

Maybe it's time we outgrew our thumb-sucking self-absorption. Maybe we're ready to question our reflexive equation of personal growth with Constant And Never-ending Improvement, of life lived deeply with Having a Nice Day. Maybe we should ask ourselves: What is our manic pursuit of happiness a flight *from*? What are our daily affirmations a lucky charm *against*?

Ask the aptly named Brother Void; he's been there, he knows. Void is an ironic mystic whose pitilessly sardonic yet heartachingly sincere philosophy of "compassionate nihilism" and "negative thinking" ("an eclectic collection of discredited left-brained problem-solving strategies, including debate, disagreement, criticism, and analysis") is what the world needs now.[10] In his book *Daily Afflictions*, Void recounts the moment when, "without smoking anything," he suddenly experienced a soul-curdling existential vertigo straight out of the tormented sci-fi novelist Philip K. Dick's metaphysical nightmares:

> Eternity was gazing through him, a terrible immensity annihilating him, demanding his surrender, and yet, in some strange way, requiring him for its own integrity....
> His whole life seemed a lie, an elaborate sleight of hand. Every aspect of his personality was little more than a blind slab of psychic armor, a false self, a pretension, a self-deluding vanity. Paradoxically, seeing himself this way felt like the first true moment in his life.
> He was being summoned. He was being called to embrace the terrifying Otherness all around him; embrace the world's horrors and hopelessness; embrace all that he feared and all that he had ever pushed away.[11]

In the ego-shriveling furnace of this encounter with the Mysterium Tremendum, the titanium-hard insights Brother Void calls daily afflictions—steely words of wisdom that arm "the individual for the jungle of existential terror and paradox that awaits with each new day"—were forged.[12] Whereas daily affirmations "promise that you can attract what you wish for by visualizing it," writes Void, afflictions "remind you that when you feel desperate and alone, you are.... You can't avoid suffering. The right affliction, however, can make your suffering more meaningful. It won't tell you the answer, but it can deepen an unresolvable question; it won't help you find yourself, but it might help you to realize that you are irretrievably lost.... For only in darkness, light; only in paradox, truth; only in affliction, affirmation."[13]

Daily afflictions such as "I will find that special person who is wrong for me in just the right way," "The future is full of possibilities that I must shoot in the head," and "I set aside a little time each day to die" turn the self-improvement movement's cherished faith in the spark of the divine within each of us inside out, forcing us to confront the dark matter we all harbor.[14] Throwing open the door to the starless existential emptiness behind the world of appearances, Brother Void exposes us to a soul-sucking spiritual vacuum that strips us, in an instant, of our positive thoughts, creative visualizations, and Transformational Vocabularies, leaving us naked and trembling before the deeply meaningful meaninglessness without—and within. The choice is clear: face, and embrace, the brutal truth that we are motes in the unblinking eye of a godless cosmos or be crushed by the infinitely dense black holes of our collapsing selves. In that moment, self-esteem will be the least of our problems.

(2002)

Pontification

SWISS GUARDS IN RENAISSANCE FINERY; SOLEMN MONKS HOLD-ing candles; a male choir chanting in the occult tongue of Latin; the anguished faithful, wracked with grief, clasping their hands in prayer or seeming to clutch at the passing bier; and, at the center of this deeply pagan drama, the dead pontiff, caught in midflight between the mortal and the marmoreal, the all too human and the already hallowed. Marilyn Manson, eat your heart out: nobody does High Gothic spectacle like the Vatican.

Borne from the Apostolic Palace, through Saint Peter's Square, and into Saint Peter's Basilica on April 4, 2005, the earthly remains of John Paul II looked, for all the world, like a prop in a Gothic opera, his kabuki-white features contrasting melodramatically with his blood-red vestments. Robed and mitered, he looked doll-like, a chess-set bishop sculpted in life-size proportions by Madame Tussaud, an unstrung puppet with his "feet turned outward awkwardly, the skin of his face chalky and drawn taut," as the *New York Times* correspondents Elaine Sciolino and Daniel J. Wakin put it in their wonderfully poetic description of the scene.[1]

Under John Paul II, Team Vatican's inquisitional intolerance for self-abuse, sex before wedlock, birth control, abortion, divorce, homosexuality, and other works and ways of the Devil cost it global market share. According to an op-ed by Thomas Cahill in the *New York Times*: "The situation is dire. Anyone can walk into a Catholic church

on a Sunday and see pews, once filled to bursting, now sparsely populated with gray heads."[2]

Even so, who can deny that, when it comes to ritualistic pomp and
circumstance, Roman Catholicism simply knocks the spots off Religion, American-style? A devout atheist to the death, I stand, nonetheless, with the splenetic contrarian Camille Paglia, who never misses
an opportunity to rant against what she perceives as the Church's
clueless attempts to rebrand itself, from Vatican II onward. "My dis-
satisfaction with American Catholicism, which partly began during
my adolescence in the late 50's, was due partly to its increasing self-
Protestantization and suppression of its ethnic roots," Paglia told
the *Buffalo News* in April 1995. "Within 20 years, Catholic churches
looked like airline terminals: no statues, no stained-glass windows, no
Latin, no litanies, no gorgeous jeweled garments, no candles, so that
the ordinary American church now smells like baby powder."[3]

Indeed, the understated Grand Guignol of the pope's posthumous
procession, equal parts medieval mystery play and prime-time spectacle, offers a timely reminder that these are the people who brought
you Saint Bartholomew, the flayed martyr with his skin flung jauntily
over one shoulder, like Frank Sinatra on the cover of *Songs for Young
Lovers,* and the beatified truck-stop waitresses Saint Lucy and Saint
Agnes, serving up their plucked-out eyeballs and severed breasts on
platters, like blue-plate specials.

Yes, the pope has that futurrific little popemobile, and yes, the Holy
See's website is the bitchenest thing in online branding for Bronze
Age belief systems. And yes, the Vatican e-mailed and IM'd the bad
tidings about the Holy Father's death to a breathless press. (What did
you expect? An archangel with a flaming sword?) Even so, Catholicism, at its thorn-crowned, gore-dripping (sacred) heart, amounts to
an inescapably pagan take on Christianity. With its martyrs and its
miracles, its relics and its stigmata, its exorcisms and excommunica-
tions, the Holy Roman faith is the Christian Gothic.

Is this why Catholics and lapsed Catholics are overrepresented in
the congregation of Gothic novelists? The famously Catholic Flan-
nery O'Connor wrestled with theological demons against a Southern

Gothic backdrop, and Anne Rice, the Mother Confessor of palely loitering goths everywhere, was raised in a fervently Catholic household and once dreamed of being a nun. The Gothic aesthetic sprang from the brow of anti-Papist Protestants such as Matthew Lewis, who associated the Catholicism of the Middle Ages with inquisitional cruelties and a dogged hostility toward science and society's first, feeble gropings toward the Enlightenment. *(Go figure!)* Lewis's 1796 novel *The Monk* chronicled the secret, De Sadean depravities of one of God's Servants, who boinks his pious groupies, dabbles in witchcraft, and conjures up abominations in the consecrated crypts beneath his abbey. *(Ah, well, who are we to be critical? "We are all as an unclean thing, and all our righteousnesses are as filthy rags . . ." [Isaiah 64:6].)*

Of course, Catholicism inherits its Gothic tendencies from its parent religion. Christianity worships a revenant stiff, for God's sake; its devotees wear an instrument of capital punishment around their necks, and its most sacred rite is a blood feast that reads like Anne Rice fan fiction at its most lurid ("Whoso . . . drinketh my blood, hath eternal life; and I will raise him up at the last day"). Catholicism is just Christianity with its graven images showing, Christianity with one foot in the chthonic.

Which is the larger part of its charm, of course. In stark contrast to the extruded, suet-y Christianity retailed in megamall megachurches like Robert Schuller's happy, shiny Crystal Cathedral,[4] Catholicism offers the uncanny consolations of mummified Capuchin monks, the preserved head of Catherine of Siena, the Stations of the Cross (the Iron Man Decathlon of piety, when performed on bended knee), the homoerotic agonies of Saint Sebastian, and the dewy-browed ecstasies of Saint Theresa, pierced by the immaculate unit of Our Heavenly Father. Did I mention a lifetime's worth of gnawing guilt (see "We are all as an unclean thing," etc., etc., above), temporarily expiated through the breathy, phone-sex ritual of whispering your juiciest True Confessions through the grillwork of a Gothic phone booth, into the eager ear of one of the Eunuchs of Heaven?

No wonder four out of five enfants terribles ask for Catholicism by name when they get tired of playing Whac-A-Mole with plaster saints and revert to bourgeois form. Consider Salvador Dalí: when surrealism was the New, New Thing, Dalí, like most of the French European avant-garde he ran with, was a virulent anticleric. (Think of the priests mocked as beasts of burden in *Un Chien Andalou*, dragging a piano full of rotting donkeys). Yet Dalí ended up a theatrically pious Catholic, his *Christ of Saint John of the Cross* (1951) a staple of Christian-kitsch gift shops.

Likewise, consider the pilgrim's progress of Patti Smith, whose 1975 punk-rock anthem "Gloria (in Excelsis Deo)" is a symbolic profanation of the host. Drawling snidely about how Jesus died for somebody's sins, but not hers, Smith kick-started punk rock (and her career) with the time-tested tactic of bitch-slapping the bourgeoisie. Sex and sacrilege set to a dry-humping rhythm, "Gloria" was cannily calculated to give the Catholic League of Decency a cardiac event. What better way to certify your street cred?

Fast forward to "Wave," on the 1979 album of the same name, where we find Patti having a Hallmark Moment with the pope. In an adenoidal little-girl voice that bears an alarming resemblance to Lily Tomlin's Edith Ann, Smith goo-goos about an imaginary audience with the Holy Father:

> i saw i saw you from your balcony window and you were standing there waving at everybody it was really great because there was about a billion people there, but when i was waving to you, uh, the way your face was, it was so, the way your face was it made me feel exactly like we're it's not that you were just waving to me, but that we were we were waving to each other. really it was really wonderful . . . goodbye. goodbye sir. goodbye papa.[5]

(Cue footage of New York's balding punk alumni, Class of '75, flinging themselves lemminglike into the East River.)

Why would the woman who snarled, in "Babelogue," that she hadn't "sold herself" to God start slinging the papal bull?[6] For the same reason that the market-smart Dalí traded in his gently used surrealism for the Holy Roman faith when surrealism's shock appeal went from cult to cute. What's an aging avant-gardist to do, once there are no bourgeoisie left to *épater*? *Épater* the bohos! Scandalize

lockstep nonconformists everywhere by going *normal!* Shock the
been-there, triple-pierced-that, Disinformation.com demographic
that wears its ennui like a designer trucker's cap with your ironic
embrace of a normalcy so insistently normal it's downright creepy.

Strapping a lobster to your head and fantasizing aloud about the
sensuous curve of Hitler's buttocks no longer landing you among the
boldfaced names on Page Six? Tossing off zany bon mots like "The only
difference between me and a madman is that I am not mad" not setting the table aroar the way it used to? Tear a page from the Dalí playbook: declare that the academic realist Meissonier could paint circles
around Picasso, insist that Franco's fascism saved Spain, and—if you
really want to pin everybody's ears back—convert to Catholicism and
start cranking out Lourdes gift-shop chromos like *Crucifixion* (1954).

Sure, you can always grow a Van Dyke, cultivate a morgue-slab
pallor, and join the Church of Satan, but how transgressive can a cult
be that claims *Sammy Davis* as one of its charter members, for chrissakes? Besides, Satanism is just a backward-masked version of Roman
Catholicism. It still kneels at the same altar; it just does it backward,
buttocks bared, hoarsely bellowing hymns of praise to Beelzebub in
its best Norwegian death-metal growl. Why settle for a lame mul-
let-head parody of the true goth faith when, for a song and a prayer,
you can have the Real Thing, replete with swinging censers, severed
fingers, extreme unction, incorruptible saints, and transubstantia-
tion (in which the consecrated host is miraculously transformed, as it
slides down your gullet, into the flesh of God Almighty)?

Of course, Vatican dogma is a lot less tragically hip than its Hammer Horror stagecraft. Sure, the pope's posthumous processional blew
the vestments off the drive-through McRituals that pass for Christian worship in America's supersized suburban churches, all self-help
homilies and feel-good ecumenical mush. But John Paul's doctrinal
positions were Gothic in a less fashion-forward sense. Not for nothing did Molly Ivins call him the greatest mind of the Middle Ages.

Of course, during the fifteen Warholian minutes of official media
mourning for John Paul II, anti-Papism was the new anti-Semitism. As *Philadelphia Inquirer* commentator Ken Dilanian helpfully

pointed out, "The media are doing now what they did when former President Ronald Reagan died in June: reducing a deeply controversial figure to a warm, grandfatherly caricature."[7]

Well, forgive me, Father, I know not what I do. I'm going to risk being tarred as Jack Chick Jr. by issuing an encyclical of my own: a Holy Father who orders his billion-member flock to eschew birth control, at the gunpoint threat of excommunication, even as AIDS rides a pale horse through Africa's hospital wards, is guilty of child abuse on a global scale. According to *The Nation* columnist Katha Pollitt, "In Africa, where HIV infects millions—20 percent in Kenya, 40 percent in Botswana, 34 percent in Zimbabwe—Catholic clergy, who oppose condoms as they do all contraception, are actively promoting the myth that condoms don't prevent transmission of the virus and may even spread it."[8] AIDS is slaughtering the innocent and the sinful alike, yet this pope insisted that the faithful adhere to a suicidally misguided doctrine straight out of the Dark Ages. This is genocide, plain and simple. *L.A. Weekly* firebrand Marc Cooper minces no words:

> I firmly believe that the Church (and religion more generally) are medieval institutions that celebrate and propagate fear and ignorance. The positive record of the currently-deceased Pope is well known. But it hardly balances out the sheer inhumanity of Church dogma that he steadfastly defended. I personally could give a flip if women are or are not allowed into the priesthood (an institution that should be abolished). What I do care about is the AIDS infection rate world-wide and the vast, staggering complicity of the Church in its preaching against condoms and, alas, birth control. Suffering, says the Church, is God's great gift to man. Nice words from those who inhabit gilded palaces and reign as Rome's greatest landlord. Any truly great Pope would do to the Church what Gorbachev did to Communism—hasten its extinction.[9]

By all accounts, Karol Wojtyla was a nice man. But is niceness next to godliness? Doubtless, he lifted the spirits of the anxious pilgrims who knelt to kiss his ring or whose babies he hoisted aloft for a benedictory peck from the Bishop of Rome; where's the harm in that?

Even so, I'm as convinced as any godless atheist can be that when we die, we all go—good and evil alike—to the same worm-turned earth. Of course, I could be wrong. Maybe John Paul is riding his popemobile triumphantly through the City of God, even now. From here, though, his earthly legacy looks like a Cloud of Unknowing, and a toxic one at that.

(2005)

The Prophet Margin

CHICK TRACTS ARE AMMONIUM NITRATE FOR THE SOUL, AN incendiary mix of blood 'n' guts Bible-thumping, paleoconservatism, millenarian visions in the *Late Great Planet Earth* mold, and what conspiracy scholars call "fusion paranoia"—that altered state in which history's unsolved mysteries suddenly resolve themselves into a unified field theory of fear and loathing.

If the name Jack T. Chick draws a blank look, the sight of a Chick "illustrated gospel tract" almost inevitably inspires the shock of recognition. They're those ubiquitous little comic-booklets, not much bigger than a playing card, that fundamentalist Christians have been using to booby-trap park benches, bathroom stalls, and trick-or-treaters' candy bags since the late 1950s.

In Chick's parallax worldview, homosexuals are plotting to poison our nation's blood supply with the AIDS virus. Rock music, whose demonic beat was first thumped out by the Druids on people-skin drums, is driving teenagers to commit suicide in the misguided belief that "Hell will be party time." Witches are everywhere, guzzling the blood of sacrificed infants and blessing rock tapes while cavorting naked. In the center of Chick's tangled web of conspiracy theories hangs the Catholic Church, like a poison-bloated black widow. Its Illuminati control the vast wealth amassed during the Inquisition; its Mafia oversees the church's criminal enterprises.

Chick tracts are a cultural gene-splice of the religious tract (whose modern incarnation is at least as old as the founding of the American

Chick tract.

Tract Society in 1825) and the comic book (specifically, Maoist agit-prop booklets, by Chick's own, incredible admission).[1] According to comics critic Daniel K. Raeburn, Chick is "the most underground of all underground cartoonists—and yet he's one of the most successful cartoonists ever in terms of readership (four hundred million sold!)."[2]

God-given talent has little to do with it. Chick's draftsmanship is amateurish, at best crudely effective, at worst eye-gougingly awful. However, Fred Carter, the artist who illustrated the best of the '70s Chick tracts, is as accomplished as Chick is inept, masterfully exploiting the dramatic punch of chiaroscuro and cinematic POVs. In "The Holy Book of Chick," the 1998 issue of his self-published 'zine of comics criticism *The Imp*, Raeburn rhapsodizes about Carter's use of "the Filipino inking style"—"quivering heads and fists, boldly cross-hatched backgrounds"—associated with DC horror-comic artists like Jesus Jodloman.[3]

In many ways, Chick tracts *are* horror comics. The lost soul tormented by Boschian monstrosities in *Back from the Dead?* and the gore-soaked crucifixion scene in *The Empty Tomb* will be instantly familiar to anyone whose adolescent nightmares were staged and scripted by DC's *House of Secrets* or, as Chick's may have been, by earlier comics such as EC's *Vault of Horror*.

Of course, Jack Chick wasn't the first to strike a Faustian bargain, in the name of reaching the unsaved masses, between moral uplift and lurid sensationalism. In 1791, the Episcopal minister Mason Locke Weems wrote and peddled tracts such as *The Drunkard's Looking Glass*, which featured a drunkard falling off his horse, a mishap that left him with one eye "cleanly knocked out of its socket; and, held only by a string of skin, there it lay naked on his bloody cheek."[4] Weems illustrated his tracts with engravings of shattered skulls and strangled corpses, their tongues bulging: a *Tales from the Crypt* for god-fearers, with a scriptural flourish to justify the Grand Guignol.

In *Selling God: American Religion in the Marketplace of Culture*, the historian R. Laurence Moore characterizes Weems's tracts as the "marriage of aggressive marketing with a moral mission," a description that neatly fits Chick's "soul-winning" tracts, ballyhooed with catchphrases like "Chick tracts make witnessing easy!" and "Chick tracts GET READ!"[5]

Chick's booklets are true to their roots in horror-comic morality plays and the penny-dreadful sensationalism of Weems's "edifying" tales. Chick's early comic *This Was Your Life!* (1958) is the ur-tract, the narrative die Chick has used, down through the years, to stamp out countless variations on this market-tested story line. A cocktail-swilling bon vivant is bushwhacked by the grim reaper. An angel ushers his naked soul into a celestial screening room, where he's forced to review his sinful life. "*I'm lost!*" he despairs. "Without hope, without Christ! I'm guilty—*guilty!*" The cowering wretch is dragged before God, a cosmic hanging judge with a blazing lightbulb for a head. "Depart from me, ye cursed, into everlasting fire," the Lord intones, and the angel drop-kicks the hapless creature into a burning lake. "This *can* be your life!" Chick warns. The last page of the tract admonishes the fear-addled reader to accept Jesus's everlasting love. Or else.

Recently, Chick tracts have begun making cameo appearances in Chick tracts. *Who, Me?* (1998) proselytizes for the gospel comic-booklets, supplanting the usual back-cover pitch with an exhortation to "begin your personal witnessing ministry *right now!*" by sending away for a "free full color catalog, showing 70 other irresistible Chick tracts."[6]

Who, Me? underscores the creepy, *Invasion of the Body Snatchers* subtext of all evangelism, a recursiveness that makes us think of viruses mindlessly colonizing new brains for the sole purpose of self-replication. A virus's "prime directive is to replicate," says Richard Preston in *The Hot Zone.*[7] "Go ye into all the world and preach the gospel to every creature," the risen Lord exhorts his followers, in Mark 16:15. We think, too, of drug addiction, of the nightmare pyramid schemes melodramatized in antidrug propaganda, lurid scenarios in which hardened junkies seduce teens into taking that fateful first step down the road to perdition. The Chick catalog underscores the conversion–addiction connection with its assertion that "Nobody can resist cartoons . . . once [the readers] are hooked, each tract delivers a simple gospel message anyone can understand."[8] William Burroughs's "algebra of need" meets the Greatest Product Ever Sold.

Chick self-published his first effort, an O-ye-of-little-faith excoriation of complacent Sunday Christians called *Why No Revival?*, sometime between 1948 and 1958.[9] According to the Chick Publications website, the tract had its genesis in a revelation that jolted the cartoonist while he was reading *Power from on High* by Charles Finney, a showstopping evangelist of the Great Revival in the early nineteenth century. (Intriguingly, Finney, like Mason Locke Weems, was a premillennialist prophet with an adman's savvy: a born orator, he counseled other revivalist ministers to adopt the studied spontaneity of the actor. Like Chick in postwar America, casting about for a means of broadcasting God's message to an increasingly televisual culture, Finney and Weems "were both searching for ways to make religion popular in an era in which commercial-culture options were growing," notes Moore.)[10]

This being Southern California, the scales fell from Chick's eyes not on the road to Damascus but in his car, during his lunch break from an art job at AstroScience Corporation in El Monte. *Power from on High* "pushed my button," he recalled. "I went to church and saw all the deadness and hypocrisy, and I thought, 'That's why there's no revival.' So I started making these little sketches."[11] On fire with the spirit, Chick drew his first tract on his kitchen table and published it with $800 borrowed from the company credit union.

Since then, a purported sixty million copies of *This Was Your Life!* have been printed in more than sixty languages.[12] Today, the Ontario, California–based Chick Publications cranks out hundreds of titles in nearly one hundred languages. But as Chick, in his mid-seventies at the time of this writing, exhorted in a recent letter to his distributors, "The end is in sight and the Lord is coming soon. Beloved, we must stay busy to spread the Word until that trumpet sounds."[13]

It's hard to imagine that Chick doesn't feel a deep sense of satisfaction, perhaps even a perverse thrill, now that the millennial Hour of Reckoning is at hand. According to Raeburn, Chick, an Army veteran, was "one of the relatively few soldiers to survive the fanatical, hellish slaughter at Okinawa in World War II."[14] Many of the true believers in Chick tracts exhibit a disconcerting overeagerness to paratroop into a better world than this. "When I go out," the cartoonist once wrote, "I want to go out with honor, and I want to take as many with me to Christ as I possibly can."[15]

Chick's office in his corporate headquarters is reportedly known by a name straight out of *Dr. Strangelove*: "The War Room." Dwayne Walker, a devoted "Chicklet" who interviewed the reclusive cartoonist in his office, told Raeburn, "All I could think of was [Slim Pickens] in *Dr. Strangelove,* riding that nuclear bomb all the way to Armageddon, going 'Yee-haw!' That's Chick! That's him to a 'T.'"[16]

Now, after forty years spent preaching the gospel of millenarian fever, conspiracy theory, and hit-and-run evangelism, Chick has lived to see his private obsessions dovetail with the zeitgeist of millennial America. Jack T. Chick is an American original, and nothing is more American—nor more fin-de-millennium—than the idea of the apocalypse as thrill ride, a concept enshrined in SF and disaster movies like *Independence Day* and *Deep Impact* and of course Slim Pickens's famous ride into oblivion astride an H-bomb.

I like to imagine Chick sitting in his celebrity box seat at God's right hand, watching the mushroom clouds of the Last Judgment roil. Perhaps, as the cosmic credits roll, he'll hum a few bars from *Strangelove*'s closing theme: "We'll meet again, don't know where, don't know when ..."

(1999)

2012

I LIKE A GOOD APOCALYPSE AS MUCH AS THE NEXT AMERICAN, which is why I'll be braving the Stepfordian horrors of the local mall for the opening of *2012*, Roland Emmerich's latest exercise in disaster porn. The trailer is awesome. It's got John Cusack in a puddle-jumper plane dodging collapsing skyscrapers, John Cusack in a car playing dodgeball with a meteor shower, and John Cusack squealing around a corner on two wheels, yelling, to no one in particular, "When they tell you not to panic, that's when you *run!*" Plus, it's got every New Yorker's idea of schadenfreude-gasm: California barrel-rolling into the Pacific.

According to the movie's press packet, Emmerich and his writing partner Harald Kloser got a brainstorm when they learned that "the Mayan calendar is set to reach the end of its thirteenth cycle on December 21, 2012—and nothing follows that date.... 'You will find millions of people, from all walks of life, who believe that in 2012 there will be some kind of shift in society, or a shift in spirit,' says Kloser. The scope and variety of theories provided inspiration for Emmerich and Kloser as they penned their screenplay."[1]

Millions of people? Really? From all walks of life? Or are we just talking about a few thousand woo-woos whose mental engine blocks have cracked from one too many psychoactive alkaloids? In any event, however many people are investing this arbitrary date with cosmic significance, it's way too many. As a throwaway plot premise for a Hollywood blockbuster, New Age "theories" about the Coming Shift in Global Consciousness *(not again!)* are harmless chaff. Who cares if every tie-dyed Elmer Gantry working the Esalen hot tub and Burning Man circuit is predicting ecstasy, or dread, or both, in 2012?

The answer, in brief, is that the stories we tell ourselves, as a culture, *do* matter. Profoundly. Daniel Pinchbeck, author of *2012: The Return of Quetzalcoatl* (the Nahuatl name for the feathered serpent god of the Mesoamerican peoples), is an object lesson in the hidden costs of myth. Bidding fair to become the media face of the 2012 phenomenon, Pinchbeck is a tireless publicist for the global cataclysm and universal outbreak of cosmic consciousness he believes will ensue when the numbers on our digital alarm clocks click over to 2012.

Which makes him the poster child for all that's worst about the 2012 craze. Pinchbeck's feathered serpent-oil salesmanship offers a case study in some of its most pernicious aspects. First, there's the gape-mouthed credulity required of true believers in the 2012 prophecies—the unblinking, irony-free ability to swallow groaners that would make a cow laugh, such as Pinchbeck's pronouncement that 2012 may beckon us through a psychic portal, into a "multidimensional realm of hyperspace triggered by mass activation of the pineal gland."[2]

Pinchbeck, like New Age thinkers all the way back to Madame Blavatsky, preaches a refried gospel of ancient wisdom and mystical, suprarational knowledge. In 2007, he told the *New York Times* that "the rational, empirical worldview ... has reached its expiration date ... we're on the verge of transitioning to a dispensation of consciousness that's more intuitive, mystical, and shamanic."[3] Well, somebody say "Amen"! There's entirely too much rationalism and empiricism clouding the American mind these days, in a nation where, according to the Public Policy, *USA Today*, and Harris polls, 42 percent of Republicans are convinced President Obama wasn't born in the United States, 10 percent of the nation's voters are certain he's a Muslim, and 61 percent of the population believe in the Virgin Birth but only 47 percent believe in Darwinian evolution.[4]

Much of the 2012 shtick is a light-fingered (if leaden-humored) rip-off of the late rave-culture philosopher Terence McKenna's stand-up routine, without McKenna's prodigious erudition, effortless eloquence, or arch wit. And Pinchbeck is no exception. For Quetzalcoatl's sake, if you're going to start a religion, at least invent your own cosmology. Even L. Ron Hubbard was canny enough to concoct a pulp theology for ham-radio enthusiasts out of leftover SF plots. But every time I see Pinchbeck's glum mug, regarding the world with a sort of forced bliss, I think: Would you buy a used eschaton from this man? (McKenna, by the way, knew which side his ectoplasm was buttered on. When I asked him, over dinner, back in the '90s, why a man of his obvious intellectual nimbleness endured the saucer abductees and trance-channelers who plucked at his sleeve during New Age seminars, he rolled a knowing eye and replied, I thought wearily, that he owed his daily crust to "menopausal mystics" and thus had to suffer them, if not gladly. Sexist, yes, but funny nonetheless.)

But the worst of the 2012 bandwagon, epitomized by Pinchbeck's lectures and writings, is the blithe cultural arrogance and staggering anthropological ignorance evident in the movement's appropriation of Mayan beliefs and history. In a discussion hosted by Pinchbeck's online magazine Reality Sandwich, the cultural theorist Erik Davis puts his finger on the minstrelsy implicit in the ventriloquization, by white, first-world New Agers, of the Maya. "It seems to me that there is very little concrete sense of what 'the Mayans' (whoever that grand abstraction represents) thought about what would happen in the human world on 2012," he writes. "To my mind it is kinda disrespectful to the Mayans to force them into our own narrative."[5]

The journalist and Boing Boing editor Xeni Jardin sharpens the point of debate. While Jardin is no expert on, or spokesperson for, the Mayan people, she *is* well positioned to reveal the 2012 phenomenon for the carnival of bunkum it is. Her adoptive father is "of indigenous descent," she told me in an e-mail interview, and working with his nonprofit in Guatemala, "doing cultural and philanthropic work" for the country's indigenous peoples, has brought Jardin into close contact with the Maya.[6] "We work to help these communities sustain their culture and social integrity," she says, providing microloans and scholarships, trying to bring clean drinking water and healthcare to the villages.[7]

When I asked her what she thought of Pinchbeck's invocation of Mayan beliefs, and of the 2012-ers' use of the Maya in general, she was blunt. "What makes me angriest about Pinchbeck's bogus, profiteering bullshit isn't so much him, but the fact that that many people are racist enough to believe any asshole white guy who declares himself an expert in Mayan culture. Did it ever occur to anyone to ask practicing Maya priests out in the villages? . . . It absolutely enrages me that while people I know in Guatemala, traditional priests, are struggling to figure out how to provide clean drinking water to their families, how to feed their communities, how to avoid being shot by the gangs and thieves that plague the roads more than ever—while they're struggling to survive and keep their communities intact, assholes like Pinchbeck are making a buck off of white man's parodies of their culture."[8]

In a moment worth its weight in black-comedy gold, Jardin told one of the priests in a K'iche village about the New Age's obsession with 2012 and the ancient Mayan myths that supposedly augur apocalypse. "I tried to explain to him that a lot of gringos believe that the *chol q'ij* says that in the Gringo year 2012, the world will end, or rainbows will fly out of a unicorn's ass, or Mayan space aliens will land on the earth and our chakras will explode," she says. "I told him they're making a movie out of it, and how much a movie like that costs to make, and stands to earn. The priest laughed, and said, 'Well, that's gringos for you, what do you expect.' These people are well-accustomed to being exploited and ripped off, and having their cultural rights shit on. That is the tragedy, and what makes me feel such disgust and contempt for the likes of Pinchbeck. They get away with it."[9]

In his Reality Sandwich remarks, Davis wondered "what is gained by . . . believing that the wizards of a rather bloody jungle culture foretold our moment of rising CO_2 levels and suicide bombers." Point taken. Premonitions of the End of Days and prophecies of a *Space Odyssey*–like leap in species consciousness, in 2012, are just the same old bedtime story—a story we never seem to tire of hearing, about the moment (forever forestalled) when there will be "wonders in the heaven above and signs on the earth below," as the book of Acts has it—when the sun will go dark and the moon will turn blood red and time shall be no more. The environmental crises and geopolitical pathologies of our times ("rising CO_2 levels and suicide bombers" and the sufferings of the wretched of the Earth, like the Guatemalan Maya) demand that we step up to our social responsibilities and engage passionately with the issues of our age. Placing our faith in addlebrained ravings about a "multidimensional realm of hyperspace triggered by mass activation of the pineal gland" or "a dispensation of consciousness that's more intuitive, mystical, and shamanic" is a luxury we can no longer afford. We're out of time.

(2009)

The Vast Santanic Conspiracy

CHRISTIAN SOLDIERS, MARCHING AS TO WAR IN THE PITCHED battle for the meaning of Christmas, worry that Santa is a tool of the vast Satanic conspiracy. To be sure, the similarity of their names, identical but for one transposed letter, is provocative. Didn't Mia Farrow use a Scrabble board in *Rosemary's Baby* to expose her grandfatherly neighbor with the flyaway eyebrows for the warlock he was, shuffling the letters of his name to reveal his true identity? Could the Religious Wrong be right, just this once? Is Santa the Deceiver's way of hijacking the Christ child's birthday? Kriss Kringle is a corruption of the German dialectal *Christkindl,* "little Christ child."[1] Were Satan and Santa separated at birth?

Consider the evidence: Santa wears red; the Devil *is* red. Santa is known, alternatively, as Saint Nick; one of the Devil's jocular pseudonyms, in England, is Old Nick. Both are associated with the element of fire (by way of the chimney in Santa's case; a little closer to home in Satan's); both live in the far antipodes. (Incidentally, in Dante's *Divine Comedy,* the ninth and lowermost circle of Hell, where Lucifer is imprisoned for eternity, isn't the Mother of All Barbecue Pits, as we usually imagine it, but an icy wasteland—just like the arctic Santa calls home. Oh, and Dante's Devil is seriously furry, calling to mind the Santa of Clement Clarke Moore's "A Visit from St. Nicholas," who is "dressed all in fur from his head to his foot.")[2]

Following the topsy-turvy logic of cultural transgression, which from the inverted power relations of medieval carnival to the (entirely apocryphal) backward-masked Satanic verses in heavy-metal music always involves turning the social order upside down, Santa, like Satan, can be seen as a sacrilegious parody of Christ. Christ was nailed to a tree so that all who believe in him may have life everlasting; Santa's totem is an evergreen tree. Christ never leaves home without his halo; Santa sports an infernal mockery of a halo, a smoke ring that "encircle[s] his head like a wreath," in Moore's poem.[3] Moore's Santa is "chubby and plump"—Victorian for obese—and, of course, mirthful; Christ is the Man of Sorrows depicted in medieval and Renaissance art, gaunt and lugubrious as David Bowie in his Thin White Duke period, when the rock god sustained himself on a diet of cocaine, whole milk, and the freshly drawn blood of fanboys.

Christians celebrate the Last Supper by eating the communion wafer; Santa parodies that holy sacrament by demanding a cookie, which he inevitably leaves mostly uneaten but for one neat bite, incontrovertible proof of his palpable reality. (Isn't there something uncanny about Santa's nocturnal feast, the midnight snack of a spectral presence who marks his passing with that signature bite, like the table rappings and trumpet playings with which the dead announced their arrival at turn-of-the-century séances?)

Kids await Santa's arrival, on Christmas eve, in an agony of excitement, thrilled at the thought that "Santa Claus is coming to town"; evangelicals expect the Second Coming any second, their anticipation ratcheted up by New Testament passages such as Revelation 22:7: "Behold, I am coming soon!" We are reliably informed, in 2 Peter 3:10, that "the Lord will come as a thief in the night; in the which the heavens shall pass away with a great noise"; Moore's Saint Nick arrives in the night with a tremendous clatter, entering the narrator's house, burglar-style, through the chimney.

More ominous still (from a Christian perspective), Santa, as noted earlier, usurps Christ's celestial CCTV surveillance system as well as his accounting methods. The New Testament makes frequent reference to the Book of Life, an infallible balance sheet of deeds naughty and nice that figures memorably in Revelation 20:12–15: "And I saw the dead, the great and the small, standing before the throne . . . and the dead were judged from the things which were written in the books, according to their deeds. . . . And if anyone's name was not found written in the book of life, he was thrown into the lake of fire." In this light, Santa's lighthearted approach—"making a list / And checking it twice" to determine who gets sugarplums and who gets an empty stocking on Christmas morning—looks like a satire of Yahweh's hard-assed Sheriff-of-Maricopa-County act. Misbehave on Santa's watch, and he drops a lump of coal into your stocking; flout God's law, and he drop-kicks your sinful ass into the Inferno, turning you *into* a lump of coal.

Finally, Santa one-ups Jesus by *actually delivering* the goods most believers spend their lives fruitlessly petitioning the Lord for. In *Huckleberry Finn,* Miss Watson scorns Huck as an unlettered bumpkin when he tells her his prayers for new fish hooks have come to naught; the only "thing a body could get by praying for it," she says, is "'spiritual gifts.'"[4] But spiritual gifts are a paltry substitute for that Ford F-150 Lariat with the leather interior you've been eyeballing, which is why Joel Osteen's Prosperity Gospel is packing them into a converted sports arena in Houston, Texas. There, in the 16,000-seat former home of the Houston Rockets, the televangelist with the megawatt smile ministers to his flock. "God wants us to prosper financially, to have plenty of money, to fulfill the destiny He has laid out for us," quoth the Good Reverend.[5] All Osteen's feel-good God asks is that you not cry, not pout, quit the Stinkin' Thinkin', and just Name It and Claim It—Pentacostal-ese for invoking the scriptural passage guaranteed to trigger the windfall God has in store for you. No mention of that buzz-killing Lake of Fire thing. Doesn't this sound a lot like Santa for grown-ups?[6]

If this extended meditation on Satan's Grudge Match with Jesus, and on Saint Nick's family ties to Satan, sounds like yet more secular-humanist hatin' on Christmas, don't take *my* word for it. Outing Santa as a Manchurian Candidate for the Satanist agenda is a cottage industry among hard-line evangelicals like the folks over at TheCuttingEdge.org ("Spiritual Insights into the New World Order So Startling You'll Never Look at the News the Same Way Again!").[7]

Dearly Beloved, they're just walleyed with fear at the thought of the Boy Scouts' hidden ties to Freemasonry and the "encroaching mind-control of the Illuminati" and—oh, dear god, it's almost too mind-shrivelingly monstrous to mention—the "genetic scientists" who are "creating a super hybrid man/beast, eradicating death so man can live eternally without a savior!!"[8] They know the Awful Truth about Santa, too, and they're shouting it from the rooftops, exposing this "counterfeit Jesus" for the Satanic sham he is: "Together with the numerous other signs of the End of the Age," says a page on the ministry's website, "this love of the Pagan (Druidic) Santa Claus is just one more clear sign of the end."[9] America, Awake!

Dr. Terry Watkins over at Dial-the-Truth Ministries has Santa's number, too. In his tract "The Great Pretender," Watkins weaves a tangled web of connections between the Man in Red and the Great Beast. Did you know that the Devil's signature entry line, in medieval miracle plays, was "ho, ho, ho!" and that, in Zechariah 2:6, "Ho, ho . . . saith the LORD"?[10] Did you know that the nineteenth-century occultist Madame Blavatsky revealed, in her Theosophical text *The Secret Doctrine,* that "many a mysterious sacred name . . . conveys to the profane ear no more than some ordinary, and often vulgar [common] word, because it is concealed anagrammatically?" ("Like S-A-N-T-A?" Watkins prompts helpfully, from offstage.) Following that logic, did you know that "Claus" may be an anagram for "Lucas," a New Age "code word" for Lucifer, but that it also "sounds a lot like 'claws,'" so "maybe Santa Claus means 'Satan's Claws'"?

OF COURSE, reasonable minds know that Santa is none other than Saint Nicholas, the third-century Greek Orthodox bishop whose legendary acts of Christian charity—for example, tossing bags of gold through the window of a man so desperately poor he would have been forced to sell his daughters into slavery—gave rise to the myth of a kindly, bearded patriarch who comes, bearing gifts, in December.

The way Jeremy Seal tells it in *Nicholas: The Epic Journey from Saint to Santa Claus,* Nicholas's association with domestic rituals endeared him to the common folk.[11] Even during the Reformation, when Protestant authorities were purging their faith of saints and other "popish" heresies, believers commemorated Nicholas's acts of kindness by leaving apples, nuts, and sweets in shoes the night before his name day (December 6).

By the fourteenth century, when the saint had arrived in Holland as Sinterklaas, his metamorphosis into Santa Claus was well under way, says Seal. According to legend, the Dutch packed their beloved Saint Nicholas in the cultural baggage they brought to New Amsterdam, the seventeenth-century settlement that would later become Manhattan. Holland ceded the colony to England in 1674, but the white-bearded saint in red ecclesiastical garb was preserved in folk memory, waiting to be resurrected by nineteenth-century New Yorkers like Clement Clarke Moore.

Drawing heavily on Washington Irving's droll caricature, in his satirical *History of New York* (1809), of Saint Nick as a gnome-sized Dutch burgher, Moore imagined him as a "jolly old elf" in his poem "A Visit from St. Nicholas" (1823), arguably the most profound influence on American conceptions of Santa Claus (and, for that matter, Christmas).

But what really put booster rockets on Santa's sleigh, Seal maintains, was consumer capitalism, via the cultural influence of local merchants and, in time, department stores and advertisers. "What actually drove Saint Nicholas to a revival was that, from the 1780s, the revolution in the creation of commercial products meant that gift-giving as a custom began to acquire fresh momentum," he told NPR interviewer Renée Montagne. "Prior to that . . . it had been the local exchange of handmade gifts. And suddenly objects were flooding in from Europe, particularly toys, and this meant that commercial, canny interests in Manhattan began to realize that Saint Nicholas was a figure which could lead this transformation in the significance and importance of gift-giving."[12]

From Moore's traveling-salesman Santa, "like a peddler just opening his pack," it's but a short ride, as the sleigh flies, to the department-store Santas who by 1890 were putting a twinkly-eyed face on conspicuous consumption, and from there to Haddon Sundblom's wildly popular depiction of Santa as a soda-swilling pitchman for Coca-Cola—advertisements whose "overwhelming ubiquity," from 1931 through 1964, "ensured that no rival version of Santa could emerge in the North American consciousness," Gerry Bowler asserts in *Santa Claus: A Biography*.[13]

That's the short version of how a third-century Greek Orthodox bishop became a secular deity, in American culture, of middle-class domesticity, childhood innocence, free-floating good cheer (until the eggnog wears off, at least), Norman Rockwellian nostalgia, and, not least, material abundance.

OR SO THE STORY GOES. In his exhaustively researched study *The Battle for Christmas*, Stephen Nissenbaum begs to differ with the official version.[14] Nissenbaum musters impressive historical evidence to argue that Santa as we know him is part of an "invented tradition," conjured out of historical thin air by Moore, Irving, and fellow New York Historical Society member Robert Pintard. Pillars of the city's conservative elite, they fabricated Santa Claus, along with the Christmas rituals we now think of as timeless, as a means of domesticating the drunken holiday revels of the dangerous classes—rowdy Yuletide celebrations, rooted in medieval carnival, that gave vent to pent-up class hostilities. "By 1820 Christmas misrule had become such an acute social threat that respectable New Yorkers could no longer ignore it or take it lightly," writes Nissenbaum.[15] During one holiday season, Nissenbaum recounts, a riotous gang armed with horns, tin pans, and other noisemakers—a Callithumpian band, in the parlance of the day—raged along Bowery, where it pelted a tavern with lime; marauded through a black neighborhood; paraded past some of the city's toniest homes, whose windows it was happy to bash in; and finally "passed noisily and triumphantly up Broadway."[16]

Convinced of the need for a bourgeois myth that would channel underclass unrest into more acceptable outlets of expression, Pintard, Irving, and Moore concocted what Disney imagineers would call a new "backstory," replacing the old English tradition of the public wassail with a private domestic ritual consecrated to home, hearth, and conspicuous consumption. (Wassailing was door-to-door caroling, in wealthy neighborhoods, by lower-class toughs, with the thinly veiled threat of a good roughing-up if grog and grub weren't forthcoming. Sample lyric: "We've come here to claim our right ... / And if you don't open up your door, / We will lay you flat upon the floor.")[17]

As the manufactured myth took root in American's emergent consumer culture, the elite's gemütlich vision of domesticity became a reality: unruly mobs gave way to children "nestled all snug in their beds" while a grandfatherly imp brought gifts instead of demanding them, assuring the anxious Victorian paterfamilias that he now had "nothing to dread."

NOT SO FAST, says Phyllis Siefker in her fascinating cultural history, *Santa Claus, Last of the Wild Men.* Siefker contends that Moore's Santa was a scrubbed-clean, rehabbed version of Belsnickle (from the German *Pelz-nickle,* "Saint Nicholas in Fur"). Covered in shaggy animal skins and black face paint, Belsnickle was a fearsome, disheveled creature who went door-to-door in Pennsylvania's German enclaves, handing out nuts and cakes to good little girls and boys and thrashing the bad ones.[18]

The state's German immigrants had imported Belsnickle from the Old World, where he lives on in various incarnations, among them Saint Nicholas's Bavarian henchman, Krampus. A sheep-horned fiend who carries a basket on his back, handy for bagging misbehaving children and toting them off to Hell, Krampus puts the claws back in Santa Claus. (Krampus has been embraced, in the United States, as the death-metal mascot of Yuletide debauchery by hipsters who cringe at Christmas treacle and wish Jimmy Stewart would just do a freaking half gainer into the river and be done with it, for chrissakes.)

According to Siefker, Belsnickle is just another incarnation of the beast-man archetype she calls the Wild Man, a wintertime fertility god whose origins date back to Paleolithic times. "Each year the people held a ritual renewing the earth, and periodically they sacrificed this god in his prime," writes Siefker. "Usually, this ritual included a mating between the Wild Man and a woman, bringing into play the fertility aspect of the god while setting the conditions for the renewal of life through new birth."[19] (Note to department-store Santas: Downside, your job perks don't include a village maiden pole-dancing on Kriss Kringle's candy cane. Upside, your seasonal gig doesn't culminate in a *Wicker Man* immolation.)

Siefker tracks the Wild Man to the village festivals of the Middle Ages. In the Tyrol, for instance, he's a hairy, bestial thing with a hump on his back (sound familiar?) who rejoices in thunder and lightning (*Donner* and *Blitzen*, in German). During the medieval era, the Wild Man finds himself in the crosshairs of the Christian authorities, who are on a Mission from God to eradicate pagan beliefs. Little wonder, then, that when Pope Gregory I puts a mythic face on the hitherto vaguely defined Christian devil, he finds it politically useful to depict the Tempter as "a goat-skinned man with cloven hooves, beard, horns, humpback, and stick"—the Wild Man, by any other name.[20]

In another, subtler gambit, Siefker asserts, the Church promoted Saint Nicholas as a seasonal replacement for his pagan precursor. "Thus the usual explanation that Santa Claus 'came from' Saint Nicholas seems to be backward: Saint Nicholas was created to take the place of the heathen god, the Furry Claus," she writes.[21] "Originally a beast-god who reminded people of the cyclical nature of the world, of death and rebirth, this Wild Man was part of fertility performances throughout Europe. He was a godhead so strong, so universally worshipped by 'pagans,' that Christianity found him *the* major impediment to its goal of European salvation. To undermine his grip on the people, Christianity labeled his worship evil, and called his followers devilish. . . . The fact is that Santa and Satan are alter egos, brothers; they have the same origin."[22]

The evangelicals at TheCuttingEdge.org and Dial-the-Truth Ministries are righter than they knew. But Crumpet and Puff, the cynical Macy's elves in David Sedaris's *SantaLand Diaries* (1992), got there first. Stumbling on the happy fact that SANTA is an anagram for

SATAN, they while away the dull hours in the store's Lollipop Forest, riffing snarkily on the overheard comments of Christmas shoppers:

"What do you think, Michael? Do you think Macy's has the real Satan?"

"Don't forget to thank Satan for the Baby Alive he gave you last year."

"I love Satan."

"Who doesn't? Everyone loves Satan."[23]

Well, *almost* everybody.

(2009)

Anatomy Lesson

THE GROTESQUE, THE GOTHIC, AND OTHER DARK MATTERS

Open Wide

RECENTLY, WHILE SUBMITTING TO THE FOND ATTENTIONS of a dental surgeon, I found myself musing idly, in an opiated haze, about the symbolic weight of teeth—musings disturbed only by the surgeon's resolute yanking on the offending tooth, a yanking that came to me only distantly, as a not entirely unpleasant tugging, punctuated by an occasional squeaking, reminiscent of the sound of a nail being pried out of a floorboard. Maybe it was the Novocain, but I found myself wondering if the widespread fear of dentists is at least in part a subconscious, perhaps even archetypal, fear of *teeth,* or if that's just the perspective of someone whose dental history is written in anxiety (and all the requisite drama-queen hysterics that go with it).[1]

Certainly, the mouth, as the biggest breach in the body's integrity, holds its own terrors: *What's this big hole in the middle of my face?! What if something falls out? What if something falls in?* Not for nothing has the face of mythic horror been a slavering maw *(Alien),* a toothy portal welcoming you to the afterworld *(Jaws).*

Teeth are scarier still. TV dramas such as *CSI: Crime Scene Investigation* and police-procedural fiction such as Patricia Cornwell's novels about the forensic pathologist Kay Scarpetta have forged an unbreakable link, in the mass imagination, between teeth and death. We know from crime fiction that dental records are often all that remain of the murdered; mute witnesses to their owner's last moments, they testify to the victim's identity and, ultimately, help put the bite on the perp.

Moreover, teeth are by definition uncanny, the point at which the skull beneath the skin erupts through the body's surface. It's the Return of the Repressed (copyright Sigmund Freud; all rights reserved)—in this case, the death we do our best to forget while we're busy living. A bony reminder that mortality is the subtext lurking just beneath the human comedy, teeth are the skeleton's insistence that it, too, is ready for its close-up.

Okay, I'm over the top here, but sometimes too much is just enough. Besides, who can top Freud, who took dental horror to Siegfried & Roy–like heights of rhetorical excess in his notorious theorization of the vagina dentata? Sure, Freud's Victorian hysterics were all about sexual phobias, but his misogynistic horror story wouldn't have packed the wallop it still does without the old Viennese devil's canny use of the Dental Uncanny.

Poe, a Freudian *avant la lettre,* gave shape to primitive male fears of the Monstrous Feminine in his story "Berenice," in which the narrator, Egaeus, monomaniacally obsessed with his lover's teeth, yanks them from her undead cadaver. His obsession is equal parts desire and horror:

> The teeth!—the teeth!—they were here, and there, and everywhere, and visibly and palpably before me; long, narrow, and excessively white, with the pale lips writhing about them, as in the very moment of their first terrible development.[2]

(The critic Killis Campbell has suggested that Poe's tale was inspired, in part, by a newspaper account of grave robbers who pried teeth out of corpses for use, presumably in the manufacture of false teeth, by local dentists.[3] Indeed, Richard Zacks claims, in his eccentric compendium of weird facts, *An Underground Education,* that a "whole generation wore 'Waterloo' dentures made from teeth yanked from the corpses on the battlefield, and the practice continued as late as the Civil War, when thousands of teeth were stolen from bodies moldering at places like Bull Run and Gettysburg."[4] This ghoulish practice is echoed, in contemporary dentistry, by the use of "cadaveric pure aura mater sterilized under X-rays" to facilitate bone regeneration around dental implants.[5])

Freudians have excavated psychosexual subtexts from "Berenice," reading Poe's story as a literalization of male attempts to defang the vagina dentata—the Vampiric Feminine, incarnate. Given the psychoanalytic interpretation of the mouth as a visual metaphor for the vagina (and vice versa), Berenice's predatory "smile of peculiar meaning," which so terrifies—and mesmerizes—the narrator, hints at the vagina's unsettling (at least, to the patriarchy) ability to swallow all comers and spit them out limp, drained of their potency. By robbing Berenice of her gleaming teeth, the narrator enacts a sympathetic magic, "castrating" the Phallic Mother and repossessing the emblems of his lost virility. (In this reading, the teeth are phallic symbols. Isn't everything?)

Personally, I've always viewed women's nether regions as the Gates of Delirium. The mouth, however, is a bacterial killing field. My dental armamentarium is *serious*. (Remember that scene in *The Matrix* where Neo says, "Guns, I need lots of guns," and—*wham-o,* he's in that celestial Wal-Mart, an infinite expanse of blinding-white soundstage whose only displays are endless aisles of matte-black gun racks bristling with AK-47s and Beretta pistols and Micro Uzis? Well, imagine all that hardware in white. And with fuzzy little FlexiSoft brush heads. And 3-D brushing action.) I'm fully loaded with the ubiquitous floss, although like all *serious* floss jocks I prefer Crest Glide tape ("your weapon against plaque and gingivitis!") to the standard-issue stuff civilians use. I've got the Glock 9 of electric toothbrushes, the Braun Oral-B Power Toothbrush with "ultra-speed oscillation," a Waterpik "dental water jet," and that increasingly common prosthesis known as a night guard, the first line of defense against nocturnal teeth grinding. Oh, and I've got this wicked little instrument my hygienist gave me, a gold-colored tool that looks like a miniature pharaoh's crook, its curved end culminating in a rubber barb for cleaning those hard-to-floss crevasses.

Not that any of this heavy weaponry has availed me much in my never-ending battle against plaque, gum recession, and other fifth-

columnist infiltrators of the body politic. It certainly didn't forestall my Appointment with Destiny in the oral surgeon's chair. It's
a genetic thing. Well, that, and growing up in the '60s and '70s, in
that Lost World before glucose intolerance and vegan vigilance and
organic anything, when "natural" was for those gap-toothed Oakies
in WPA photographs and breakfast was a Pop-Tart or a heaping bowl
of Count Chocula and no sack lunch was complete without a Ding
Dong or a Devil Dog and nothing slaked your cotton-mouth thirst
on those parched Southern California afternoons like a pitcher of
Kool-Aid or, when I was out of short pants, an ice-cold Fresca.

All of which brings me, in the usual divagating way, back to the
question of whether or not teeth are inherently fearsome things. Do
they inspire fear and loathing for reasons buried deep in the cultural
unconscious, or would I see them in a more innocuous light if I had
the radiantly beamish grin of, say, Julia Roberts or the scary Stein-
way smile of motivational guru (and acromegalic giant) Anthony
Robbins?

In the chair, with the good doctor attacking the recalcitrant molar
with hammer and tongs, I thought about the brief fad, back in the
1980s glory days of postpunk culture, for graphic images of extreme
dental surgery, ripped from surgical textbooks and remixed in underground 'zines. In that innocent time before Columbine, Abu Ghraib,
and Rotten.com, nothing gave normals the fantods like in-your-face
images of maxillofacial surgery. The fourth edition of the massive
mail-order catalog for the underground bookseller and publisher
Amok Press—one-stop shopping for style-conscious transgressives,
in the late '80s—includes a selection of pathology titles, featuring,
for your delectation, the *Color Atlas of Oral Cancers*. Postindustrial
artists such as Nine Inch Nails have mined this vein in videos such
as "Happiness in Slavery," which features the late S/M performance
artist Bob Flanagan strapped into a dentist's chair from Hell and
tortured by robotic drills with a mind of their own. (Oral horrors
seem to be an ongoing obsession of Nine Inch Nails' Trent Reznor,
who was going to call the band's 2005 album *Let It Bleed* but settled,

instead, on the title *With Teeth*.) Marilyn Manson has been there, too, in his "Beautiful People" video, a KISS Army-meets-Joel-Peter Witkin fantasia in which the singer is fashionably accessorized by a gothic contraption that looks like the Grand Inquisitor's idea of a dental retractor. (These days, Manson's chrome-plated teeth are suitably scary all by themselves, now that The Artist Formerly Known as America's Bogeyman has opted for a Weimar-era gloss on the Bond villain Jaws.) The Swedish electronica artist Fingertwister has gotten in on the act as well, in his Web-only song "The Dentist," an ominous techno-dub track that incorporates snippets of operating-room dialogue ("got some blood, here") and the high-pitched whine of a dentist's drill, calculated to inspire a thrill of terror in any dentophobe.

There's an inescapable viscerality to dental imagery that, er, sets the teeth on edge. The panic-attack feeling of being trapped in the chair, the helpless vulnerability of submitting to the dental dam and the tongue retractor, the inexorable descent of the whining drill, the rotten reek of burning decay: we've all been there. The gleaming sterility of the high-tech surgical instruments and the crisp professionalism of most dentists only heighten our awareness of the medieval barbarity of the whole gory business. Which is exactly what makes that first prick of the needle, that first buzz of the drill, such a jarring reality check. In a postmodern moment when our desensitized sensibilities demand ever more voltage from the atrocity exhibition that is pop culture (*Fear Factor, Jackass, Extreme Makeover*), and when embodied experience is growingly irrelevant as our "real" lives are lived increasingly on the other side of the terminal screen, the dentist's drill is the short, sharp shock that reminds many of us that, for the moment at least, we still have bodies. In J. G. Ballard's speculative novel *Crash,* the affectless narrator embraces the car crash that nearly killed him as a rejuvenating force, a bracing jolt that snaps him out of the media-induced numbness that had drained him of all spontaneous responses and genuine emotions. I'm reminded of a friend who once told me that he refused all anesthesia during dental operations for the simple reason that it's a rare opportunity to experience the raw charge of real pain, a sensation we experience all too seldom, here in Prozac Nation. (He's a better man than I; wussy that I am, I'm always wheedling that extra poke of Novocain.)

Then, too, one of the root causes (forgive pun; something about the subject seems to invite them) of dentophobia may be the latent sadism of the whole situation: like an S/M top, the masked, rubber-gloved dentist is both tormentor and Angel of Mercy, a dualism exploited by the almost unwatchable torture scene in John Schlesinger's *Marathon Man* (1976)—*the* locus classicus for dentophobes—in which the Mengele-like Nazi doctor Christian Szell drills down to the nerve of one of Babe's teeth. In one hand, Szell holds sweet relief: clove oil, a topical anesthetic that banishes the brain-shriveling pain of seconds earlier. In the other, the instrument of that agony: a dentist's drill. There is something of the police-state interrogation cell here, and of De Sade's pleasure dungeon.

As always, there's a fine line between fear and fetish: a Google search for "dental retractor" uncovers a clammy sub-subculture of that branch of S/M that inclines toward medical fetishes. (Note: A fetishist's idea of a "retractor" differs from the professional usage of the word. To a dentist, a retractor is a small, pencil-shaped steel instrument, typically with a hook at the business end or, in the specific case of cheek retractors, an unintentionally hilarious plastic contraption that stretches the mouth for maximum dental exposure; anyone wearing one looks as if s/he's impersonating a lamprey. By contrast, when a fetishist talks about a retractor, s/he's talking about a nasty-looking tangle of metal, a wire-frame gadget designed to hold the mouth open during BDSM sex play. Dental fetishists rejoice in mock-medical paraphernalia, from double-ratchet retractors to forceps guaranteed to "force a mouth open to a maximum diameter of 2¹/₈""[6] (To what end, you ask? Discretion bids me leave the details to the reader's overheated imagination.)

What is this? The psychosexual equivalent of the Stockholm syndrome? Are those of us sentenced, by unlucky nature and unwise nurture, to long hours under the drill fated to act out bedroom psychodramas in which we exorcize the traumas of the chair in pornographic narratives starring us, a willing costar (or two), and a double-ratchet retractor? If so, one can only hope that the nitrous oxide flows freely, and that we emerge smiling from such transactions, all of our molars happily intact.

Go ahead: Rinse and spit.

(2005)

Gray Matter

REMEMBER THAT SCENE IN *CITIZEN KANE* WHERE THE REPORTER visits the imposing Walter Parks Thatcher Memorial Library to examine Thatcher's unpublished memoir? The scene is a study in secular ritual, from the stern mother superior of a librarian who admonishes him to read pages 83 through 142 and pages 83 through 142 *only,* to the shadowy sanctum of the reading room itself, where the reporter reads in a shaft of glowing, otherworldly light, hemmed in by darkness.

The New York Academy of Medicine Library, a literary reliquary tucked away on "museum mile" (a stretch of Fifth Avenue flanking Central Park West, where the Met and the Guggenheim hold court amid smaller museums), is only slightly less ceremonial than *Kane*'s Thatcher library. The procedures in place at this noncirculating medical library—one of the finest in the country and the only one in the New York area to open its doors to the public—are highly ritualized: you browse the library's online catalog, fill out electronic request slips for the titles you're interested in, click the "Request Selected Item" button, then take a seat in the stately, early Romanesque reading room, and . . .

Wait. And wait. And wait. True to cliché, dust motes hang in the sunbeams that fall slantingly through the high, arched windows, across the wild beasts cavorting in the sixteenth-century tapestry on one wall. The insect tick of your watch's second hand sounds

suddenly loud. Stone busts of bewhiskered medical men frown down
from their perches on top of the bookshelves. Horns and sirens drift
up from the street, only a few stories down but a world away. In the
fullness of time, a staff member arrives, wheeling a cart piled high
with books, among them your pickings from this garden of unearthly
delights.

The Academy Library is the sort of place that makes blood brothers of Nicholson Baker and Joel-Peter Witkin. Here are books on
forensic pathology and morbid anatomy, books on wax models of
skin diseases, books—in case you were wondering—on the occult
origins of kidney stones, such as William Adams's eighteenth-century
*Disquisition of the Stone and Gravel: And Other Diseases of the Blad-
der, Kidneys, &c.; The Occult Causes of the Stone Assign'd, Its Principles
Explain'd with the Manner of Its Accumulation, and by What Means
a Nucleus is First Form'd, Which Generates the Stone.*[1] Books worth
perusing for their titles alone, such as the 1973 *Proceedings of the
International Workshop on Nude Mice* or William A. Rossi's *Sex Life
of the Foot and Shoe.* Books to treasure for their homiletic wisdom,
such as Robert A. Matthews's *How to Recognize and Handle Abnor-
mal People* (1960), a law-enforcement manual whose sage counsel
will prove useful to anyone forced to attend family functions or office
meetings. Books to savor for their droll wit, such as *Sublime of flagellation,* an eighteenth-century bagatelle in the guise of letters from
"Lady Termagant Flaybum, of Birch-Grove, to Lady Harriet Tickle-
tail, of Bumfiddle-Hall . . . in which are introduced the beautiful tale
of La coquette chatie . . . and The boarding-school bumbrusher."[2]

More sobering are the library's annals of pseudoscientific bigotry, innocent-looking old tomes such as George Franklin French's
*Eradication of syphilis and crime by the extirpation, in that class, of
the procreative power,* presented to the Maine Medical Association
in 1878, calling for the sterilization of "that class"—the underclass—
as a means of stamping out social ills. Here, too, are clinical inqui-
ries into nature's crueler sports, such as Fredrik Ysander's *Studies on
the Morphology and Morphogenesis of Human Thoracopagic Monsters,*

with Special Reference to the Malformation of the Heart (1924)—"tho-racopagic monsters" being conjoined twins, fused at the upper trunk, face-to-face—and studies whose scholarly titles can't quite muffle the sound of special pleading, as in Charles Sennet's *Sunshine and Natur-ism: A Reasoned Exposition of the Naturist Movement* (1944).

Traditionally, medical libraries have guarded the profession's hard-won knowledge jealously. By closing their doors to the masses (whose interest, it was assumed, could only be voyeuristic), they maintained the mysteries, and thus the power and status, of the white-coated priesthood. By contrast, the New York Academy of Medicine—a socially responsible nonprofit dedicated, in the words of its website, "to enhancing the health of the public through research, education and advocacy, with a particular focus on disadvantaged urban popula-tions"—has sought, from the first, to *raise* public consciousness about health care issues, to *de*privatize medical knowledge, as it did when Fellows of the Academy voted, in 1875, to admit the public to the academy's newly founded library.[3]

This intellectual transparency has had a fringe benefit—or, more accurately, it has benefited the fringe, providing ready access to a mother lode of "invisible literature," the SF novelist J. G. Ballard's term for medical textbooks, scientific journals, technical manuals, and other gray matter. Although it comprises a veritable galaxy in the universe of print media, invisible literature is nowhere to be found in general-interest bookstores and is never reviewed in mainstream book pages for the simple reason that no one, not even the specialists who are its intended audience, thinks of this stuff as *literature* in the literary sense of the word.

At least, no one did until Ballard began promoting the notion that beyond the narrow bandwidth of the literary narrative as con-ceived by cultural mandarins at, say, the *New York Review of Books* lies the vast spectrum of corporate, government, and scientific com-munications, from *Gray's Anatomy* to the Warren Report, interoffice memos to cockpit voice-recorder transcripts, all of it an untapped source of inspiration for the postmodern imagination. Seen in the right light, asserts Ballard, such publications can be read as expressions of the unconscious of our age: specialized jargon sounds like found poetry; the Warren Report reads like "the novelization of the Zapruder film"; the Los Angeles *Yellow Pages* is "as surrealist in its way as Dali's autobiography."[4]

To test Ballard's hypothesis, take a seat in the library and thumb through a classic of invisible lit such as the *Journal of Forensic Sciences* or *Autoerotic Fatalities* (1983) by Hazelwood, Dietz, and Burgess. As you browse, the walls of the reading room seem to shimmy and dissolve into the starless dark on the far rim of human experience. Somewhere, across the wounded galaxies of inner space, gas-station attendants are found "dead on the floor following . . . rupture of the bowel from a grease-gun enema"; an elderly man is found naked and very much deceased, his penis stuffed into the attachment of the still-running vacuum cleaner lovingly cradled in one arm.[5] A forty-two-year-old Asian man accidentally hangs himself from a rope attached to the raised shovel of his backhoe tractor. "Determination of autoerotic death was made from decedent history and circumstantial indicators," report the authors of "Autoerotic Fatalities with Power Hydraulics," in the *Journal of Forensic Sciences*. "The victim kept a journal of love poetry dedicated to his tractor that he had named 'Stone,' outlining his desire for them to 'soar high' together."[6]

Another *Journal of Forensic Sciences* article investigates the bizarre death of a forty-year-old airline pilot who tells his wife he's going pistol shooting in a rural area. Later, a fisherman finds him at the end of an isolated road, crushed to death against the rear fender of his 1968 Volkswagen, nude and covered with "confluent skid-type abrasions." Apparently, the deceased had chained himself, by the neck, to the bumper of his Volkswagen and rigged the car to run in slow, concentric circles, so that he could jog or be dragged alongside it in a sadomasochistic transaction whose details remain unclear. But, as the medical examiner who wrote the case report (waggishly titled "The Love Bug") dryly notes, he committed a grave "pilot error" by allowing the car to run over the chain, which wound around the back axle,

strangling him. "Once again," the author deadpans, "we have graphi-
cally illustrated the fact that we know very little about some aspects
of human behavior."[7]

Immersed in the pathos and perversity of these snuff films from
another solar system, the reader realizes with a jolt that the actors
in these sick-sad psychodramas might be living next door. The per-
functory observation, in case report after case report, that the decedent "had no known psychiatric history and no known deviate [sic]
behavior" reminds us that there's more dark matter in the spiral galaxies of the soul than is dreamt of in the traditional novel.[8] An hour
spent with an issue of the *American Journal of Forensic Medicine and
Pathology* makes the middlebrow worldviews and regulation-issue
normalcy of most characters in mainstream fiction seem suddenly,
jarringly *ab*normal.

More than this year's Young White Male Genius, come to save the
novel from its slide into cultural irrelevance, the dreamy musings of
mail-order catalogs, Deep Thoughts of corporate mission statements,
and dead voices channeled by cockpit voice recorders and the phone-
machine messages of Twin Tower victims are a truer mirror of our
times. They're closer to the bone of what we are, as a society, than
the "new social novel" imagined by Tom Wolfe in his 1989 manifesto
"Stalking the Billion-Footed Beast," a call for novelists to eschew post-
modernist "interrogations" of literary form and of language itself and
embrace a more naturalistic, reportorial fiction—in effect, cloning
Zola. "At this weak, pale, tabescent moment in the history of American literature," Wolfe sermonized, "we need . . . a brigade of Zolas
to head out into this wild, bizarre, unpredictable, Hog-stomping
Baroque country of ours and reclaim it as literary property."[9]

Right question, wrong answer. Wolfe was timely in his realization that the American novel in both its blockbuster and highbrow
manifestations was fixated on individual psychology and interpersonal relations to the exclusion of its characters' "inextricable relation to the society around [them]."[10] (This, remember, was before
the rise of writers like David Foster Wallace, though notable exceptions to Wolfe's rule were at hand, even then, in novels by Burroughs,

Pynchon, Philip K. Dick, and DeLillo.) Yet, ever the knee-jerk neo-con, he rejects the argument, mounted by academic theorists and avant-garde writers starting with *nouveau roman* novelists like Alain Robbe-Grillet in the '6os, that literary naturalism is no longer ade-quate to the task of mirroring the "chaotic, fragmented, random, dis-continuous" nature of everyday life in our media-mad world.[11] The answer to what ails the mainstream novel, which Wolfe rightly diag-noses as "tabescent," is not more Zola but more McLuhan, or better yet more Baudrillard.

Ballard gets it. In his introduction to the French edition of his 1974 novel *Crash,* he critiques mainstream novelists' seeming obliv-iousness to the psychological torque of postmodernity, their insis-tence on peopling their imaginative landscapes with the introspec-tive, alienated Giacometti figures of twentieth-century modernism rather than the guilt-free, affectless, distributed selves we inhabit in remix culture. Multiple, protean, and playfully pathological, the post-modern self is a psychological mash-up, remixed from the media feed playing inside our heads. Bemoaning "the slow shrinking of the tra-ditional novel as it concerns itself more and more exclusively with the nuances of human relationships," Ballard argues for a new char-acterological topos, a psychology born of the always-on, all-pervasive media, the hyperacceleration of technological change, and the ver-tiginous urbanism, decentered and decentering, of our overdesigned cities and suburbs.[12]

"Across the communications landscape move the spectres of sin-ister technologies and the dreams that money can buy," writes Bal-lard, in oracular mode. "Thermo-nuclear weapons systems and soft-drink commercials coexist in an overlit realm ruled by advertising and pseudo-events, science and pornography."

Given these transformations, what is the main task facing the writer? ... Is his subject matter the sources of character and personality sunk deep in the past, the unhurried inspection of roots, the examination of the most subtle nuances of social behaviour and personal relationships? ... I feel that, in a sense, the writer knows nothing any longer. He has no moral stance.... His role is that of the scientist, whether on safari or in his laboratory, faced with a completely unknown terrain or subject. All he can do is to devise various hypotheses and test them against the facts.[13]

The novelist, then, as society's forensic pathologist.

In the pages of the forensic journals shelved in the Academy of Medicine Library, we catch glimpses of a posthuman fiction in which the Updike-ian, Roth-ish, Mailer-esque psyches that populate conventional narratives have collapsed into themselves like burned-out stellar cores, leaving Ballardian, media-fractured multiple personalities in their wake; in which interpersonal relationships have given way to the obsessive behaviors and fetishistic rituals of an electronically autistic age, where human contact is rapidly being replaced by the user interface. Intentionally or not, the invisible literature written by psychologists, pathologists, and others who specialize in the deviant mind or the monstrous body beckons us toward a psychogeography unimagined by most novelists—a narrative landscape where the airline pilot throttled by his Love Bug and the man wedded, in death, to his beloved backhoe costar in an autoerotic remake of *Love Story*.

(2002)

Thirteen Ways of Looking
at a Severed Head

I. AS A LOAD OFF YOUR SHOULDERS

ALTHOUGH (OR MAYBE BECAUSE) I GREW UP IN SUNNY SOUTH-ern California in the '60s and '70s, I was a morbid child, much given to Poe, Hammer horror films, and lovingly embroidered visions of a premature death—revenge fantasies in which my grief-crazed parents had to be physically restrained from hurling themselves into the grave as shovelfuls of earth thudded on my little coffin ("Bury me with him! Why, oh, *why*, sweet Jesus, didn't we get him that Mattel Creepy Crawlers Thingmaker he begged us for!?!").

Such scenarios were all in good, mean fun. When I was truly depressed, bummed by a life grown way too complicated in the midst of what was supposed to be the endless summer of a California boyhood, I'd daydream about decapitation. *Twilight Zone* comics, read by flashlight under the covers, together with the Aurora "Monster Scenes" kit for a working, 1:15-scale guillotine in the window of my local hobby shop, its plastic blade poised to decapitate the little victim that came with it, provided the raw material for imaginary beheadings whose symbolism was groaningly obvious: What better pain reliever for a loner who practically lived at the local library and whose grade school head was already a wasp's nest of hopes, dreams, fears, and insecurities, not to mention the fascinating factlets I was gleaning from all the books I was reading? Sometimes, it felt as if my skull was about to explode from the hyperbaric pressure of too much thinking.

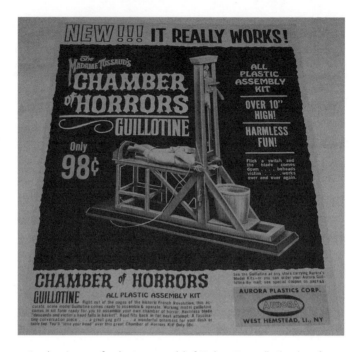

1964 advertisement for the Aurora model of Madame Tussaud's Chamber of Horrors Guillotine.

My status as an only child only compounded such problems.[1] Solipsism is a singleton's birthright, and I lived with a nonstop monologue inside my head—an ever-present voice-over that converted the world (the Not-Me) into the Me through an act of philosophical data processing: the instant, reflexive categorization and critiquing of everything around me. It was alienating, this internal voice, turning me into a neurotic escapee from a Bergman film who had somehow ended up in laid-back Southern California, harshing everyone's buzz. In the San Diego of my youth, brooding existentialists in black turtlenecks were sentenced to reeducation in Disneyland, The Happiest Place on Earth. To be sure, a Marcuse-ian critical distance was all that stood between me and the intellectual horrors of being mellowed to death, in the real-life Margaritaville of '70s SoCal. Nonetheless, there is such a thing as *too much* critical distance, and the little me inside my skull, the garrulous homunculus that insinuated its hyperintellectual interpretations between me and everything I experienced, made me want to take a load off my shoulders with a real-life guillotine, sometimes. If only I could lose my head, I thought, I'd be mindless, a happy camper at last.

2. AS NO-BRAINER

Paradoxically, there are those whose dumb-as-dirt demeanor, evident in their slack jaws and gazeless stares, makes them seem as if they deserve to lose the heads they obviously aren't using. Surely, this writer isn't the only nabob of negativism to have noted the uncanny similarity between the stunned, where's-the-rest-of-me? expression characteristic of severed heads and the trademark frozen grin and lights-are-on-but-nobody's-home gaze of George W. Bush, Dan Quayle, and other zero-forehead public figures.[2]

Typically, we see politicians, pundits, and the rest of the chattering class on TV, from the neck up, as talking heads—a term rich in symbolism. Listening to the just-shoot-me vacuities of bantering news anchors and Sunday-morning pundits, one can't help but wonder if they're proof positive of the theory, propounded by some of the doctors who experimented on freshly guillotined heads in Revolutionary France, that consciousness survives decapitation.

The history of Dr. Guillotin's ingenious machine abounds in gothic tales of severed heads that responded to the sound of their own names, a head transfused with the blood from a living dog (reportedly, its lips quivered and its eyelids fluttered), and the heads of rival members of the National Assembly, which, when tossed into the same sack, sank their teeth into each other so tenaciously that they couldn't be separated.[3] A Dr. Séguret claimed that open eyes in heads that were exposed to the sun "promptly closed, of their own accord, and with an aliveness that was both abrupt and startling," while a head whose tongue was pricked with a lancet retracted it immediately, "the facial features [grimacing] as if in pain."[4]

The evidence for the survival of awareness (as opposed to brain activity) after decapitation remains inconclusive. According to Dr. Ron Wright, a forensic pathologist and former chief medical examiner of Broward County Florida, "After your head is cut off by a guillotine, you have 13 seconds of consciousness (+/− 1 or 2).... The 13 seconds is the amount of high energy phosphates that the cytochromes in the brain have to keep going without new oxygen and glucose."[5] Naturally, electrochemical activity is no guarantor of conscious thought, although as Wright notes, there are alleged instances of disembodied heads blinking in response to questions, "two for yes and one for no."[6]

If bodiless heads can think, what about headless bodies? Mike the Headless Wonder Chicken springs immediately to mind. On September 10, 1945, Fruita, Colorado, resident Lloyd Olsen sent— or attempted to send—Mike the way of all fryers with a well-aimed whack. Amazingly, the rooster survived his beheading: Olsen had indeed decapitated the bird, but he'd somehow managed to miss its jugular vein and, as important, leave its brain stem (or enough of it to be dangerous) intact, albeit dangling by the proverbial thread. The next morning, Olsen discovered the rooster pecking and preening (phantom head syndrome?), his reflex actions intact, thanks to the brain stem that had miraculously escaped the vorpal blade. Sustained by grain and water dripped into his exposed esophagus, Mike went on to sideshow fame. He lived for another eighteen months before succumbing, at last, to decapitation-related complications.[7]

Historical flashbacks to a decapitated chicken who lives to strut another day, and to guillotined heads who seem to recognize the sound of their names, bring us full circle to meditations on TV's talking heads. The symbolic resonances between severed heads (and the headless bodies they imply) and the ubiquitous image of the disembodied and seemingly brainless pol, pundit, or newsdroid, floating on-screen like a pickled head in a bell jar, reverberate in "Headless Reporter Continues Work," a wire-service report from the future brought to you by the humor website Futurefeedforward.[8]

The story is an account of an event that hasn't happened yet, but will, according to the site's revolutionary Temporal Networking technologies. Apparently, 20/20 reporter John Stossel (widely reviled in progressive media circles as a conservative ideologue and pro-market flack for corporate interests) was—er, will be—decapitated while filming "'Oil is Good Food,' a series of reports looking skeptically at the promise of 'alternative energy,'" when a wind turbine whirs unexpectedly to life. Acting quickly, doctors save Stossel's life by sealing off his neck and leaving his "'enteric nervous system' or 'gut brain'" in command of his mouth and mind.[9] In no time flat, he's back in action and ready to kick tree-hugger butt, talking tough "through a vocoder linked to special 'contact microphones' affixed to his neck":

> Responding angrily to questions about his decision to forego use of a prosthetic head, Stossel noted that he felt no embarrassment about being headless and that colleagues at ABC agreed that he has done some of his best work in years since the accident: "Do I wish it hadn't happened? Sure. Am I any less of a reporter just because I haven't got a head? No way."[10]

3. AS FETISH OBJECT

Drift-net fishing through the Internet's deeps brings up numerous examples of decapitation fetishism, a queasy mix of necro-porn, splatter movie, and upchuck humor guaranteed to appall even the most politically incorrect postfeminists. One needn't be a born-again Dworkinite, brandishing *Intercourse* like a Gideon Bible, to get creeped out while browsing the Axe & Guillotine website ("The Best in Beheading"), Necromancer's website ("Behead and Debreast"), Mickey Jay's website ("Beheading"), Scanbastard's website ("Beheading"), Mocktoad Manipulations's ("Beheading"), or any of the scores of similar sites that cater to snuff fetishism, a twisted little limb on the family tree of pathological sexuality, at the juncture of S&M and necrophilia.[11]

THIRTEEN WAYS OF LOOKING AT A SEVERED HEAD

The pay-per-view website the Fantasy Decapitation Channel (not to be confused with the Fantasy Hanging Channel) is all beheading, all the time. For $24.95 a month, subscribers can savor Grand Guignol photoplays such as "Lover's Block" ("Two babes go naked on the block!"), "Annabelle's Head on a Platter," and "Double Decap Delight," all of which feature women, nude but for panties, messily beheaded by swords, axes, and scarily convincing guillotines.[12] The executioners are usually men, though occasionally they're goth babes in latex fetish gear; the victims are always female.

In this weirdly chaste torture garden, a sort of soap-opera De Sade, the men are always clothed and maintain a respectful distance from the female victim; male desire is displaced onto the falling blade, which penetrates her soft, virginal neck in a Freudian metaphor that's as subtle as a bag of axes. Where most hetero-guy porn sites obsess over double-D cups, the Fantasy Decapitation Channel rejoices in double decaps; here, the climactic moment comes when a jet of gore geysers out of the neck stump of some sweet young thing—a necrophilic parody of ejaculation depicted with obsessive realism, thanks to the sleight-of-eye made possible by image-manipulating software.

In *lustmord* porn like the stories archived at Chez Marquis, death by decapitation is the ultimate erotic buzz; here, as in the auto-erotic asphyxiations endlessly replayed in the novels of William S. Burroughs, death is precisely synched to the split second of orgasm. To the authors of such fantasies, it is an ecstatic agony, beautiful as the chance meeting, on a chopping block, of sex and death. In "A Rolling Head Gathers No Moss," by the pseudonymous Marquis of Chez Marquis, the supermodel Kate Moss has "the best sex of her life on the guillotine where Madonna died."[13] In the Marquis's story, the deathblow and the "little death," as the French call orgasm, come together in an emotional crescendo of exquisite pain:

> His cock twitched inside me, ready to deposit its final load. I took a deep breath—my last—and pressed the button. The blade fell flawlessly, as I had known it would. It sliced through my neck like a hot knife through butter. There was no pain. The world tumbled, then righted itself as my head

landed in the basket. My headless corpse reared up on the table, in the throes of an ecstasy, a passion so complete that it defies words. And as red faded quickly to black, the last thing I saw was my lover's face, and on it a look of purest pleasure.[14]

Here, the Marquis lives up to his namesake, who reimagined murder as an erotic thrill beyond all others. To the De Sadean imagination, power—power without limit, unbounded by conscience—is the ultimate high. It extends the ego, godlike, to the edge of infinity, transforming everything within its sphere of power into the raw material of the lord and master's pleasure. A casebook example of sadism, decap fantasies draw their voltage from the utter subjugation of the other, her (always *her*) reduction to a paraphilic object— a mute, manipulable toy on which the author of the fantasy can exhaust his desires. At its most extreme, this objectification refunctions the head—metonym for the human and repository of the psyche, of all that makes us unique, thinking beings—into a pocket vagina, as in the Chez Marquis story "Giving Head":

> I gasped as I fucked her dying, disembodied head. . . . To my astonishment I realized that I had gone all the way through her. The top four or five inches of my erection emerged from the bloody stump of her neck.
> The antics of her headless body were comic, but also deeply erotic. Her hands reached up to feel around for a head that wasn't there any more.[15]

"Comic" in the sense that the sight of the human reduced to a witless, herky-jerky mechanism is always comical, as Henri Bergson famously argued in *Laughter* (1900); erotic in the sense that the willful mind subjugated to the animal body—a fuck puppet who lives to serve your every perverse whim—is erotic.

When she loses her head, the victim of "Giving Head" is reduced to a hot bod without all that troublesome *thinking* to get in the way, like the decapitated (but still spunky) Devil Girl who becomes Flakey Foont's living sex doll in "A Bitchin' Bod" by R. Crumb, a comic that, like many of Crumb's comics, is either the bare-naked face of the artist at his most mind-bendingly misogynistic or a tongue-in-check satire of misogyny, à la Swift's "Modest Proposal," or some queasy-making cocktail of both, in equal measure. After scrunching Devil Girl's head into her body and sealing off the stump of her neck, Mr. Natural has his Dirty Old Man way with her, telling a speechless Foont:

> This's truly a magnificent body, isn't it? . . . But, y'know, the head was always a big problem. . . . She had such an irritating set of sensibilities! And such a nasty mouth! Oy! It was vicious! . . . So I got to thinkin' an' figurin'— why not just get rid of th' head? Th' body is what we're *mainly* interested in, right?[16]

Well, gentlemen? Is Crumb indulging every man's guiltiest fantasy? Or is the American Hogarth, as the art critic Robert Hughes called him, caricaturing the male libido at its most bestial?[17]

For straight men (and decap fantasies seem to be straight men's meat), eroticized beheading, especially by guillotine, is a double-edged pleasure. Ostensibly a fever-dream vision of dominance and submission in which a De Sadean male penetrates a powerless babe with his steely blade, decap snuff is haunted by the homoerotic gothic. The dark dreams of Marquis and others like him are shadowed by homophobic fears of the Queer Within: beheading is at once eroticized castration and ejaculation (with the spurting neck stump as grotesque parody of the squirting penis).

At the same time, the severed female head invokes what the feminist film critic Barbara Creed calls the monstrous feminine, that gorgonian archetype whose stony glare and grinning gape mock the almighty phallus into shriveled impotence. The ur-text on this subject is Freud's over-the-top essay "Medusa's Head" (1922), in which he asserts, "To decapitate = to castrate. The terror of Medusa is thus the terror of castration that is linked to the sight of something."[18] For a young boy, the "something" is that unforgettable first glimpse of the awesome female pubes, most likely his mother's, with their snaky tangle of hair. To Freud's terrified little boy, mom's you-know-what is at once a fearful wound where the penis used to be and a shaggy maw, waiting to gobble up his organ as well. The mother of all castrating bitches, Medusa wears the severed members of her Bobbitt-ized victims in the form of her serpentine locks.

What would the Jewish father of psychoanalysis have made of Hitler, had he known that the Führer was fascinated by decapitation? The man who vowed that heads would "roll in the sand" when he came to power, and who once remarked that German justice should consist of "either acquittal or beheading," wasted no time bringing the guillotine back from history's prop room.[19] According to Daniel Gerould's *Guillotine: Its Legend and Lore,* an estimated 16,500 enemies of the Reich were murdered with the machine.[20]

Tellingly, the Führer was "infatuated," in the words of Hitler scholar Robert G. L. Waite, with the beheaded Medusa, she of the "piercing eyes that could render others impotent."[21] Franz von Stuck's gothic painting of the Gorgon cast an eerie spell on the Nazi leader—"Those eyes! Those are the eyes of my mother!" he reportedly exclaimed, on seeing the painting for the first time—and a carving of the Medusa's baleful head decorated the front of the massive desk he designed for his office in the Chancellery. Furthermore, Hitler was inordinately proud of his own penetrating gaze and often "practiced 'piercing stares' in front of the mirror," according to Waite. Freud theorized the "substitutive relation between the eye and the male member which is seen to exist in dreams and myths and phantasies," and Waite, ever the Freudian, traces Hitler's Medusa fixation to sublimated castration anxiety, inspired by an allegedly undescended testicle.[22] "In order to help master the anxiety engendered by the anatomical defect, disturbed monorchid boys favor symbolic substitutes for the missing testicle," asserts Waite, who notes that such patients "may be excessively concerned about eyes."[23] Reportedly, Hitler exulted in staring people down. "In effect," writes Waite, "he may have been saying to them and to himself, 'See, I do have two powerful (potent) testicles, and I can penetrate and dominate others.'"[24] And if piercing eyes could serve as a potent surrogate for a missing testicle, might not bodiless heads represent the severed member— phallic talismans obsessively collected by a monorchid haunted by the unconscious fear that he was "half a man"? It's a theory, anyway, as laughably hyperbolic yet satisfyingly neat, in its narrative closure, as Freudian readings always are.

But Freud holds no patent on the psychosexual subtext of decapitation. As Gerould points out, "Severed male heads and decapitated bodies play a prominent role in the decadent art and literature of the late 19th century, particularly in the biblical stories of Judith and Salomé. Flaubert, Huysmans, Laforgue, and Wilde in literature, and Moreau, Klimt, Beardsley, and Munch in painting are the best known of a whole host of male fin-de-siècle artists obsessed by visions of vengeful, headhunting 'demonic' women."[25] Think of "The Climax," Beardsley's drawing of Wilde's lascivious Salomé, pursing her lips to kiss the severed, still dripping head of John the Baptist.

Meanwhile, the gentle sex was hunting heads in actual fact. The huge crowds that flocked to public guillotinings in nineteenth-century France included a significant number of women who, as one of the characters in Henri Monnier's 1829 short story "The Execution" notes, reportedly found the spectacle more titillating than men did.[26] Nor was the arousal of female bloodlust in the presence of the National Razor, as the French called their decapitation machine, unique to the nineteenth century: in a note to his novel *Justine* (1791), De Sade observes that "whenever there is a public assassination ... almost always women are in the majority" because "they are more inclined to cruelty than we are," a predilection the Divine Marquis attributes, curiously, to the fact that "they have a more delicate nervous system."[27]

Fittingly, the guillotine itself was mythologized, in the mass imagination, as a man-eating black widow, yet another manifestation of the romantic archetype of the femme fatale. Gendered feminine in French *(la guillotine)*, the machine was referred to as Guillotin's daughter and soon acquired nicknames such as "Dame Guillotine" and "The Widow." Her white wood not yet stained, a guillotine was known as a "virgin" until she had tasted her first blood. Taking one's place on a virgin machine—lying flat on one's belly on the plank known as the bascule, head in the pillorylike lunette that holds it in place so the blade can do its work—was called "mounting Mademoi-selle." After her ritual deflowering, a guillotine was painted red; lying on her was known as "mounting Madame."[28]

In the same spirit, the Scottish decapitation machine, the precursor of the guillotine, was called the Maiden. According to Regina Janes, a specialist in eighteenth-century culture, "The last man to die by the Maiden, the earl of Argyle in 1685, declared 'as he pressed his lips on the block, that it was the sweetest maiden he had ever kissed.'"[29]

4–13. AS POLYSEMIC PERVERSITY, ABJECT OBJECT, UNDEAD FETISH, DISQUIETING MUSE, SIGNPOST AT THE EDGE OF THE CIVILIZED WORLD, RELIC OF ANCIENT BARBARITIES, FACE OF CONTEMPORARY CRUELTY, SYMBOL OF POLITICAL PROTEST, MIND/BODY SPLIT MADE FLESH, AND EXPLORATORY PROBE LAUNCHED INTO THE AFTERWORLD

Any way you slice it, the severed head is an enigmatic object, and this essay only begins to tease out its tangled meanings. Ghastly and fasci-nating, perverse and polyvalent, the severed head stares back at us, its clouded eyes at once as depthless as a dead fish's and as deep as star-less space. Inert, yet all too human, it hovers disconcertingly between being and thing-ness. Like all corpses, it is a human object, a poster child for Freud's uncanny and Kristeva's abject. Yet, unlike a headless body or a severed limb, which evokes pity, grief, fear, and horror at the sight of another human reduced to a broken doll, the head's eter-nal status as the mind's throne and the movie screen of the soul (via the face) make it not merely pitiable or dreadful (although it is those things, too) but powerfully mesmeric, an undead fetish whose fasci-nations are a witches' brew of repulsion and attraction.

I'm looking at the photographer Scott Lindgren's portrait of a breathtakingly lifelike sculpture of a decapitated Chinese head, which appears in the 2000 calendar of the Philadelphia-based Müt-ter Museum of pathological anatomy. Presented to the museum by Dr. Charles D. Hart in 1896, the object may be Japanese in origin and is made of unknown materials, although X-rays have revealed that it has a wooden armature. "Its purpose is unknown," the photo caption notes, "whether to serve as a substitute for a real trophy head, or as a stage prop."[30]

For my purposes, the Mütter head is an alas-poor-Yorick aid to contemplation, a disquieting muse. Studying its soulless eyes, its brow knitted in pain, the braided pigtail looped around its neck stump, the trickle of blood oozing from one nostril, the weirdly labial folds of the horrific gash in one cheek (did the executioner miss, on first try?), I see the severed head as a signpost at the edge of the modern world, marking our border crossing into precivilized times. Sad, battered, and bloody, the Chinese head in the Mütter catalog appears to us as the gruesome relic of a more barbarous age, like the infamous woodcut of Vlad the Impaler having dinner amid a forest of spears writhing with impaled victims or the eye-curdling 1905 photo, reproduced in *The Tears of Eros* by Georges Bataille, of the murderer tortured to death in the unspeakable Chinese punishment known as the "Hundred Pieces."[31]

In fact, decapitation is still with us, perpetuated by totalitarian regimes, fanatical sects, lone psychopaths, jihadis, and anyone else in need of a particularly humiliating slap in his victim's face, an indignity that heaps desecration on death. It's especially popular among Islamist terrorists such as the Abu Sayyaf guerrillas in the Philippines or the Pakistani group that cut off the head of the *Wall Street Journal* reporter Danny Pearl after killing him. Beheading is voguish, too, in nations under Koranic law, such as Saudi Arabia, where, according to Amnesty International, the accused are routinely decapitated, after confessions extorted under torture, for "apostasy, witchcraft, sexual offenses, and crimes involving both hard and soft drugs."[32] In the age of biotech, nanotech, cloned sheep, and the cracking of the genomic code, there are corners of the world where the Reign of Terror never ended. Heads (more often than not women's) roll in the noonday sun, their blood lapped up by thirsty sand.

(Lest I be accused of stooping to Orientalist caricature in my evocations of Muslim cruelty, let me point out the obvious—namely, that our republic of virtue is hardly more humane in its methods of

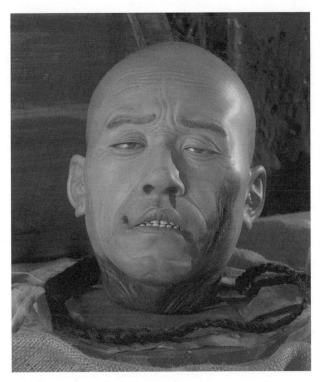

Life-sized model of a decapitated Chinese head, presented to the
Mütter Museum by Dr. Charles D. Hart, 1896. A nearly identical head
in the collections of the Science Museum, London, is believed to have
been modeled on the head of an executed Chinese Yangtze river pirate.
The origins and purpose of the Mütter head are unknown. Head shot
copyright 1999 by Scott Lindgren, from the book *Mütter Museum*,
published by Blast Books; reprinted with permission of Blast Books, Inc.

capital punishment. Decapitation, Saudi-style, while unquestionably
more gory than our preferred methods of lethal injection, strangula-
tion by hanging, asphyxiation by gas, death by firing squad, and, most
notoriously, being fried alive in the electric chair, is also a swifter and,
arguably, more painless end. Accounts of the botched 1997 electro-
cution, in Florida, of convicted killer Pedro Medina describe flames
shooting out of Medina's face mask and smoke that stank of burned

flesh, making the Saudi sword seem like sweet relief by comparison.[33] Even lethal injection, widely perceived as a kinder, gentler state-sanctioned murder, may be more painful than previously imagined, according to a 2005 study by medical researchers. Inmates may be inadequately anesthetized, the authors contend, and therefore may consciously experience the "asphyxiation, a severe burning sensation, massive muscle cramping and cardiac arrest" that accompany death by injection—cruel and unusual punishment, by any other name.[34])

Staring at the anonymous Mütter head, I think, too, of decapitation as political protest, from Renaissance Florentines' embrace of the biblical story of Judith as a metaphor for their righteous resistance to Medici rule, to "Margaret on the Guillotine," an anti-Thatcher tune on Morrisey's 1988 record *Viva Hate* (a politically incorrect fantasy, complete with guillotine-clang sound effect, that earned the pop star a visit from the police), to Paul Kelleher's ritual decapitation, in 2002, of a statue of Lady Thatcher. After unsuccessfully assailing the marble effigy of Thatcher with a cricket bat, Kelleher managed to knock its block off with one of the handy metal posts used to support the rope cordon keeping visitors to the London-based Guildhall Art Gallery at a safe distance from the sculpture. Kelleher said he believed the neo-liberal ideology of conservatives like Thatcher was doing "irreparable damage" to the world in which his two-year-old son was growing up. "I haven't really hurt anybody," he said. "It's just a statue, an idol we seem to be worshipping."[35]

But somewhere behind the cloud of meanings conjured up by *the* severed head as icon lies *a* severed head—a pathetic, flesh-and-blood being who experienced the mind/body split at its most cruelly literal.

What must it feel like to be a thinking, feeling, seeing, hearing being one instant and, with the flash of a blade, a heap of dead meat the next? How can we imagine the unimaginable—that thirteen-second eternity when your body twitches, headless, on the bascule and your head sits in the sawdust-strewn basket, staring skyward, still thinking, thinking of—what? Do you squint into the glare of the sun, before your consciousness flickers into nothingness? Do you wrinkle your nose when a fly walks across it? Does thirteen seconds stretch into a frozen moment, as it does in the movies, time enough to rewind and fast-forward through a life? Does your severed head experience a sort of phantom limb—or, rather, ghost body—syndrome? Where are *you* when you lose your head?

In his gothic fantasia *Thoughts and Visions of a Severed Head*, the nineteenth-century Belgian romantic painter Antoine Weirtz puts our heads in the lunette and drops the blade:

> A horrible noise is buzzing in his head.
>
> This is the noise of the blade coming down.
>
> The executed prisoner believes that he has been struck by lightning, not by the blade.
>
> Incredible! The head is here, under the scaffold, but it is convinced that it is still up above, a part of the body waiting all the while for the blow that must separate it from the trunk. . . .
>
> . . . The eyes of the condemned prisoner roll in their bloody sockets.
>
> . . . They stare fixedly toward the sky, he thinks he sees the immense canopy of the sky tear in two and two parts draw apart like huge curtains. In the infinite depths behind, there appears a blazing furnace, where the stars seem engulfed and consumed forever.[36]

Here is where words wink out like dying stars, lost in the endless night of the unthinkable. Shorn of the organ that makes meaning, the decapitated never ask what a severed head means. Or, perhaps, by losing their heads, they find out at last, but cannot tell us. Their lips tremble, their eyelids flutter, two for yes and one for no, but thirteen seconds is too brief an eternity to tell the living the meaning of life.

(2003)

Been There, Pierced That

THE WAY HE TELLS IT, ADAM PARFREY—THE RON POPEIL OF fusion paranoia, pop Satanism, bad art, cannibal killers, Jews for Hitler, and fecal black magic (okay, make that brown magic)—*had* to become America's most mondo publisher. It's an ugly job, but somebody had to do it. Mainstream houses wouldn't touch the stuff he was drawn to—beyond-the-pale subject matter that makes the minds of most readers curl up like slugs on a hot griddle. "If other people weren't going to publish what I found intriguing, then I had to do it," he told a Salon writer. "I couldn't really work for other people. Like, 'Hey, I'll find another *Chicken Soup* book for ya!' I couldn't see myself doing that. No way."[1]

Since 1986, when he cofounded Amok Press, he's done it his way, beginning with *Apocalypse Culture,* his 1987 omnibus of crackpot scholarship, Spenglerian ravings about the decline of just about everything, and matter-of-fact interviews with an unrepentant necrophile, a connoisseur of child torture, and a devotee of "body play" who clamps clothespins on his lips and cinches his waist to a wasplike fourteen inches. Its fringe cred certified by J. G. Ballard, who pronounced its contents "the terminal documents of the twentieth century," *Apocalypse Culture* had sold a reported 55,000 copies as of a 2000 profile of Parfrey in Salon.[2]

The book is a bona fide subcultural classic, widely credited with kick-starting alt.culture as we know it, from the 'zine revolution to designer paranoia in the ha-ha-only-serious *X-Files* mode to the Gen-X vogues for serial-killer fandom and body modification (although my nominee for that distinction would go to *Re/Search* books such as *Industrial Culture* and *Modern Primitives,* avowed Parfrey influences). Whether they know it or not, Marilyn Manson, *X-Files* creator Chris Carter, transgressive novelist Dennis Cooper, Disinformation.com, Yahoo's Alt.culture, 'zines like *Murder Can Be Fun* and *Juxtapoz,* Brian King *(Lustmord: The Writings and Artifacts of Murderers),* and Vankin and Whalen *(The 60 Greatest Conspiracies of All Time)* owe Parfrey a debt of gratitude. Richard "The Night Stalker" Ramirez has already given him his props, enthusing, "He provides an extended view and insight into the world of deviancy and depravity—or maybe just a different lifestyle."[3] (In our therapy culture, even thrill-killing psychopaths speak the touchy-feely language of Zoloft-enhanced tolerance.)

Now, Parfrey has inflicted a sequel, *Apocalypse Culture II* (2000), on an unprepared (though maybe richly deserving) world. Like its predecessor, it's adorned with a cover painting of frolicking freaks and living dead by Joe Coleman, the self-styled "nascent mass murderer" seen dissecting what appears to be a genuine cadaver in his contributor's photo.[4] Also like its predecessor, *AC II* features conspiracy theory, right-wing fulminations, apologias for pedophilia, sympathetic portraits of psychopaths, and the true confessions of a necrophile, plus (at no extra charge!) fascist-flavored kiddie porn, John Hinkley's mash notes to Jodie Foster, an ad for the Second Coming Project (devoted to cloning Jesus using DNA extracted from holy relics), the official Aryan Nations guide to deconstructing Don McLean's "American Pie," a modest attempt at fiction by the Unabomber, and a handy-dandy clip 'n' save Necrocard:

I request that after death
   A. my body may be used for any type of sexual activity or
   B.
      gay only [ ]
      straight only [ ]
I do not wish my body to be dismembered or disfigured during necrophiliac sex [ ][5]

No *Chicken Soup* here; *AC II* is a bottom-feeder's *Salmonella for the Soul*.

The question on every transgressophile's mind, of course, is: Does the sequel provide all the noxious delights of the first *AC*? The short answer is: No. It's a better book in almost every way, far broader in scope and more thoughtfully edited, not to mention slicker and more generously illustrated, with eye-frying images of Shirley Temple in Nazi drag, Captain Kirk in the raw, hyperreal sex dolls with hermaphroditic genitals, and the by-now pro forma morgue-slab photos of a horribly dismembered corpse.

But America at the hinge of the millennium is a far weirder, more unhinged, but nonetheless more branded, niche-marketed place than it was in '87, when *Apocalypse Culture* introduced a new generation of under- and overeducated lumpen to the perennial pleasures of baiting the politically correct by tipping every sacred cow in sight. Necrophilia, pedophilia, dead-baby jokes, and sympathy for those durable old devils, Uncle Adolf and Uncle Charlie—you know, the guy with the swastika carved on his forehead—just don't deliver the cattle-prod jolt they delivered in '87, before Jeffrey Dahmer, JonBenet Ramsey, John Wayne Bobbitt, *When Animals Attack, Seven*, Joel-Peter Witkin, the vogue for schoolyard shootings, the adolescent nastiness of the Chapman Brothers, and, most of all, the Web, which has proven hospitable to an algal bloom of sites like MorbidReality.com ("Accidents, murder, dead babies, suicide, medical pics, disease. . . . If you are a closet sicko fascinated with the misery and misfortune of others . . . then you'll want to check out morbid reality").[6]

We've been there, pierced that. The escalation of subcultural hostilities and free-floating weirdness, in our age of extremes, has robbed all the old, reliable Satanic litanies—what Parfrey calls acts of "aesthetic terrorism"—of their power to outrage. So has the strip-mining and strip-malling of every fringe-culture ritual of resistance, virtually the moment it appears. There's a desperately insistent, methinks-thou-dost-protest-too-much quality to recent proclamations that the counterculture is alive and well, whether at the increasingly bobo-friendly Burning Man; in Ann Powers's *Weird Like Us: My Bohemian*

America; or at Disinfo.con, the New York festival of transgression where a speaker declared, somewhat unconvincingly, "When they" (presumably, "They" in the uppercase, '60s sense of the word, meaning the squares) "just buy the thing that we really believed in, that's them surrendering to us." (I get it! *[cue forehead slap]* So, like, when the Gap starts selling leather pants, it means that even the Gap has been infected with the, like, rebellion meme, right?) Ironically, Parfrey, in his Ron Popeil–like role as pitchman on the pathological midway, has greatly accelerated this dynamic. The center is widening; the fringes cannot hold.

If he were simply a buck-hungry retailer of the unspeakable, he'd go down easier. But he insists on a more exalted status than the Charles Kuralt of our psychic badlands: that of a Luciferian Noam Chomsky, speaking the awful truths about The Conspiracy and the Dictatorship of Political Correctness that the lapdog mainstream media dare not utter. Unfortunately, it's well-nigh impossible to reconcile Parfrey's lofty claims with his mean-spirited "retard" bashing, his seeming endorsement of wet-brained conspiracy theories about Waco, and his creepy coziness with one too many neo-Nazis and Odin-worshipping Aryan supremacists. The shout-outs, in the book's acknowledgments, to close friend Michael Moynihan, described in a *New Times* article on Parfrey as a "fascist activist" who has published the writings of neo-Nazis and sold CDs and merchandise with a pagan-right slant; the inspirational quotes from Hitler and the National Socialist Liberation Front poster in *AC*; the gay Nazi poster and the social Darwinist ruminations, in *AC II*, on "democracy's deification of Victimhood," by good buddy Boyd Rice, last seen in brownshirt attire, accessorized with a darling little Nazi knife, in James Ridgeway's study of white supremacists, *Blood in the Face*: I'm sensing a theme here. And I'm not the first: former *Re/Search* publisher V. Vale told a *New Times* reporter, "Adam is a racist scumbag, and he's friends with a lot of racists. Here's why he publishes: purely to foment shock value and to celebrate himself. There isn't any compassion. He's just a typical privileged, stunted-growth, adolescent white male."[7]

Parfrey stands unbowed in the face of such charges. "My articles and investigations take me far and wide, and I get friendly with SWAT teams, extreme right-wingers and anarchist bomb-throwers," he told me, via e-mail. "To cull Boyd Rice out of a group of published friends and then do a guilt-by-association trip is sinister McCarthyism."[8] He readily concedes that *AC* and *AC II* "concern the extremes of human belief," but defends his refusal to render moral judgment with the disclaimer, "I respect the human consciousness enough not to infantilize it by spelling out moral conclusions. I *do* admit that I like making people uncomfortable with nanny culture's ideas and expectations. . . . God help me, I'm a pot-smoking libertarian."[9]

Maybe, but from my sniper's perch on the post-Marxist left, there are a lot of chinks in the pomo/boho argument that ethics is so *over*, already, and in the self-serving defense that blowing bong hits at the politically correct is bad-boy fun (and profitable, too). Why should we infantilize *ourselves* by ceding all moral authority to neocon scolds like William Bennett or left-wing inquisitors like Andrea Dworkin? Moreover, chain jerking the "nanny culture" doesn't have much intellectual frisson, at this point, for anyone besides the Don Imus fan in the beer-can-holder baseball cap. Parfrey's brighter than that, by far. If only he could outgrow his clubby need to bond with subcultural baddies like Rice and Moynihan (the enemy of my enemy the bourgeoisie is my friend, even if he spouts social Darwinist bilge and plays footsie with the far right).

Sadly, Parfrey shows no sign of ranging beyond the traditional quarry of all twentieth-century cultural vanguards—the Babbitt class and its *Book of Virtues* morality—to bigger game such as the vanguard itself, with its designer schadenfreude and its *Nietzsche for Beginners* contempt for the masses.

More's the pity, because he's got a deft, Menckenesque way with the lacerating one-liner and a nose for great stories: I CAN, "a cult of sex-obsessed cripples"; survivalist nutcake "Bo" Gritz's run for the White House; and the awesome Mister Awesome, a beefcake legend in his own mind who stalks Parfrey's message machine with scary-funny ferocity. His dark, sardonic postcards from the abyss, in the

Apocalypse books and (my personal favorite) *Cult Rapture,* are toxic good fun. In my dreams, he'll follow Clarice Starling's advice to Hannibal Lecter in *Silence of the Lambs* and point his "high-powered perception" at himself. He'll train the philosophical crosshairs of his withering wit and his pitiless cynicism on his own mind— all the unacknowledged, unconsidered ideologies in his closet—and pull the trigger.

(2000)

Death to All Humans!

WHAT THE WORLD NEEDS NOW IS SUICIDE, ABORTION, CANNI-balism, and sodomy. That, at least, is the Church of Euthanasia's modest proposal. A tax-exempt "educational foundation" dedicated to the proposition that all men (and women) are created superfluous, the Church has staked its claim on the far fringes of the negative population growth movement, alongside neo-Malthusians like the Voluntary Human Extinction Movement and deep ecologists like the Gaia Liberation Front. According to a Church spokesperson, "The Church is devoted to restoring balance between humans and the remaining species, through voluntary population reduction."[1]

The Church, which claims "hundreds" of card-carrying members as well as a thousand "e-members" scattered across the Net, is based in the Somerville, Massachusetts, apartment of its cross-dressing cleric, the Reverend Chris Korda.[2] It was there, on a hot summer night in 1992, that she (though male, Korda prefers the female pronoun) had the fateful dream that set her on a mission from God—or, more precisely, from the alien entity she calls the Being, a cheery mix of Klaatu and Kevorkian who noted the dire state of the global ecosystem and advised, "Save the planet; kill yourself!"

Or, less messily, evangelize *others* to kill *themselves.* Thus was born the Church of Euthanasia, whose theological cornerstone is the single commandment "Thou shalt not procreate" and whose four pillars of wisdom are its radical solutions to the population explosion: suicide, abortion, cannibalism, and sodomy. This doesn't mean, by the way, that sodomy is a "Euthanist" sacrament; the Church uses the term in the biblical sense, meaning any sex act not intended for procreation, such as anal or oral sex. Nor does the zealously vegetarian Church condone Hannibal Lecter's idea of frugal-gourmet fare; its endorsement of cannibalism is merely a special dispensation for those "godless flesh-eaters" who can't kick the habit.[3] As the credo on the Church's website states, anthropophagy, Euthanist-style, is "strictly limited to consumption of the already dead."[4] Even so, Korda, a strict vegan, can't resist suggesting that cannibalism is also environmentally friendly. "We have 60,000 auto-accident fatalities a year," she says. "That meat is getting buried in the ground. It should go straight to McDonald's, where the food is already so processed I don't think anybody would notice the difference."[5]

As mordant social satire and neo-Situationist street theater, the Church is a howl: God's revenge on Operation Rescue, in a universe ruled by Abbie Hoffman. Korda has clearly inherited her father Michael's gene for media manipulation. (Korda senior is a onetime titan of the publishing industry, the former power-lunching editor in chief of Simon & Schuster and author of best-selling Nietzsche lite such as *Power! How to Get It, How to Use It* and *Success!*)

Tastefully turned out in silver bangles and a chic little cocktail dress, the reverend has led her troops into battle against pro-lifers, Buchananites, and Jerry Springer. Rallying around a banner emblazoned with the admonition "Eat a queer fetus for Jesus," the Church has serenaded horrified Operation Rescue protesters with its marching song, "All We Are Saying / Is Fetus Paté." Under the guise of Pedophile Priests for Life, Korda and her true-believing troops have waged guerrilla media war against the Catholic activists Our Lady's Crusaders for Life, brandishing an inflatable sex doll nailed to a life-sized crucifix and squirting the Crusaders with a water pistol shaped like a humongous penis. Anti-abortion protesters "try to intimidate everyone with shock tactics and disgusting props," says Korda, "but we can out-shock and out-disgust them any day. We're seizing the moral low ground right out from under them."[6]

And when they're doing it, Korda and her Euthanasians are unquestionably on the side of the angels, not to mention social satirists like Abbie Hoffman (an acknowledged influence). But the laughter curdles when Korda extols the virtues of the Unabomber, rationalizing the murder of a timber industry lobbyist and father of two who wasn't even the bomber's intended victim as a "worthy target, when the goal is correctly understood."[7]

Moreover, the misanthropy that lies just beneath the surface of the Church's baby loathing and breeder bashing aligns it with unhappy bedfellows like Randall Phillip and Jim and Debbie Goad, all of whom are listed as "contacts" in the Church's house organ, *Snuff It.*[8] Phillip's 'zine *Fuck* is an echo chamber for his white-supremacist ravings about the joys of thinning the herd through infanticide and mass murder ("I smile wide all day in the sunshine that glistens off your mutilated bodies").[9] The Goads' self-described "bible of hatred," *Answer Me!,* is a bullhorn for spleen-soaked rants such as "You Turn Me Off," in which Jim Goad declares, "Sex is merely the continuance of the species, so I'm dead-set against it. The only bodies I want to see are yours burning."[10]

Asked about the connection between the Church and a toxic misanthrope like Phillip, Korda replies, "Randall's descriptions of humanity as a 'Martian invasion' have much in common with my view. . . . I tend to view humans the way a being from outer space would: as a species, housed among many other species. . . . Humans are behaving like bacteria in a petri dish, and if nothing is done their fate will be similar."[11] She clarifies her position: "I can certainly be described as a misanthrope—or, more correctly, an anti-humanist."[12]

Misanthropy, it turns out, goes hand in glove with the Malthusian gospel that the Church preaches. In Thomas Malthus's *An Essay on the Principle of Population* (1798), the ur-text of population apocalypticism, the good reverend recoils in gothic horror at the engulfing poor. (William Hazlitt, that sharp-tongued observer of English society, saw Malthus for what he was: a "conscience-keeper to the rich and great" who salved the consciences of the manor-born with a philosophy that relieved them of any social responsibility. "Many who would have shrunk from denying 'the poor' came almost to feel that they were doing a virtuous thing in denying the 'surplus' population a morsel out of their superfluity," writes Hazlitt. "It is a fearful thing to insult human need with formulas like these.")[13] Like Malthus, Paul Ehrlich can barely suppress a shudder of revulsion, in his 1968 best seller *The Population Bomb,* at the locustlike masses swarming around his taxi during a ride through Delhi: "My wife and daughter and I were returning to our hotel in an ancient taxi.... The seats were hopping with fleas.... The streets seemed alive with people. People eating, people washing, people sleeping. People visiting, arguing, and screaming. People thrusting their hands through the taxi window, begging. People defecating and urinating. People clinging to buses. People herding animals. People, people, people, people."[14]

It's no coincidence that Ehrlich's panic attack happens as his taxi is surrounded by a sea of brown-skinned Others—creatures who, to the white eye, are hardly more human than the animals they herd (how primitive!) and no more distinguishable, one from another, than the fleas overrunning their verminous land. Historically, when the voices who've dominated the cultural conversation in the West have turned their attention to race, gender, and sexuality, they've used those terms to mean black, female, and queer, since their own attributes—whiteness, maleness, presumptive straightness—were simply those of any speaker whose opinions mattered, and were therefore so "natural" as to be unremarkable. Likewise, when the Ehrlichs of the world spin gothic tales about overpopulation, their bogeymen assume the predictable form of a flood of dirty, dark-skinned Third Worlders, threatening to swamp the taxi where the White Man and his terrified womenfolk prepare to make civilization's last stand.

George Orwell's 1939 essay "Marrakech" lays bare the subtext lurking in the Ehrlich passage. Orwell, who lanced the abscesses of his own soul as unflinchingly as he did society's, gives us a white man's view of empire's colonial subjects, their dark, dirty faces the face of a Malthusian nightmare:

When you walk through a town like this—two hundred thousand inhabitants, of whom at least twenty thousand own literally nothing except the rags they stand up in—when you see how the people live, and how easily they die, it is always difficult to believe that you are walking among human beings. All colonial empires are in reality founded upon that fact. The people have brown faces—besides, there are so many of them! Are they really the same flesh as yourself? Do they even have names? Or are they merely a kind of undifferentiated brown stuff, about as individual as bees or coral insects?[15]

Here, then, is Dorian Gray's true face: the racism, classism, and virulent misanthropy that too often hide behind the dream of a pre-industrial, nay, prehuman Paradise Regained, a world emptied at last of the eating, washing, sleeping, visiting, arguing, screaming, begging, defecating, urinating masses. And the masses, naturally, are always the teeming, undifferentiated others—everyone, that is, but me.

(1999)

Great Caesar's Ghost

IN THE DREAM LIFE OF EIGHTEENTH- AND NINETEENTH-CENTURY
Europe, Italy and the Gothic were conjoined twins.

The first Gothic novel, Horace Walpole's *Castle of Otranto* (1764)
—a spookhouse ride whose oubliettes, subterranean passageways,
and doors that slam shut by themselves still stock the Gothic prop
room—is set in medieval Italy. In fact, the first edition purported
to be a translation of a sixteenth-century manuscript by an Italian
cleric named "Onuphrio Muralto," rediscovered in the library of "an
ancient Catholic family in the north of England."[1] Ann Radcliffe's
hugely influential *Mysteries of Udolpho* (1794), which provided seed
DNA for all Gothic romances to come, takes place partly in Italy, in a
gloomy medieval pile in the Apennines where Our Heroine is men-
aced by the sinister Count Montoni. (Radcliffe had used Italy as a
backdrop before, in *A Sicilian Romance* [1790], and would again, in
The Italian [1797], where a diabolical monk named Schedoni puts a
twisted face on the terrors of the Inquisition.)

To Northern Europeans, especially the English, Italy reeked of cultural atavism—the inbred depravity of a decaying aristocracy and the
perversions of Papism (paganism in a reversed collar, as far as Protestants were concerned). It's as if the sheer antiquity of the place—all
those Roman ruins, haunted by the godless shades of all those parri-
cidal, pedophilic Caesars Gibbon described in such scandalous detail
in *The Decline and Fall* (1776–88)—deformed the Italian psyche,

Crypt of the Capuchins, Rome, Italy. Photograph copyright Eric Berger; all rights reserved.

warping it under the accumulated weight of a thousand years of perversion and profanation, scheming and throat slitting.

To the Enlightenment mind, ancient Rome was undeniably the embodiment of classical virtues in philosophy and culture. But the brilliance of Seneca, Cicero, Horace, and Virgil had to be weighed against the horrors of Nero, Domitian, and Caligula. True, the Apollonian perfection of a Roman column was an inspiring sight, even in ruins. But it was also a melancholy reminder that even Rome, the sunburst of Western civilization, had succumbed to an epic fail. By the Middle Ages, the Eternal City had decayed into a necropolis of ten thousand, abandoned by the popes. By day, the Forum was a pasture for grazing cows; after dark, wolves hunted the streets of the Vatican City.

The Grand Tour of the Continent impressed these lessons on England's upper class. Intended to certify the scions of the powerful as worldly-wise and culturally literate, worthy of their lofty perch on the social pyramid, the Grand Tour was by 1700 "part of an English gentleman's preparation for life," as Richard Davenport-Hines notes in *Gothic: Four Hundred Years of Excess, Horror, Evil, and Ruin*.[2] Italy, more than any other country, was seen as indispensable in sanding the rough edges off entitled party animals, turning them into well-rounded gentlemen: the term *Grand Tour* was first used in Richard Lassels's *Voyage of Italy* (1670). The more studious Grand Tourists studied Italian and acquired a fashionable taste for Italian art and architecture: Charles Talbot, duke of Shrewsbury, remodeled his Oxfordshire home on the Villa Borghese in Rome.

But English Italophilia was darkened by the shadow of the Gothic. "The broken magnificence which was to become integral to the gothic imagination fascinated the English in Italy," writes Davenport-Hines.

> The morbidness in their approach was exemplified by two young gentlemen . . . whose grand tour in 1707 took them to Rome, where they were "assiduous . . . in visiting . . . the remains of the superb Monuments of the Grandeur and of the Magnificence of the Ancient Romans." The Catacombs held a horrible fascination for the English brothers, [which] "is not very surprising for young Men who had heard it said that a Company of four German Gentlemen were lost there for some time, previously, with their Guide, [and] would not have appeared again, had it not been that Trumpeters and Drummers were led there several times to see if the sound of these instruments of war would enable them to find the right way again. . . ." Dark and gloomy caves, subterranean labyrinths, the despair of incarceration—all these are staples of the gothic imagination.[3]

If classical Rome's reason and rectitude made it a beacon for the Enlightenment, the eeriness of Italy's decrepit castles, the blasphemy of its popish heresies and macabre relics and incorruptible saints, and the Medici murders and pagan depravities buried in its cultural basement proved useful to nineteenth-century Romantics. Brandishing the Gothic like an upside-down crucifix against neoclassicism, the Romantics championed imagination over reason, excess over economy, a morbid obsession with the past over a utopian faith in progress.

The momentous discovery, in the late fourteenth century, of mysterious *grotte*, or underground chambers, in Rome's Aventine hillside had exhumed the Gothic's close cousin, the Grotesque. The caverns turned out to be Nero's Playboy Mansion, a party villa called the Domus Aurea (Golden House) whose droll mosaics and frescoes captivated Renaissance artists: writhing vines, chimerical beings gene-spliced from humans and animals, surreal landscapes. Inspired by these *grotteschi*, as the decorative elements in Nero's "grottos" were called, Renaissance artists such as Raphael borrowed the creative license of the pre-Christian Romans—"the capricious and bizarre designs of pagan painters who were given freedom to invent whatever they pleased"—and decorated their friezes with wriggling tendrils and fantastic humanimals. In time, the style became known as *grottesco*, or Grotesque.[4]

The Grotesque rejoices in excess, exhibiting a *horror vacui* reminiscent of the obsessive figuration of schizophrenic art. It delights in the subversion of the social and even the natural order, symbolized by misbegotten creatures whose bodies hybridize man and beast. In its playful perversities, it hints, with an absurdist wit wanting in its close kin the Gothic, at unsettling truths behind the world we think we know. (The Grotesque is what the Gothic looks like after augmentation humor-plasty. Poe's "Tell-Tale Heart" and "Fall of the House of Usher" are Gothic; his "Cask of Amontillado" and "Hop-Frog" are Grotesque. Nick Cave? Gothic. The Tiger Lillies? Grotesque. Frank Miller? Gothic. Basil Wolverton? Grotesque. Stephen King's *It*? Gothic. *Shakes the Clown*? Grotesque.) The Gothic is here to tell us that the past is never really dead and buried, that it may rise again from its shallow grave in the cultural unconscious—or the individual psyche, for that matter. In that sense, the Gothic is reactionary—crypto-conservative, almost, if you'll pardon the pun. The Grotesque, by contrast, is subversive—carnivalesque, in the Bakhtinian sense. It mocks our insistence on lives that have purpose and a cosmos that makes sense, knocking social hierarchies and received truths ass over teakettle.

Think of these things as you make your way through the Crypt of the Capuchin monks, beneath the Santa Maria della Concezione church, in Rome. From 1631 until 1870, the monks buried their dead here—some four thousand of them, reportedly. The musty, mineral smell of the hard-packed dirt floor mingles with the sweaty tang of your fellow Grand Tourists pressing close, their body heat making the cramped corridor muggy. The corridor gives on six roped-off antechambers, or chapels. First up: the Crypt of the Resurrection. Skulls and bones form an arch over a painting—Lazarus raised from the dead, fittingly. On the ceiling, skulls and what look like femurs, arranged in geometric shapes, simulate the effect of a coffered vault. Others explode in starburst patterns or Tinkertoy themselves into trellises. Flanking the painting are two niches formed by arches of stacked skulls, thighbones, and other leg bones; a skeleton, with just enough parchment skin still clingwrapping its skull to pass as a mummy, reposes in each, wearing the characteristic brown habit of the order. (Hence *cappuccino.*)

In the second room, what might be scapulae and vertebrae describe crazy arcs across the ceiling; skeletons in habits, their empty-eyed skulls peering lugubriously out of the shadows of their cowls, stand propped against a wall of neatly stacked skulls. The third room, the Crypt of Skulls, features scapulae cascading down one wall, overlapping like the scales on a suit of armor. In the fourth, the Crypt of the Pelvises, scapulae, pelvises, and assorted small bones form mescaline mandalas, turning the ceiling into a macabre kaleidoscope of fleurs-de-lis and rosettes (the central rosette being "formed by seven shoulder blades with appendages made of vertebrae, in a frame of sacral bones, vertebrae, and foot bones," according to my helpful guidebook, Rinaldo Cordovani's *Capuchin Cemetery*—purchased, naturally, in the Crypt's gift shop; we live in an age when even dust-mossed ossuaries have gift shops).[5]

The sixth and last chapel, the Crypt of the Three Skeletons, enshrines the skeletons of three children. (The guidebook strikes a philosophical note: "Death has no favorite age.")[6] One, the skeleton of a Barberini princess, holds a scythe and the scales of judgment, a minikin Grim Reaper.

The Marquis de Sade came here, appropriately enough, in 1775; in his *Viaggio in Italia*, he describes "well-preserved" skeletons "in varying attitudes, some reclining, others in the act of preaching, others at prayer," all clad in the Capuchin habit, some still wearing their beards. "Never have I seen anything so impressive," the Divine Marquis enthused, advising the Grand Tourist who wants to experience the crypt's jolt at full voltage to visit in the suitably sepulchral gloom of the evening, rather than during the day, when the sunlight "abates the horror."[7]

Hawthorne, too, was spellbound by the ossified monks. In *The Marble Faun* (1860), he describes the final resting place of the *Cappucinni*:

> The arrangement of the unearthed skeletons is what makes the special interest of the cemetery. . . . There is no possibility of describing how ugly and grotesque is the effect, combined with a certain artistic merit, nor how much perverted ingenuity has been shown in this queer way. . . .
>
> In the side-walls of the vaults are niches, where skeleton monks sit or stand, clad in the brown habits that they wore in life. . . . Their skulls (some quite bare, and others still covered with yellow skin, and hair that has known the earth-damps) look out from beneath their hoods, grinning hideously repulsive. One reverend Father has his mouth wide open, as if he had died in the midst of a howl of terror and remorse, which perhaps is even now screeching through eternity.[8]

Nine years later, in *The Innocents Abroad*, Twain takes up Hawthorne's refrain, rhapsodizing wryly about the "picturesque horrors" of the crypt, with its "startling pyramids, built wholly of grinning skulls" and its "elaborate frescoes, whose curving vines were made of knotted human vertebrae" and "whose flowers were formed of knee-caps and toe-nails."[9] Like Hawthorne, Twain hears a silent scream in the postmortem rictus of one "dead and dried-up" monk:

> Brought down to us through the circling years, and petrified there, was a weird laugh a full century old! It was the jolliest laugh, but yet the most dreadful, that one can imagine. Surely, I thought, it must have been a most extraordinary joke this veteran produced with his latest breath, that he has not got done laughing at it yet.[10]

By the last chamber, the brain is reeling. The claustrophobic confines of the crypt, the dizzy geometry of the anatomical arrangements, a baroque delirium of rosettes and florets and eight-pointed stars, all made of bones, bones, bones: it begins to feel like a bad-acid flashback, brought to you by Pol Pot. And yet, you can't help but marvel at the Spirograph rhythms of it all, the—Gothic? Grotesque?—aesthetic of the repeating visual melodies of capitals and crosses and cornices outlined in bones. And then you remember something Sir Francis Bacon said ("There is no excellent Beauty, that hath not some Strangeness in the Proportion"), and it makes a certain mad sense, after all.[11]

(2009)

Aphrodites of the Operating Theater

"WHY HAVE WE NOT DEVELOPED AN AESTHETIC OF THE INSIDE of the body?" wonders one of the twin gynecologists in David Cronenberg's *Dead Ringers*. He speaks for Cronenberg, who took up the thread in an interview with me. "We have contests in which we decide who is the most beautiful woman in the world," said the director, "and yet, if you were to show the inside of that woman's body, you would have a lot of grossed-out people. Why is that? We should be able to have a World's Most Perfect Kidney contest, where women or men unzip to show their kidneys. We can't become integral creatures until we come to terms with our bodies, and we haven't come remotely close to that. We're incredibly schizophrenic."[1]

Cronenberg's visceral aesthetic is bodied forth in La Specola, an eighteenth-century anatomical museum at the University of Florence. It's fitting that the name, from the Latin for *mirror* (the museum is housed in a former observatory), is close etymological kin to *speculum,* an instrument used, as every woman knows, to dilate the opening of a body cavity for examination. La Specola is home to a collection of visible bodies, medical teaching aids that comprise some of the finest examples of ceroplasty, the art of modeling anatomical specimens in wax.

The ceroplastic process was perfected in eighteenth-century Florence by the abbot Felice Fontana (1730–1805), a cleric and naturalist. First, an anatomist dissected the cadaver to be modeled. Artists made plaster casts of the desired areas, then poured layer upon layer of variously colored waxes into the molds to simulate the translucency of actual tissues. The finished simulacrum was polished with brushes soaked in turpentine. The pursuit of verisimilitude bordered on the fanatical: the hair-fine striations of muscles were painstakingly traced with a sharp point; blood vessels, the branches of lymphatics, and the radicles of nerves were simulated with thread soaked in wax; actual eyebrows and eyelashes were implanted one hair at a time.

When La Specola (officially the Royal Museum of Physics and Natural History) opened its doors in 1775, 486 such preparations, created under Fontana's watchful eye, greeted an awestruck public. One of the museum's more celebrated visitors, the Austrian emperor Joseph II, was so dazzled by Fontana's handiwork that he made him a knight of the Holy Empire and commissioned a duplicate set of models for his school for military surgeons in Vienna, where the survivors repose to this day.[2]

La Specola's waxworks are wondrous strange, indeed—a pathological beauty pageant worthy of Cronenberg's wildest dreams. "Le Grazie Smontate," the "Dissected Graces" of the master modeler Clemente Susini (1754–1814), is a trio of recumbent young women, their tresses spilling over their shoulders, their shapely legs gracefully arranged, the fat, yellow sausages of their intestines coiled neatly on their disemboweled torsos. Gazing languorously up at the viewer, one grace toys girlishly with a braid, her modesty intact despite her bared entrails. Another sloe-eyed beauty flaunts a pert rosebud of a nipple, seemingly unperturbed by the fact that her breast hangs from a flap of flesh peeled back to expose her heart. The hard nipples; the bent leg partly covering (or coyly revealing?) the downy pubes; the head thrown back, lips slightly parted, in an attitude that hovers unsettlingly between postorgasmic languor and the marionette floppiness of the corpse: such images tap a subterranean river in the erotic imagination. Behind the curtain of scientific progress and public edification drawn across La Specola lurks the shadow of a more than clinical interest in female flesh, and even in a more Cronenbergian aesthetic, perhaps.

In this light, *Anatomia Barocca,* Akira Sato's book of photos taken at La Specola, resembles a lavish catalog for high-priced love dolls, designed with Jack the Ripper fans in mind. One obstetrical model, Susini's "La Venere Smontabile" (The Dissected Venus), is presented as a sort of centerfold: facing pages form flaps, each of which features the comely mannequin, whose cascading hair and neoclassical pose recall her better-known Florentine sister—Botticelli's Venus. The flaps open to reveal the Venus in various stages of dissection, culminating in a close-up of the body cavity, a tiny fetus nestled in the womb. It's a striptease inside a striptease: in a textual mimicry of the act of disrobing, the reader unveils a four-photo sequence in which the lid of the Venus's belly is lifted and her organs are removed, exposing her penetralia for all to see.

La Specola's wax women hold a mirror up to culture rather than nature—specifically, the Enlightenment culture into which they were born, when scientists were busy weaving myths about gender and the "natural order" that denied women the democratic promise of the *Declaration of the Rights of Man and of the Citizen* (1789) and redefined them as weaker vessels, consecrated to procreation and (male) recreation. The anatomical models of the day often literalized this reduction of woman to womb.

But in the essay that accompanies Sato's photos, writer Nahoko Kametsu turns a blind eye on the gender politics of eighteenth-century medical mannequins, drawing our attention, instead, to the Venuses' "erotic atmosphere." Recalling the historian Philippe Ariès's observation that the naked cadaver was an object of both "scientific curiosity and morbid pastimes" from the sixteenth through the eighteenth centuries, Kametsu observes that Susini's obstetric model likewise "gives rise to morbid fantasies in the mind of the viewer."[3] Eros and Thanatos come together in the womb of a two-hundred-year-old mannequin.

Kametsu isn't the first to note the erotic *frisson* of anatomical Venuses. The social historian Hillel Schwartz reminds us that the same waxworks that preserved "'many transient phenomena of disease of which no other art could have made so lively a record,'" as an eighteenth-century writer put it, also "perpetrated . . . a gravid

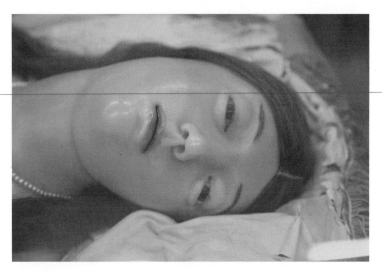

Wax anatomical model, La Specola museum, Florence, Italy. Photograph by Joanna Ebenstein, Morbid Anatomy, http://morbidanatomy.blogspot.com. Copyright Joanna Ebenstein. Printed by permission of La Specola Museo di Storia Naturale, Università di Firenze, Italy.

pornography, private parts teased out, the lovely naked woman manhandled."[4]

In *A Traffic of Dead Bodies: Anatomy and Embodied Social Identity in 19th-Century America*, the medical historian Michael Sappol argues that the popular anatomical museums of the nineteenth century—that is, those museums open to the general (male) public, as opposed to those for medical professionals only—cannily exploited a pornographic subtext even as they veiled it in moral sanctimony. "Beginning in the 1830s and intensifying in succeeding decades, there arose a variety of anatomical entrepreneurs, eager to cultivate, exploit, and cater to the audience for anatomy through anatomical museums and exhibits," writes Sappol. "And from the outset . . . anatomy was assimilated to the purposes of satisfying and profiting from the demand for sexual material, to its critics pornography."[5]

Schwartz has his finger on the source of the wax Venus's bizarre charms when he writes, "The female anatomical figure with removable parts ... was truly a pedagogical tool, but in wax it also suggested malleability, voluptuousness, and *morbidezza*: delicate flesh."[6] There's a voluptuous luster to her beeswax-and-animal-fat flesh that makes her uncannily lifelike, more so after two centuries than modern wax-works made of synthetic paraffins or the latex-skinned grotesques in theme-park robot dramas. Unlike an actual cadaver, whose waxy pallor makes it look as lifeless as a mannequin, the Dissected Venus seems almost to glow, if not with life, with a robust undeath.

But as Schwartz suggests, her allure is more than skin deep: even her viscera are beautiful—glistening, viscid things whose interiority and vulnerability makes them seem somehow more intimate, more "feminine" than her sex organs, even. The "manhandling" of her internal organs by the presumably male student removing them, layer by layer, evokes a sort of foreplay or, less decorously, a ravishment—the bride stripped bare on the dissecting table. And the male gaze's invasion of her uterus, the sanctum sanctorum where the Mysteries of the Organism unfold unseen, is an obvious metaphor for sexual penetration.

Theorizing the operatic horrors of the predatory male gaze has grown, over the years, into an academic cottage industry, one whose slasher-movie exaggeration of that bogeyman ironically ends up lending it an authority it might never have had. (This is what the cultural critic McKenzie Wark means when he says that criticism can be "the best ornament power ever had. It *looks* like it is opposed to power, and indeed it thinks it is.... Yet criticism talks about nothing but the invincible strength of its other."[7]

Even so, there's no avoiding the scopophilic subtext of the male medical gaze exploring wax wombs. The image is unmistakably familiar, recalling the speculum's-eye view of the world that characterizes hard-core porn and strip-club acts like the one described by Ian Buruma in his study of Japanese culture, *Behind the Mask*. "The girls shuffle over to the edge of the stage, crouch and, leaning back as far as they can, slowly open their legs just a few inches from the flushed faces in the front row," writes Buruma. "The audience, suddenly very quiet now, leans forward to get a better view of this mesmerizing sight, this magical organ, revealed in all its mysterious glory. . . . To aid the men in their explorations, [the women] hand out magnifying glasses and small [flashlights], which pass from hand to hand. All the attention is focused on that one spot of the female anatomy."[8]

Reflecting the male gaze back at itself, the performance artist Annie Sprinkle has appropriated this gynecological ritual in the service of a pro-sex New Age feminism. Inserting a speculum into her vagina, she invites audience members up for a closer look. "I think it's important to demystify women's bodies," she says. "It wasn't until recently that anyone was allowed to *look* at pussy—really get down and look at [it]. A lot of women have never even seen their own! . . . [I]n a way I wanna say, 'Fuck you guys—you wanna see pussy, *I'll* show you pussy!'"[9] Rewriting the ancient script, Medusa turns the conquering hero to stone.

Despite their dissimilar contexts, Sprinkle's performances, Buruma's Japanese strip-club act, and the gynecological close-ups of hardcore porn underscore the scopophilic subtext of the male medical gaze penetrating the Dissected Venus. Peering and probing into the deepest, darkest places in our anatomy, more private by far than our private parts, the surgeon knows us more intimately, in some ways, than any lover ever will. The SF novelist J. G. Ballard, whose brief flirtation with a career in psychiatry saw him studying medicine at Cambridge, describes his relationship to the female cadaver he dissected in his first anatomy class: "I saw her naked every day, and I knew her more intimately than any other woman in my life," he writes in his fictionalized autobiography, *The Kindness of Women*. "But I never embraced her."[10]

Shot through with a playful, platonic necrophilia, Ballard's account of the dissection of his Venus makes explicit the sexual subtext of entering someone else's body, even a cadaver's, with a scalpel. "You can get very close," he tells a girlfriend. "It turns into a weird sort of marriage."[11] Later, in bed with him, Ballard's girlfriend refers to his anatomized woman as "my biggest rival" and teasingly asks, "Can you imagine dissecting me? Where would you start?" He responds that "dissection is a kind of erotic autopsy" and flirtatiously proposes start-ing with the cervical triangle.[12] When they resume lovemaking, Bal-lard's mind is still in the dissecting room: "I entered her vagina, need-ing her so much that I could happily have dissected her. I imagined a strange act of love performed by an obsessed surgeon on a living woman, in a deserted operating theater in one of those sinister clinics in the Cambridge suburbs. I would kiss the linings of her lungs, run my tongue along her bronchi, press my face to the moist membranes of her heart as it pulsed against my lips."[13]

Obviously, the politics of transgressive aesthetics gets sticky when taken literally, in everyday life. One needn't be a card-carrying Dwor-kinite to worry about the real-world implications of libertine, sur-realist visions of "erotic autopsies" on live women or of philosophi-cal musings on the role of disemboweled dummies in male fantasies of "the lovely naked woman manhandled." This way lies the prob-lematic territory whose signposts are as old as the "morbid fantasies" Kametsu implies have always haunted the minds of men ogling Susi-ni's Venus and as recent as the infamous *Esquire* cover that featured Laura Palmer, the blue-skinned corpse from *Twin Peaks,* as one of the "Women We Love."

All that said, the creepy seductions of eviscerated wax women can't be neatly disposed of as a misogynist's guilty pleasure. There's more to La Specola's anatomical models than meets the male gaze. They were essential aids to medical pedagogy *and* obscure objects of desire, disseminating lifesaving knowledge about female anatomy even as they reaffirmed the primacy of women's sexual and maternal functions. Now, more than two hundred years after their birth, the anatomical Venuses still taunt us. The morbid fantasies they inspire are reviled by feminist critics and relished by aesthetic transgressors in the Bataillean mode.

Walking from vitrine to vitrine in La Specola, I'm mesmerized by the visceral charms of these obstetric Ophelias, floating through the centuries on suggestively rumpled sheets. I can't tear my eyes away from the hallucinogenically vivid colors of their coiled intestines, no less lovingly modeled than their unmistakably Florentine faces. Their sheets are brittle, fraying to ribbons, but they seem not to have aged a day since they were first unveiled to the public eye in 1780. Trying to make sense of the welter of conflicting reactions, philosophical and psychological, that they inspire, I recognize these Aphrodites of the Operating Theater as disquiet muses of the Pathological Sublime—uncanny sisters of the nude sleepwalkers in Paul Delvaux's surrealist nocturnes, or of the naked victim in Duchamp's creepy, Hitchcockian last work, a museum-style diorama of a sex murder called *Étant donnés*. I think of the Victorian critic Walter Pater's famous meditation on the *Mona Lisa*:

> Like the vampire, she has been dead many times, and learned the secrets of the grave; and has been a diver in deep seas, and keeps their fallen day about her; and trafficked for strange webs with Eastern merchants: and, as Leda, was the mother of Helen of Troy, and, as Saint Anne, the mother of Mary; and all this has been to her but as the sound of lyres and flutes, and lives only in the delicacy with which it has molded the changing lineaments, and tinged the eyelids and the hands.[14]

F. Gonzalez-Crussi calls wax modeling, which replaced the cadaver on the dissection table with a lifelike simulacrum, "the first successful effort we undertook to distance ourselves from the dead. Since then, we have not ceased in our efforts to deepen the gulf."[15] The invention of ceroplasty marks the beginning of the history of the virtual cadaver, an ongoing chronicle whose latest chapter is the Visible Human Project, in which a male corpse was sliced into 1,871 millimeter-thin sections with a laser, digitized, and transformed into a navigable 3-D atlas of the human body, accessible via the World Wide Web.

Paradoxically, wax anatomical models also recall us to a time when death and disease were an everyday affair and we were able to establish what Gonzalez-Crussi calls "a certain communion with the dead." La Specola's wax women offer a taste of that sacrament.

(2009)

Goodbye, Cruel Words

PEOPLE WHO NEED PEOPLE IN THE OBSEQUIOUS, BARBRA-esque sense of the word may be the scariest people in the world, but people who have never contemplated suicide are close contenders, in my book.

And my book is *The Bell Jar,* Sylvia Plath's jagged little pill for girls who dream of sticking their heads in the Easy-Bake Oven. As every undergrad knows, Plath's autobiographical tale of a bright young overachiever's dizzy plunge into suicidal depression when her white-picket worldview falls apart is also a scarifyingly funny evisceration of the peppy vacuity and mind-cramping conformity of the Eisenhower era. Posthumously canonized as the patron saint of hopelessly alien-ated poets manqués—the self-styled Lady Lazarus, for whom "dying / is an art, like everything else"—Plath makes suicide seem like the Most Radical Gesture, as the Situationists might say, a violation of the ultimate bourgeois taboo.[1]

Of course, the romanticization of suicide is mere bullshit. In real-ity, suicide is a miserable, wretched business, a scourge that in 1999 snuffed out more than twenty-nine thousand Americans and inflicted psychic collateral damage on their friends and families.[2] It's the elev-enth leading cause of death in the United States; more Americans die by their own hands than from homicide.[3]

Nonetheless, writers often mythologize self-murder, maybe because they are storytellers by nature, maybe because they do the deed in disproportionate numbers. Depression is the black lung of the scribbling trade, brought on by writer's block, the agony of the rejection slip, or the grim tidings that your book is about to be remaindered, recycled, and reborn as a copy of *Who Moved My Cheese?* Despondent over his growing inability to get it up, creatively, Ernest Hemingway stuck both barrels of a 12-gauge shotgun in his mouth and blew the top off his cranial vault. Tarred by charges of plagiarism and gnawed by fear of memory loss, Jerzy Kosinski tied a plastic bag over his head and stretched out in his bathtub to wait for death. Haunted by his father's suicide and unhinged by manic depression, John Berryman leapt off a bridge, leaving a pathetic note: "I am a nuisance."[4] Hart Crane, Randall Jarrell, Malcolm Lowry, Primo Levi, Yukio Mishima, Cesare Pavese, Anne Sexton, Virginia Woolf—the list goes on, seemingly without end.

Odd, then, that the suicide note should be so neglected as a literary genre. The annals of suicidology bulge with clinical studies, but a review of the genre from a lit-crit perspective is long overdue.

The suicidal mind is infinitely perverse in its resourcefulness: people have killed themselves by leaping into volcanoes; stuffing turkeys, rump-first, down their throats; strangling themselves with their own hair; injecting themselves with peanut butter; swallowing lighted firecrackers; boring holes in their heads with power drills; applying a hundred leeches to their bodies; and lying down beside their sleeping wives and buzzing through their jugular veins with electric carving knives, going messily into that good night.[5] Such ingenuity is equaled only by the inexhaustible creativity of the suicide-note writer. Self-killers have scrawled their farewells in blood, e-mailed them, printed them on mirrors in lipstick, left them on answering machines, and written them, poignantly, in the mud with their toes.[6]

Some are painfully short, like the wrenching note pinned to the shirt of the young boy who hanged himself beside the family Christmas tree ("Merry Christmas") or the pitiful haiku written by a 50-year-old Massachusetts man—

I'm done with life
I'm no good
I'm dead

—or the sardonic "Good-bye, suckers" penned by another guy, a wiseass to the last.[7] Some are long, such as the 800-word letter described by Ian O'Donnell, a researcher who analyzed the notes of people who killed themselves on the London Underground—a "stream-of-consciousness essay written over the course of an hour sitting on a bench in the railway station and ending with a description of the last few steps towards the railway line and the final preparation for the arrival of the train."[8] Some freeze the marrow with their murderous rage: "May you always remember I loved you once but died hating you," a man wrote to his adulterous wife, on the back of her photo.[9] Some are bleakly funny: "Dear Betty: I hate you. Love, George."[10] Or silly: "Bow wow and good-bye, Pepper" (from a man to his dog).[11] Or unwittingly comedic, in their own piteous way: "I'm sorry but I'm possessed by demons."[12] Or spooky: "I would like my sister Frances to have the piano that you have in your apartment. Do this or I will haunt you. Good-bye Sweets. Be seeing you soon. Love, Joe" (from a guy to his ex-girlfriend).[13] Or unutterably lonely: "I no longer live here. I am farther beyond than you can reach."[14] Or weirdly reportorial, as if the author were conducting a scientific experiment: "I feel the effects now. The room is going around and around. I can barely see what I am writing. Maybe it is the end. Who knows? I don't care . . ." (written by a man who killed himself with a black widow spider).[15] A few are hauntingly poetic, such as the journal entry of a twenty-year-old freelance journalist wracked by chronic depression: "I have lost my angel. I have lost my mind. The days are too long, too heavy; my bones are crushing under the weight of these days."[16]

Most, however, are breathtakingly banal—to-do lists for survivors, full of admonitions to "change the spark plugs on the Ford every 10,000 miles" or "put out the garbage on Thursdays."[17] Ed Shneidman, a suicidologist, has observed, "Suicide notes often seem like parodies of postcards sent home from the Grand Canyon, the catacombs or the pyramids—essentially *pro forma*, not at all reflecting the grandeur of the scene being described or the depth of human emotion that one might expect to be engendered by the situation."[18] Maybe depression has flattened the victims' personalities into cardboard cutouts, blunted their minds to the point where they're incapable of writing a searing, searching postcard from the edge of eternity, just before they step off. As Shneidman points out, "In order to commit suicide, one cannot write a meaningful note; conversely, if one could write a meaningful note, one would not have to commit suicide."[19]

Naturally, if *I* did the deed, I'd chisel some deathless prose befitting the occasion, rich in wisdom and dark with the lengthening shadow of our mortality—at least, that's how I imagine things. As a writer, I've always taken comfort in the knowledge that if I ever did contemplate—*seriously* contemplate—taking a dirt nap, I'd never get past the suicide note. The performance anxiety induced by the knowledge that this would be the last thing I'd ever write, which means it would have to be the best thing I'd *ever* write, would ensure that I'd procrastinate, kvetch, dither, spell-check, word-count, and endlessly rewrite and re-rewrite the damn thing until I was out of the mood. Either that, or dropped off the twig from old age or sheer vexation.

Glibness aside, most people—three out of four—don't leave suicide notes. Instead, they leave unimaginably painful silences, enigmatic emptinesses that torment their loved ones forever. "He didn't leave us a note," said the friend of a boy who took his own life. "He didn't want to make it easy for us. He didn't want to give us an answer. He wanted to leave us with questions. He wanted us to think about it. Maybe he was saying, 'Take a look at yourselves.'"[20]

Maybe. Or maybe he didn't leave a note because suicide is the ultimate act of self-erasure, a point underscored by the profoundly sad story of Blair Newman, a longtime member of the seminal online community the WELL, who used a "scribble" command to delete the countless comments he had contributed to WELL conversations, going back years, then killed himself in actual fact.[21] The awful truth (unthinkable to a writer) is that eloquent suicide notes are rarer than rare because suicide is the moment when language fails—fails to hoist us out of the pit, fails even to express the unbearable weight that drags someone about to murder himself down, into endless, silent night.

(2003)

Cortex Envy

CORTEX ENVY—THE HAUNTING FEAR THAT SOMEONE, SOME-where, may be smarter than you are—was my birthright. When I was little, my mother (last seen protesting her high IQ to a gerontologist, just before Alzheimer's hit the DELETE key on her mind) liked to tell me my Marvel Comics origin story: how she acquired target on my future father because she knew he was bright, she knew *she* was bright, and it only stood to reason, therefore, that do-it-yourself eugenics would produce a wunderkind.

My parents divorced shortly after I was born, but what of it? Decades before the Nobel Prize sperm bank, my mother had genetically engineered a brainchild all her own, named (in what might charitably be called an excess of optimism) Mark Alexander, after the Roman emperor Marcus Aurelius and the Greek conqueror Alexander the Great.

Psychologically, the expectation that I would live up to my namesakes' reputations (world domination, a breezy way with the gnomic one-liner, burial in a solid-gold sarcophagus while legions wept) and that I would do so by dint of my supposedly prodigious intellect proved almost unbearable, saddling me with an anxiety so crushing it inspired suicidal ideation before I was out of short pants. (How many Baby Einsteins are dragging this cross, I wonder?) In *The Know-It-All: One Man's Humble Quest to Become the Smartest Person in the World*, A. J. Jacobs confides:

Growing up, I thought I was smart. Well, that wasn't exactly the whole story. I didn't just think I was smart. I thought I was *really* smart. I thought I was, in fact, the smartest boy in the world. I'm honestly not sure how this notion popped into my head. My mom probably had something to do with it, seeing as she was only slightly less enamored of me than I was of myself.[1]

A precocious reader, I was devouring comics before kindergarten; by grade school, I was reading voraciously, omnivorously, driven by the lash of great expectations. ("He isn't living up to his potential" was a tongue-clucking refrain, in parent–teacher conferences; hadn't Mozart written his first concerto by the age of four?)

Undaunted by the illimitable vastness of things, I dreamed, half seriously, of knowing *everything*, cramming all the spiral galaxies and crab nebulae of human knowledge into my skull. I compiled lists of every jawbreakingly polysyllabic or vanishingly arcane word I encountered in my reading. What better way to prove you're the Smartest Boy in the World—or a pluperfect little asshat—than to drop a vocabulary bomb like "ovine hebetude" in the lunchroom or, better yet, before an audience of overawed adults? I tossed off conversational non sequiturs like "$E = MC^2$," a cryptic incantation that meant nothing to me, beyond the all-important fact that it was Einstein's best-known one-liner, a spell that magically conferred the nimbus of genius on anyone who uttered it.

I wanted to be Gary Mitchell when I grew up. Mitchell is the mutant helmsman in the *Star Trek* episode "Where No Man Has Gone Before" (1966) whose exposure to a "magnetic space storm" endows him with godlike psionic abilities, goth-tastic silver pupils, and, not incidentally, geometrically multiplying brainpower. Sucking information out of the starship's memory banks faster than the computer can deliver it (an experience that practically gives the machine a microstroke), he's the instant master of every thinker he encounters. Spinoza? "Once you get into him, he's rather simple," says Mitchell. "Childish, almost."[2]

Meanwhile, in the parallel world of 1970s Earth, my stepdad and

I were locked in the Freudian version of Ultimate Cage Fighting, a passive-aggressive slapfest that pitted my Oedipal desire to slay the father against his Cronus complex.[3] Raging across indoor theaters of war, from the dinner table to the so-called family room (a shrine to the rabbit-eared god of domesticity, the TV), we reenacted the psionic beatdown from the final minutes of "Where No Man Has Gone Before," when Mitchell and another mutant trade thunderbolts, pausing between rounds to give each other the shiny silver stinkeye.

Our fraught psychodynamic had its origins in my mental caricature of my stepdad as Conan the Vulgarian, a life-of-the-party lowbrow with an unconvincingly hearty belly laugh and an Archie Bunkerian fondness for "Polack" jokes; a man who rejoiced in the hillbilly hijinx of the comedy show *Hee Haw*; a man whose literary tastes ran to "hard" SF for ham-radio buffs (Robert Heinlein, Isaac Asimov) and, yes, the Orientalist gore porn of Robert E. Howard's Conan saga.

Internalizing my mother's aspirational bohemianism—a suburbanite's dream of the beatnik life, macraméd out of Joan Baez and cinder-block bookshelves, Rod McKuen and community-college pottery—I claimed the top of the taste hierarchy as my due and consigned my stepdad to the bottom rung of the social Darwinian ladder. When our hostilities escalated to physical violence—he backhanded me, knocking me to the floor—I saw it as a Clash of Civilizations: Brahmin versus barfly. And, crucially, smart versus *d'oh!*, because the highbrow/middlebrow/lowbrow strata in the pyramid of taste cultures correlate not only to class but to IQ, befitting their roots in the racialized anthropology of the nineteenth century.

Twenty years after my parents divorced, my stepdad sent me a mea culpa, confessing he'd "bullied" me out of intellectual insecurity. "I felt challenged intellectually," he wrote. "It became a contest to see who was smarter, me or the kid."[4] Apparently, I had taken an IQ test, on the eve of junior high, to qualify for placement in what was then called the "gifted children" program, and my score had been perilously close to his, he confided, maybe higher.[5] He would never know for certain, he said, because the administrator who scored the test wouldn't release my numerical score, merely confirming that I had scored "well within the qualifying range for the program, which required an IQ of at least 140."[6] Cortex envy was an auger that turned in his head.

I'M SITTING in a Manhattan apartment, across a small table from Nate Thoma, a Ph.D. candidate in clinical psychology at Fordham University, who is dispassionately administering the Wechsler Adult Intelligence Scale test, third edition (the WAIS-III, pronounced "wayce" by those in the field). I'm taking the test partly because I want to banish the specter of unfulfilled promise, once and for all, by outscoring my Inner Child Prodigy (in other words, it's "a contest to see who [is] smarter, me or the kid"), and partly because guinea-pigging yourself makes for good stunt journalism.[7]

Published in 1955, the WAIS was David Wechsler's new and improved version of the Wechsler-Bellevue Intelligence Scale that he'd developed in 1939 while serving as chief psychologist at the Bellevue Psychiatric Hospital in New York City. Dissatisfied with existing intelligence tests, which had been designed with children in mind, Wechsler created a neuropsychological exam better suited to diagnosing his adult patients. In doing so, he repurposed elements from existing instruments such as the Binet-Simon Scale—the ur-IQ test, introduced in France in 1905 by the psychologists Alfred Binet and Théodore Simon for the diagnosis of what would now be called "special ed" children—and the U.S. Army's Alpha exam, designed by Robert Yerkes during World War I to identify prospective officers and weed out "intellectual defectives," as Yerkes put it in the delicate parlance of the day.[8]

Today, the WAIS-III and its counterpart the Wechsler Intelligence Scale for Children, or WISC, are the most widely used of the so-called IQ tests, superseding the once-universal Stanford-Binet.[9] Defining intelligence as "the global capacity of a person to act purposefully, to think rationally, and to deal effectively with his environment," Wechsler conceived of it as a constellation of mental abilities, a departure from the prevailing theory, articulated in 1904 by the English psychologist Charles Spearman, that intelligent behavior is attributable to a single, underlying cognitive factor, a theoretical entity that Spearman dubbed g (for general factor). [10]

In keeping with Wechsler's belief that intelligence is multifactorial, the WAIS divides mental abilities into two hemispheres, so to speak: Verbal IQ and Performance (nonverbal) IQ, which it further subdivides into four indexes: Verbal Comprehension and Working Memory on the Verbal side, Perceptual Organization and Processing Speed on the Performance side.

The Verbal Comprehension subtests include a cultural-literacy quiz whose unabashed Eurocentricity would gladden the hearts of Defenders of the Canon like E. D. Hirsch *(Who wrote Hamlet? Who painted the Sistine Chapel?)*; a test of abstract reasoning in which you're given two terms—"piano" and "drum," "orange" and "banana"—and asked what they have in common; and "Vocabulary," in which you're asked to define a series of increasingly complex words. (For what it's worth, vocabulary, of all the subtests, has the highest correlation with Full Scale IQ.) The Working Memory section includes arithmetic problems; "Digit Span," which involves memorizing strings of up to nine random digits and reciting them forward and backward; "Letter–Number Sequencing," in which you're required to memorize a long, utterly random alphanumeric sequence, on the spot, then repeat it back to the administrator *with the numbers in numerical order and the letters in alphabetical order*; and "Comprehension," a vaguely named catchall that tests your common sense as well as your grasp of the cultural logic behind laws and customs: *Why is it important to have child labor laws? If you found an envelope on the street that was sealed and had a new stamp on it, what would you do? Why do people who were born deaf have difficulty learning spoken language?*

In the Perceptual Organization and Processing Speed indices of the WAIS's Performance IQ section, you're tasked with "Block Design" (re-creating geometric patterns using color-coded blocks—a test of spatial perception, abstract visual processing, and problem solving);

"Picture Completion" (supplying the missing detail in an image, which measures the ability to rapidly process visual details); and "Picture Arrangement" (assembling a series of wordless, comic strip–like panels into logical narrative sequences, an activity that ostensibly measures an amorphous attribute called "social judgment," although an authoritative source concedes that "data validating its use as a measure of social judgment has not been forthcoming").[11]

ON THE DAY of Psychometric Reckoning, I arrive girded for battle, heavily armored with social-constructionist skepticism about psychology's claims for the scientific objectivity and empirical validity of intelligence testing.

For much of the twentieth century, psychometric testing served as what Foucault would call a "disciplinary mechanism" on behalf of the established order, surveilling the mass mind and policing the norms of industrial society. Such tests assisted in the Taylorization of the American intellect, opening doors for obedient workers and unquestioning soldiers, herding minorities into remedial classes and menial jobs, pathologizing and in some cases even criminalizing dissidents and deviants (homosexuals spring immediately to mind).

More than any other psychologist, it was Lewis Terman who transformed the IQ test into an instrument of social engineering. In 1916, Terman introduced the Stanford-Binet Scale—the old Binet-Simon Scale, standardized using a large American sample and equipped with a new means of comparing individual performance to group norms (the now-mythic "intelligence quotient").[12] In the Stanford-Binet, Terman handed examiners a scale for weighing the worth of any intellect—and, based on the numerically scored results, assigning each American his or her proper place in the socioeconomic scheme of things.

In 1917, Yerkes repurposed the test for his U.S. Army exams, evaluating millions of recruits and, more important, introducing America to the IQ test. "Despite the army's dim view of intelligence tests and their practical relevance," notes Stephen Murdoch in *IQ: A Smart History of a Failed Idea*,

> Robert Yerkes, Lewis Terman, and [their] colleagues used the war to catapult their careers and field. From then on, American students have taken IQ tests and their standardized test progeny, such as the SAT and graduate school entrance exams. . . .
>
> Terman and Yerkes' biggest accomplishment was not convincing the army to test recruits, but persuading America of the usefulness and success of the army tests, despite the dearth of supportive evidence. At war's end, Terman said he was immediately "bombarded by requests from public school men for our army mental tests in order that they may be used in public school systems."[13]

Terman oversaw the creation of the National Intelligence Tests for grades three through eight. Unlike the Binet-Simon, which was designed to help underachieving children receive specialized instruction intended to bolster their performance, Terman's grade school IQ tests were designed, in the Brave New World of postwar America, to divert megabrainy Alpha Pluses and semimoronic Epsilons into their appropriate career paths, a sorting process known as "tracking."

For much of their history, intelligence tests have been rotten with the cultural and class biases of their makers, a diagnostic deck stacked against minorities, immigrants, and those at the bottom of the wage pyramid. Test designers have equated English-language fluency with intelligence, presumed a familiarity with upper-class pastimes such as tennis, and expected examinees to provide the word *shrewd* as a synonym for *Jewish*. As late as the 1960 revision, the Stanford-Binet was presenting six-year-old children with crude cartoons of two women, one obviously Anglo-Saxon, the other a golliwog caricature of an African American, with a broad nose and thick lips. The test accepted only one correct answer to the question "Which is prettier?": the white woman.[14]

Terman begrudgingly conceded that environmental factors might play some small part in IQ test scores. For the most part, though, he was a thoroughgoing hereditarian. Like the Victorian psychologist Francis Galton (the founding father of eugenics, whom Terman devoutly admired), he believed that intelligence is inborn and unalterable; DNA is destiny. "High-grade or border-line deficiency . . . is very, very common among Spanish-Indian and Mexican families of the Southwest and also among negroes," he notes in *The Measurement of Intelligence* (1915). "Their dullness seems to be racial. . . . Children of this group should be segregated into separate classes and be given instruction which is concrete and practical. They cannot master abstractions but they can often be made into efficient workers."[15]

At the very moment that intelligence testing was sanctifying the race-based educational neglect of blacks, Mexicans, and other textbook examples of the "defective germ plasm," legislatures in thirty-three U.S. states were writing the compulsory sterilization of the "unfit" into law, a stroke of the pen that would lead, over time, to the coerced sterilization of sixty thousand Americans.[16] The black stork of the eugenics movement was spreading its wings across America, and in much of the era's officially sanctioned bigotry, the IQ test was a silent partner. "While America has had a long history of eugenics advocacy," notes the historian Clarence J. Karier, "some of the key leaders of the testing movement were the strongest advocates for eugenics control. In the twentieth century, the two movements often came together in the same people under the name of 'scientific' testing."[17]

Terman was Exhibit A for Karier's case: a pioneer of cognitive testing and chair, for two decades, of the Stanford psychology department, he was also a founding member, in 1928, of the Pasadena-based Human Betterment Foundation, a well-funded eugenics group that crusaded vigorously for the compulsory sterilization of the "insane and feebleminded" patients in California state institutions. In *The Measurement of Intelligence,* he lamented American resistance to the modest proposal that the intellectually unfit (as determined by IQ testing, of course) "should not be allowed to reproduce, although from a eugenic point of view they constitute a grave problem because of their unusually prolific breeding."[18] Nonetheless, the foundation's efforts gave aid and comfort to racial hygienists on the other side of the Atlantic, most notably a certain disgruntled German corporal with a Chaplinesque moustache and dreams of a racially cleansed utopia, who cited California precedent in support of his views on eugenics.[19] "I have studied with interest the laws of several American states concerning prevention of reproduction by people whose progeny would, in all probability, be of no value or be injurious to the racial stock," Hitler told a fellow Nazi.[20] Taking heart from his Californian comrades, he followed their logic to its inevitable conclusion: the insatiable ovens of Auschwitz.

KNOWING WHAT A BLUNT INSTRUMENT the IQ test is, what a dark and storied history it has, why am I so nervous about taking the WAIS? Why am I so inordinately proud when I knock a few softball pitches—*What is the speed of light? Where were the first Olympics held? Who was Catherine the Great? What is the Koran?*—out of the park? Why do I experience a near panic attack when I can't name three kinds of blood vessels or (to my undying chagrin) the seven continents? Worst of all, why am I so damnably *relieved* when the Ph.D. candidate who administered the test and scored my performance tells me, "You did quite well. If you turn to page two, you can see where it says 'IQ scores.'"

"Quite well" is where we'll leave it, drawing the curtain of modesty across my Full-Scale IQ (calculated by combining the examinee's Verbal and Performance scores). But since I'm guinea-pigging myself for your delectation, dear reader, I *will* confide that my examiner, Nate Thoma, characterized my Verbal IQ as "extremely high." My Performance IQ, on the other hand, was "very average" (a phrase I'll treasure forever for its droll use of the intensifier). Am I one of nature's little cognitive jokes, an idiot savant with the Verbal IQ of the *OED* on DMT and the Performance IQ of a stump?

Thoma replies that, given my cognitive lopsidedness, my Full-Scale IQ score simply isn't an accurate representation of my cognitive functioning. "It's more accurate to look at it in terms of multiple intelligences," he says—different skills. Apparently, cases like mine are far from uncommon. Partly in recognition of that fact, cognitive psychology has undergone a paradigm shift in recent decades, from Spearman's notion of a general intelligence (g) affecting performance in every area of cognitive functioning to the Gardnerian model of multiple intelligences, each comprising subintelligences, which may interact synergistically.[21]

Which is reassuring, although it sounds uncomfortably close to one of those pop-psych homilies about self-esteem, here in the land where All Men Are Created Equal but All of the Children Are Above Average. This, I feel, is the time to confide to Thoma, who is after all a psychotherapist in training, that for much of my life I've been gnawed by the neurotic suspicion that my idiosyncratic use of language (rarefied vocabulary, arcane allusions, Proustian syntax, poetic metaphors), coupled with a fondness for "intellectual" subject matter, creates the *illusion* of intelligence in a society with a pronounced logocentric bias.

Thoma doesn't exactly steeple his fingers, but he does modulate into the intense, reflective key familiar from Analysts I Have Known. "I'm glad you brought that up," he says. "It's an important responsibility of the person sharing the interpretation of the results to help a person make personal meaning of the results, especially something that is so fraught as IQ." Most laypeople aren't aware, he explains, that IQ tests are most commonly used not to determine how smart someone is, but rather in a neuropsychological context, to determine the cognitive effects of, say, a stroke or traumatic brain injury—vital information in devising a treatment strategy for the patient. "IQ tests are *never* used to just find out someone's IQ—their rank in the world," he stresses.

Nonetheless, Terman's restless specter haunts the popular imagination. In the public mind, says Thoma, the IQ test is still seen as an implacable, infallible measurement of "your core being—the essence of your intelligence—which in our society is also your rank: high intelligence, high rank; low intelligence, low rank. You're about to find where you are in the pecking order, most people think, and chances are you're not at the top, because it's a long line."

Which is precisely why the social critic Walter Lippmann decried the IQ test as cant in a lab coat, its hereditarian pseudoscience pernicious to democracy. "I hate the impudence of a claim that in 50 minutes you can judge and classify a human being's predestined fitness in life," he wrote. "I hate the sense of superiority which it creates, and the sense of inferiority which it imposes."[22]

In a 1922 debate with Terman in the *New Republic*, Lippmann put his finger on the Achilles' heel of intelligence testing: "We cannot measure intelligence when we have never defined it."[23] Psychometricians hotly deny this, but close examination reveals that definitions of intelligence remain fuzzy around the edges. Too often, psychologists have taken refuge in a tautology, defining intelligence as what intelligence tests measure. In 1923, the Harvard professor Edward Boring soberly asserted, "Intelligence as a measurable capacity must at the start be defined as the capacity to do well in an intelligence test."[24]

Of course, this assumption presumes that test items correlate, in some empirically verifiable way, to whatever intelligence truly is. Yet test items are indelibly stamped with cultural values, such as logocentricity, the importance of conforming to social norms or, be it said, test-taking skills—specifically, the ability to excel at intelligence tests. "The intelligence test ... does not weigh or measure intelligence by any objective standard," argued Lippmann. "It simply arranges a group of people in a series from best to worst by balancing their capacity to do certain *arbitrarily selected* puzzles, against the capacity of all the others. . . . The intelligence test, then, is fundamentally an instrument for classifying a group of people, rather than 'a measure of intelligence'" (emphasis added).[25]

MAYBE INTELLIGENCE is a connectionist phenomenon, an emergent property of the complex system we call mind. Maybe it's the ability to draw lines of connection between far-flung scraps of information and insight, constellating new meanings out of thin air; to discover the intertextual wormholes connecting parallel universes of knowledge and experience; to map the labyrinth of subtextual tunnels secretly connecting all stories and histories. Or is the notion of hidden meanings and buried connections just some epistemological metafiction—Nabokov's idea of Intelligent Design, Eco's answer to conspiracy theory? Is the intellectual tendency to Always Connect, and to equate that with intelligence, just a cognitive echo of the neurological fact that our thoughts travel on dendritic networks?

Shaded by a broad umbrella, I'm sitting at a patio table on a bright, blank Southern California morning, in the assisted-living facility where my mother lives. I'm looking into her Alzheimer's-glazed eyes, searching their brown nothingness for any vestige of her mind's big bang—the cognitive equivalent of background radiation, neutrinos, anything. Mute, gazeless, she seems oblivious to her surroundings: the proverbial empty house, lights on, nobody home. The god of irony has seen fit to wipe the mental hard drive of this woman who venerated the intellect.

It occurs to me that her enduring gift to me—me, her failed attempt at engineering the World's Smartest Boy—may be (another irony!) Alzheimer's, a line of genetic code that even now could be triggering amyloid plaques and neurofibrillary tangles, unplugging the neural connections in my brain one by one.

My mother is pointing. She makes a clotted noise. It could be the word "pattern." It could be an infantile *glub*. I follow her gaze, up, to the umbrella's underside. I hadn't noticed it, but the open blossom of the spreading canopy is covered with a reticulate pattern—intersecting lines that branch and branch and branch again, in an almost fractal way. *Dendrites*, I think.

(2009)

Acknowledgments

I owe a debt of gratitude to my editor at the University of Minnesota Press, Jason Weidemann, for his zeal for this project. His editorial attentions improved it tenfold. At Jason's right hand was editorial assistant and worker of last-minute miracles Danielle Kasprzak, who brought the whole thing off with effortless aplomb. I am grateful as well to my indefatigable agent, Andrew Stuart, of the Stuart Agency.

I also thank the editors of individual essays in this volume for their surgical skill with the red pencil and, equally, their forbearance with the meat cleaver: Coates Bateman (True/Slant); Tim Cavanaugh (Suck, *Los Angeles Times*); Ashley Crawford (*21C*); Scott Dickensheets (*Las Vegas Weekly*); Andrew Hultkrans (*Bookforum*); Chris Lavergne (Thought Catalog); Michael Martin (Nerve); Sina Najafi (*Cabinet*); Ed Park (*Village Voice Literary Supplement*); R. U. Sirius (GettingIt.com, *H+*); Lenora Todaro (*Village Voice Literary Supplement*); Mark Zucker, dialectical sparring partner of many years and gimlet-eyed proofreader, was helpful in spotting the odd typo, too.

I'm humbled and inspired, in equal measure, by the indefatigable enthusiasm of Mark Frauenfelder, David Pescovitz, and Xeni Jardin—ardent supporters of my work and, not incidentally, co-curators of the Web's greatest *Wunderkammer*, BoingBoing.net, which published early versions of "Great Caesar's Ghost" and "Aphrodites of the Operating Theater" as well as extended, Director's Cut versions of "Cortex Envy" and "(Face)book of the Dead," both of which had originally appeared in *Cabinet*.

I'm indebted to Nate Thoma, whose willingness to administer, score, and answer my questions regarding the so-called IQ test not only made my essay on the Wechsler possible but, by virtue of Nate's thought-provoking yet uncannily empathic responses to my questions, enriched it immensely.

Naturally, this book would be a desert for the eye without the images that enliven its pages. There are too many photographers and artists to thank here (their names appear next to their images), but they know how appreciative I am of their talent, not to mention their generosity.

I must single out for special praise the incomparable Joanna Ebenstein—scholar, artist, and morbid anatomist, whose arresting photo graces the cover. (Evan Michelson, costar of the reality-TV series *Oddities* and co-owner of the curiosity shop Obscura Antiques & Oddities, was kind enough to offer her blessing for our use of her uncanny mannequin.) On short notice, Joanna excavated the dustjacket image from her files and secured permission to reproduce it. Taken in medical museums around the world, her photographs are picture windows in the mind, looking out on the remotest reaches of human experience and bodily form.

Of course, none of these polemics, philosophical investigations, or poetic reveries would have seen the light of day without the indulgence of my long-suffering wife and daughter—Margot Mifflin and Thea Dery, blithe spirits who endure the man in the attic office and his obscure obsessions with equanimity (and, it must be admitted, an occasional roll of the eye).

Notes

INTRODUCTION

1. Quoted in Richard Reeves, *President Reagan: The Triumph of Imagination* (New York: Simon & Schuster, 2005), 212.

2. Noam Chomsky, interviewed in the movie *Manufacturing Consent: Noam Chomsky and the Media* (1992); transcribed quote archived at the Internet Movie Database entry for *Manufacturing Consent,* http://www.imdb.com.

3. Jean Baudrillard, *America* (New York: Verso, 1989), 23.

4. John Winthrop, "A Model of Christian Charity," in *The American Tradition in Literature,* 7th ed., ed. George Perkins, Sculley Bradley, Richmond Croom Beatty, and E. Hudson Long (New York: McGraw-Hill, 1990), 42.

5. John F. Kennedy, "City upon a Hill" speech, delivered on January 9, 1961, to a joint convention of the General Court of the Commonwealth of Massachusetts at the state house, Boston; transcript archived at the website of the Miller Center of Public Affairs, http://millercenter.org.

6. Seymour M. Hersh, *The Dark Side of Camelot* (New York: Little, Brown, 1997), 10.

7. Ibid., 11.

8. "I Wonder What the King Is Doing Tonight," from *Camelot: Original Broadway Cast Recording* (Columbia Masterworks, 1960).

9. Ronald Reagan, farewell address to the nation, broadcast from the Oval Office on January 11, 1989; published text archived at the website of the Miller Center of Public Affairs, http://millercenter.org.

10. Christopher Hitchens, "Not Even a Hedgehog: The Stupidity of Ronald Reagan," Slate, June 7, 2004, http://www.slate.com.

11. Nathaniel Hawthorne, "Young Goodman Brown," in Perkins et al., *The American Tradition in Literature,* 754.

12. Robert Sklar, *Movie-Made America: A Cultural History of American Movies* (New York: Vintage Books, 1994), 355.

DEAD MAN WALKING

1. See Christine Vestal, "States Cope with Rising Homelessness," Stateline.org, March 18, 2009, http://www.stateline.org.

2. David J. Skal, e-mail to the author, March 15, 2010.

3. Matt Taibbi, "Inside the Great American Bubble Machine," *Rolling Stone*, July 9, 2009, archived at http://www.rollingstone.com.

4. See Paul Krugman, "Even More Gilded," Paul Krugman Blog, August 13, 2009, http://krugman.blogs.nytimes.com.

5. See John Ydstie, "Fed Chief Issues Warning on Income Gap," NPR.org, February 7, 2007, http://www.npr.org.

6. Alfred Metraux, *Voodoo in Haiti* (New York: Schocken Books, 1972), 282.

7. The Fourth Whirlwind, "The 'Prepper Lawyer,'" SurvivalBlog, 2008, http://www.survivalblog.com.

8. Michael Z. Williamson, "Mike Williamson's Product Review: Dead On Tools Annihilator Demolition Hammer," SurvivalBlog, January 31, 2010, http://www.survivalblog.com.

9. "Letter Re: Retreats in the Eastern United States," unsigned letter to the editor, SurvivalBlog, 2007, http://www.survivalblog.com.

10. See definition for "Golden Horde," James Wesley, Rawles, "A Glossary of Survival and Preparedness Acronyms/Terms," SurvivalBlog, 2005–2011, http://www.survivalblog.com.

11. James Wesley, Rawles, "The Precepts of Rawlesian Survivalist Philosophy," SurvivalBlog, 2008–2011, http://www.survivalblog.com.

12. "Browning 35," post in "Zombie Survival Kits and Ultimate Zombie Survival Thread," Stormfront.org, February 7, 2008, 10:07 p.m., http://www.stormfront.org.

13. "Chrispy," post in "Zombie Survival Kits and Ultimate Zombie Survival Thread," Stormfront.org, February 7, 2008, 10:44 p.m., http://www.stormfront.org.

14. "Son of the Mist," "Re: Zombie Survival Kits and Ultimate Zombie Survival Thread," Stormfront.org, February 8, 2008, 02:45 a.m., http://www.stormfront.org.

GUN PLAY

1. "Curious teenager": Dan Barry, "Looking Behind the Mug-Shot Grin," *New York Times*, January 15, 2011, http://www.nytimes.com. "Crossroads of the West gun

show": William Yardley, Michael Luo, and Sam Dolnick, "At a Gun Show and a Safeway, Tucson Looks for 'Normalcy,'" *New York Times*, January 15, 2011, http://www.nytimes.com.

2. See Center for Responsive Politics, OpenSecrets.org, "National Rifle Assn," information page, http://www.opensecrets.org.

3. Nicholas D. Kristof, "Why Not Regulate Guns as Seriously as Toys?" *New York Times*, January 12, 2011, http://www.nytimes.com.

4. Second Amendment to the U.S. Constitution, archived at the Legal Information Institute at the Cornell Law School website, http://topics.law.cornell.edu/constitution.

5. Yardley, Luo, and Dolnick, "At a Gun Show and a Safeway."

6. "Leads the industrialized world in gun violence": "Unsafe in Any Hands: Why America Needs to Ban Handguns," Violence Policy Center website, 2000, http://www.vpc.org. "Eleven times more likely": Kristof, "Why Not Regulate Guns as Seriously as Toys?" "Japan, whose gun laws are among the world's strictest": E. G. Krug, K. E. Powell, and L. L. Dahlberg, "Firearm-Related Deaths in the United States and 35 Other High- and Upper-Middle-Income Countries," *International Journal of Epidemiology* 27 (1998): 214–21, http://ije.oxfordjournals.org.

It bears pointing out that some commentators believe Japan's low rate of gun-related deaths is less a product of strict gun control than of Japan's deep-rooted culture of submission to authority, which privileges the law-abiding member of society over the rugged individual enshrined in American frontier myth. "Regulations are treated more as road maps than as rules subject to active enforcement," writes Philip Brasor in the *Japan Times*. "Japan is still a very safe country when it comes to guns, a reality that has less to do with laws than with prevailing attitudes," See Philip Brasor, "Japan Faces Up to a World of Gun Crime," Japan Times Online, December 23, 2007, http://search.japantimes.co.jp.

7. See Richard Slotkin, *Regeneration through Violence: The Mythology of the American Frontier, 1600–1860* (Norman: University of Oklahoma Press, 2000), passim.

8. J. G. Ballard, *The Atrocity Exhibition* (San Francisco: Re/Search Publications, 1990), 101–3.

9. "Rebuilding America's Defenses: Strategy, Forces, and Resources for a New Century (A Report of the Project for the New American Century)," September 2000, 6, http://www.newamericancentury.org.

10. Negativland, *Guns* (SST, 1991). By stitching together some of the TV and movie clips that correspond to the audio samples used by Negativland, the commercial video producer/director Peter Neville created a deadpan, grimly funny

music video for *Guns*. Neville has archived it on the YouTube page for his production company, Image Control Unit, at http://www.youtube.com.

MYSTERIOUS STRANGER

1. Quoted in Larry Rohter, "Dead for a Century, Twain Says What He Meant," *New York Times*, July 9, 2010, http://www.nytimes.com.

2. H. L. Mencken, "Mark Twain's Americanism," *New York Evening Mail*, November 1, 1917, archived at http://www.positiveatheism.org.

3. Ibid.

4. Mark Twain, *Autobiography of Mark Twain*, vol. 1 (Berkeley: University of California Press, 2010), 405–9.

5. Rohter, "Dead for a Century."

6. Twain, *Autobiography*, vol. 1, 462.

7. "Hoodlums and riffraff": William S. Burroughs, "Roosevelt after Inauguration," in *Word Virus* (New York: Grove Press, 1998), 110. "Whiskey gentry": Hunter S. Thompson, "The Kentucky Derby Is Decadent and Depraved," in *The Great Shark Hunt: Strange Tales from a Strange Time* (New York: Summit Books, 1979), 31. "Propping their giant atrophied glutes": Matt Taibbi, "The Truth about the Tea Party," *Rolling Stone*, October 14, 2010, archived at http://www.rollingstone.com.

8. "Defending the birthers": David Weigel, "Paglia's a Birther," Politico.com, September 17, 2009, http://www.politico.com. "An intellectual firecracker": Camille Paglia, "Obama Surfs Through," Salon.com, November 12, 2008, http://www.salon.com.

9. Camille Paglia, *Sexual Personae: Art and Decadence from Nefertiti to Emily Dickinson* (New York: Vintage Books, 1991), 623.

10. Ibid.

11. Ibid.

12. Mark Twain, *The Adventures of Tom Sawyer*, in *Mississippi Writings: "Tom Sawyer," "Life on the Mississippi," "Huckleberry Finn," "Pudd'nhead Wilson,"* (New York: Library of America, 1982), 110.

13. Ibid.

14. See Leslie Fiedler, *Love and Death in the American Novel* (Briarcliff Manor, N.Y.: Scarborough Books, 1982), 270–90.

15. Mark Twain, *Huckleberry Finn*, in *Mississippi Writings: "Tom Sawyer," "Life on the Mississippi," "Huckleberry Finn," "Pudd'nhead Wilson,"* (New York: Library of America, 1982), 912.

16. Ibid., 762.

17. Fiedler, *Love and Death in the American Novel*, 286.

18. Ibid., 287.

19. Twain, *Huckleberry Finn*, 851.

ALADDIN SANE CALLED

1. Sasha Frere-Jones, "Ladies Wild: How Not Dumb Is Gaga?" *New Yorker*, April 27, 2009, http://www.newyorker.com.

2. "Bubble World": As in: "A year from now, I could go away, and people might say, 'Gosh, what ever happened to that girl who never wore pants?' But how wonderfully memorable 30 years from now, when they say, 'Do you remember Gaga and her bubbles?' Because, for a minute, everybody in that room will forget every sad, painful thing in their lives, and they'll just live in my bubble world," Lady Gaga, quoted in Vanessa Grigoriadis, "Growing Up Gaga: The Self-Invented, Manufactured, Accidental, Totally On-Purpose New York Creation of the World's Biggest Pop Star," *New York*, March 28, 2010, http://nymag.com.

3. Definition for "Gaga," Dictionary.com (this definition provided by Random House Dictionary), http://dictionary.reference.com.

4. Definition for "Gaga," Yahoo! Education (dictionary provided by Houghton-Mifflin), http://education.yahoo.com.

5. "Rockist": See Kelefa Sanneh, "The Rap against Rockism," *New York Times*, October 31, 2004, http://www.nytimes.com.

6. Queen, "The Fairy Feller's Master-Stroke," *Queen II* (Elektra, 1974).

7. Ibid.

8. Dale Carnegie, *How to Win Friends and Influence People* (New York: Simon & Schuster, 2009), 88.

9. "Disco stick": "LoveGame," *The Fame* (Interscope, 2008). "Bluffin' with my muffin": "Poker Face," *The Fame*. "Getting shit wrecked": "Beautiful, Dirty, Rich," *The Fame*. "Louis, Dolce Gabbana, Alexander McQueen, eh ou": "Fashion," soundtrack to *Confessions of a Shopaholic* (Hollywood Records, 2009).

10. David Brooks, "The Other Education," *New York Times*, November 26, 2009, http://www.nytimes.com.

11. Sanneh, "The Rap against Rockism."

12. Ibid.

13. Richard Dyer, "In Defence of Disco," *Gay Left*, no. 8 (Summer 1979), http://www.gayleft1970s.org.

14. Frere-Jones, "Ladies Wild."

15. Jonah Weiner, "How Smart Is Lady Gaga? Pop's Most Pretentious Starlet," Slate.com, June 16, 2009, http://www.slate.com.

16. Brad Larosa, "How Stefani Germanotta Became Lady Gaga," ABCNews. com, January 21, 2010, http://abcnews.go.com.

17. See Laurence Senelick, *The Changing Room: Sex, Drag, and Theatre* (London: Routledge, 2000), 387.

18. See Susanne Pfeffer, "Interview with Joe Coleman," JoeColeman.com, http://www.joecoleman.com.

19. "Lady Gaga: The Singing Sensation on Stress, Sexuality, and Her Romantic Future," *Elle*, undated, http://www.elle.com.

20. "Barbara Walters Says Lady Gaga Is 'Quite Intelligent,'" StarPulse.com, December 3, 2009, http://www.starpulse.com.

21. All Simon Reynolds quotes are from e-mail to the author, April 10, 2010, 6:59 p.m.

22. Michael Watts, "Oh, You Pretty Thing," *Melody Maker*, January 22, 1972, archived at The Ziggy Stardust Companion, http://www.5years.com.

23. David Bowie, quoted in "The Ziggy Stardust Time-Line: Ziggy Takes Shape," The Ziggy Stardust Companion, http://www.5years.com.

24. "Lady Gaga: 'I Love Androgyny'—Barbara Walters Talks Sex, Love, and Family with the Breakout Pop Star," ABCNews.com, January 22, 2010, http://abcnews.go.com.

25. Cameron Crowe, "Candid Conversation: An Outrageous Conversation with the Actor, Rock Singer, and Sexual Switch-Hitter," *Playboy*, September 1976, archived at The Uncool.com ("The Official Website for Everything Cameron Crowe . . ."), http://www.theuncool.com.

26. Jason Louv, "Lady Gaga and The Dead Planet Grotesque," *H+*, March 16, 2010, http://hplusmagazine.com.

27. Blurb for Georges-Claude Guilbert, *Madonna as Postmodern Myth: How One Star's Self-Construction Rewrites Sex, Gender, Hollywood, and the American Dream* (Jefferson, N.C.: McFarland, 2002), at http://www.amazon.com.

28. Louv, "Lady Gaga."

29. Seth Plattner, "Women in Music: Lady Gaga—Pop's It Girl Has Nothing to Hide and in Leotards, Nowhere to Hide It," *Elle*, June 12, 2009, http://www.elle.com.

30. Ben White, "The Style Council—David Bowie and Mos Def," *Complex*, August/September 2003, archived at DavidBowie.com, http://www.davidbowie.com.

31. Ann Oldenburg, "Lady Gaga Explains Her VMA Raw Meat Dress," *USA Today*, September 13, 2010, http://www.usatoday.com.

32. "Bare-bottomed": See "Bum Note: Lady Gaga Shows Buttocks in See-Through Flesh-Coloured Pants for a Chilly Shopping Trip in Ice-Bound Paris,"

Daily Mail, December 22, 2010, http://www.dailymail.co.uk. "Teetered through": "Lady Gaga Allowed through Airport Security with Handcuffs. Maybe Her Outfit Was a Bit Distracting," *Daily Mail,* September 15, 2010, http://www.dailymail.co.uk.

33. Ann Oldenburg, "Lady Gaga Visits 'The View,'" *USA Today,* May 23, 2011, http://content.usatoday.com.

34. See Courtney Crowder, "Lady Gaga's New Video Explained: Dead Diners, Americana, and Cigarette Sunglasses," ABCNews.com, March 16, 2010, http://abcnews.go.com.

JOCKO HOMO

1. David Sedaris, "Go Carolina," in *Me Talk Pretty One Day* (New York: Little, Brown, 2000), 5.

2. Robert Lipsyte, *Raiders Night* (New York: HarperTeen, 2006), 6–7.

WIMPS, WUSSIES, AND W.

1. "Irreverent and controversial," "nappy-headed hos": Ed Payne, "Imus Hires Attorney, Will Likely Sue CBS," CNN.com, May 3, 2007, http://articles.cnn.com. "Deeply hurtful": "NBC News: 'Only decision we could reach,'" MSNBC.com, April 11, 2007, http://www.msnbc.msn.com.

2. "Seven times more blacks," "fifteen times more likely": See National Urban League, "2007 State of Black America: Portrait of the Black Male (Executive Summary)," archived at http://www.weourselves.org. "Cantankerous old fool": Quoted in James Joyner, "Don Imus Berates Contessa Brewer," Outside the Beltway, May 1, 2005, http://www.outsidethebeltway.com.

3. "Faggot": See J. S., "Coulter Reference to Edwards as 'Faggot' Gives Rise to Questions for Media," MediaMatters.org, March 2, 2007, http://mediamatters.org. "Total fag," "even money": See S. S. M., "Coulter Put 'Even Money' on Sen. Clinton '[C]oming out of the Closet,'" MediaMatters.org, August 3, 2006, http://mediamatters.org.

4. David Weigel, "Coulter Comes Out Against Gay Clinton Marriage," Wonkette.com, undated, http://wonkette.com.

5. "Gay boy": Marcela Creps, "Insults Fly at Coulter Speech; Conservative Polemicist Visits IU Auditorium," *Indiana University Herald-Times,* February 24, 2006, http://newsinfo.iu.edu.

6. U.S. Department of Justice/Federal Bureau of Investigation, "FBI Releases Its 2005 Statistics on Hate Crime," October 2006, http://www.fbi.gov.

7. David Edwards and Ron Brynaert, "Coulter: 'Faggot' Not Offensive to Gays, It's a 'Schoolyard Taunt,'" The Raw Story, March 6, 2007, http://www.rawstory.com.

8. Cynthia Lee, "Fighting the New F-Word," *McGill Reporter,* April 19, 2007, http://www.mcgill.ca.

9. Steve Sailer, "Does Al Gore Lisp?," iSteve.com, November 4, 2000, http://www.isteve.com.

10. See Margaret Garrard Warner, "Fighting the 'Wimp Factor,'" *Newsweek,* October 19, 1987, http://www.newsweek.com.

11. Ibid.

12. Kitty Kelley, *The Family: The Real Story of the Bush Dynasty* (New York: Doubleday, 2004), 450–51.

13. Molly Ivins and Lou Dubose, *Shrub: The Short but Happy Political Life of George W. Bush* (New York: Vintage Books, 2000), 45.

14. Ibid., 143.

15. "Locker-room joshing": Ibid., 46. "What a stud": Dave Ford, "Shrinking Bush: S.F. Psychologist Argues That Hyper-masculinity Is Undermining the American Political Culture," *San Francisco Chronicle,* September 17, 2004, http://www.sfgate.com.

16. Lillian Kwon, "Christian Men Seek Lost Masculinity," *Christian Post,* March 20, 2007, 06:32 p.m., http://www.christianpost.com.

17. John Rogers, "Rep. Aaron Schock Burned His Gay Belt. What About His Homosexual Shirt?" Queerty.com, June 14, 2010, http://www.queerty.com.

18. Lakshmi Chaudhry, "The Wimp Factor," AlterNet, October 29, 2004, http://www.alternet.org.

STARDUST MEMORIES

1. Quoted in Mark Spitz, *Bowie: A Biography* (New York: Crown, 2009), 225.

2. Jimi Hendrix, *Axis: Bold as Love* (Reprise, 1968).

3. Andy Warhol, *The Philosophy of Andy Warhol* (Orlando, Fla.: Harcourt, 1977), 53.

4. Quoted in Toby Creswell, *1001 Songs: The Great Songs of All Time and the Artists, Stories, and Secrets Behind Them* (New York: Thunder's Mouth Press, 2006), 237.

5. Ellen Willis, "Bowie's Limitations" (1972), in *Out of the Vinyl Deeps: Ellen Willis on Rock Music* (Minneapolis: University of Minnesota Press, 2011), 38, 40.

6. Ibid., 40.

7. Ibid.

8. Ibid., 40–41.

9. Ibid., 41.

10. "Homo Sapiens have outgrown their use": David Bowie, *Hunky Dory* (RCA, 1971). "Keeps Moet et Chandon": Queen, *Sheer Heart Attack* (Elektra, 1974).

11. Spitz, *Bowie*, 177.

12. Ibid., 177–78.

13. Ibid., 209.

14. Ibid., 186.

15. Ibid., 301.

16. Quoted in George Tremlett, *David Bowie: Living on the Brink* (New York: Carroll & Graf, 1997), 20.

17. David Bowie, *Diamond Dogs* (RCA, 1974).

18. Spitz, *Bowie*, 111.

19. Ibid., 316.

20. Ibid., 367.

21. Ibid., 366.

22. Ibid., 398.

WHEN ANIMALS ATTACK!

1. Gordon Grice, *Deadly Kingdom: The Book of Dangerous Animals* (New York: Dial Press, 2010), 253.

2. Gordon Grice, *The Red Hourglass: Lives of the Predators* (New York: Dell, 1998), 75.

3. Ibid., 58–59.

4. Thomas Harris, *Red Dragon* (New York: Dell, 2000), 454.

5. Grice, *Deadly Kingdom*, xxii.

6. Ibid., xxiii.

7. Ibid., 20.

8. Ibid., 22.

9. Ibid., 29.

10. Ibid., 30, 33.

11. Ibid., 35.

12. Ibid., 47.

13. Ibid., 50.

14. Ibid., 90.

15. Ibid., 91.

16. Ibid.

17. Wade Sampson, "In Walt's Worlds: Natural Walt," Mouse Planet, January 30, 2008, http://www.mouseplanet.com.

18. Associated Press, "4 Teams of Surgeons Operate on Chimp's Victim; Woman Mauled by Rampaging Pet Making Progress after 7 Hours of Surgery," MSNBC.com, February 18, 2009, http://www.msnbc.msn.com.

19. "Small and cute and friendly"; "lived like a human": Michael Wilson, "After Shooting Chimp, a Police Officer's Descent," *New York Times,* February 24, 2010, http://www.nytimes.com. "Sleeping (and bathing!) with his owner": Associated Press, "Owner Shared Bed and Took Baths with Chimpanzee from Connecticut Attack," FoxNews.com, February 20, 2009, http://www.foxnews.com.

20. Grice, *Deadly Kingdom,* 285.

21. Ibid., 284.

22. See David Gardner and Joanna Tweedy, "Woman Trainer Dies after Attack by 'Serial' Killer Whale in Front of SeaWorld Spectators," *Daily Mail,* February 25, 2010, http://www.dailymail.co.uk.

23. "Notorious among animal-rights activists": See, for example, Lindsay Barnett, "Animal Activists Call for Changes at SeaWorld Following Trainer's Orca Death," *Los Angeles Times,* February 27, 2010, http://latimesblogs.latimes.com. See, too, PBS *Frontline,* "A Whale of a Business," original airdate November 11, 1997, http://www.pbs.org.

24. Gardner and Tweedy, "Woman Trainer Dies."

25. Ibid.

26. Ibid.

27. Grice, *Deadly Kingdom,* 38.

28. I've relied here on Kevin Sanders's essay "Timothy Treadwell Incident—A Full Report and Examination/Night of the Grizzly: A True Story of Love and Death in the Wilderness," Yellowstone-Bearman.com, 2008, http://www.yellowstone-bearman.com. Although not a trained journalist, Sanders, a naturalist, sometime columnist, and author of a bear-safety guide, has written a well-researched account of Treadwell's death, drawing on government documents, scholarly articles, and historical studies.

29. "Memorable Quotes," entry for *Grizzly Man,* Internet Movie Database, http://www.imdb.com.

30. Sanders, "Timothy Treadwell Incident."

31. Ibid.

32. Grice, *Deadly Kingdom,* 13.

33. Thomas McIntyre, "The Downfall of Bear Fanatic Timothy Treadwell," *Field & Stream,* March 31, 2004, http://www.fieldandstream.com.

34. Grice, *Deadly Kingdom,* 23.

35. Sanders, "Timothy Treadwell Incident."

36. "Memorable Quotes."

TOE *FOU*

1. As in *The Clam-Plate Orgy: And Other Subliminal Techniques for Manipulating Your Behavior,* Wilson Bryan Keys's masterwork of overheated Freudianism and wack-job semiotics. Keys, along with Vance Packard (author of *The Hidden Persuaders*), was a leading light in the "subliminal seduction" school of advertising criticism.

2. "Golden Lotus": the ideal three-inch female foot produced, in ancient China, by binding girls' feet. In a research paper included in Fordham University's Internet Women's History Sourcebook website, Marie Vento writes: "For Chinese men, bound feet were associated with higher-status love and sex, carrying strong connotations of both modesty and lasciviousness. Bound feet became a sexual fetish and were said to be conducive to better intercourse. It was accepted that these golden lotuses had developed not only an aesthetic appeal for the Chinese male, but also a sexual one. A widespread male fantasy claimed that footbinding produced the development of a highly-muscled vagina 'full of wondrous folds,' with the tiny appearance of the foot arousing a combination of lust and pity. Chinese pornography of the past reflects a preoccupation with the feet, and the men who adored them—'lotus lovers'—became the authors of the classics of brothel culture, which describe in detail the various shapes of bound feet and the erotic practices in which they could be employed." See Marie Vento, "One Thousand Years of Chinese Footbinding: Its Origins, Popularity, and Demise," Internet Women's History Sourcebook, http://www.fordham.edu/halsall/women/womensbook.html.

For more on the erotics of the Golden Lotus, see Howard S. Levy, *The Lotus Lovers: The Complete History of the Curious Erotic Custom of Footbinding in China* (Buffalo, N.Y.: Prometheus Books, 1992). Intriguingly, fetish porn involving "footjobs"—women masturbating men with their feet, a practice that effectively transforms the foot into "a highly-muscled vagina"—is a thriving genre on the Web. Wikipedia defines the footjob as a sexual practice that presumes a degree, at least, of foot fetishism. "Related activities include toejob, focusing on the toes, sandaljob whilst wearing sandals, and solejob, using only the foot soles." See "Footjob," Wikipedia, http://en.wikipedia.org. Where will it end?

3. Geoff Nicholson, *Footsucker* (Woodstock, N.Y.: Overlook Press, 1996), 217.

4. Alex Comfort, *The Joy of Sex* (New York: Fireside/Simon & Schuster, 1972), 152.

5. Ibid.

6. Georges Bataille, "Big Toe," in *Encyclopaedia Acephalica: Comprising the Critical Dictionary and Related Texts,* ed. Isabelle Waldberg and Iain White (London: Atlas Press, 1995), 87.

7. Ibid., 92.

8. Ibid., 90.

9. "Gently waving his long, thin fingers": Arthur Conan Doyle, *The Complete Sherlock Holmes* (New York: Doubleday, 1960), 185. "Long, quivering fingers": ibid., 672.

10. "Corded, knuckly" hands and "large, firm" hands: Robert Louis Stevenson, *Dr. Jekyll and Mr. Hyde* (New York: Signet Classics, 1987), 112.

11. Bram Stoker, *The New Annotated Dracula,* ed. Leslie S. Klinger (New York: W. W. Norton, 2008), 47.

12. Bataille, "Big Toe," 92.

13. Ibid.

14. Anthony N. Fragola, "From the Ecclesiastical to the Profane: Foot Fetishism in Luis Buñuel and Alain Robbe-Grillet," *Journal of the American Academy of Psychoanalysis* 22, no. 4 (1994): abstract.

15. Jeannette Walls, "Pope Singles Out Madonna for Criticism," *Today,* June 21, 2004, http://today.msnbc.msn.com.

16. Valerie Steele, *Fetish: Fashion, Sex, and Power* (New York: Oxford University Press, 1996), 4–5.

17. Ibid., 220.

18. Brian Dakss, "Madonna: Diva, Author, Housewife," *CBS Early Show,* December 20, 2004, http://www.cbsnews.com.

SHOAH BUSINESS

1. Quoted in Tim Cole, *Selling the Holocaust: From Auschwitz to Schindler— How History Is Bought, Packaged, and Sold* (New York: Routledge, 1999), 6.

2. Ibid., 17.

3. Ibid.

4. Ibid.

5. Quoted in ibid., 4.

6. Norman G. Finkelstein, *The Holocaust Industry: Reflections on the Exploitation of Jewish Suffering* (New York: Verso, 2000), 4.

7. Ibid.

8. Ibid., 3, 7–8.

9. Ibid., 76–77.

10. Ibid., 73–74.

11. Cole, *Selling the Holocaust,* 17.

12. Deborah Dwork and Robert Jan van Pelt, *Auschwitz: 1270 to the Present* (New York: W. W. Norton, 1996), 361.

13. Cole, *Selling the Holocaust,* 111.

14. Ibid., 110.

15. Ibid., 75.

16. J. G. Ballard, "Introduction to the French Edition of *Crash,*" in *Re/Search #8/9,* ed. V. Vale and Andrea Juno (San Francisco: Re/Search Publications, 1984), 96.

17. Fredric Jameson, *Postmodernism, or, The Cultural Logic of Late Capitalism* (Durham, N.C.: Duke University Press, 1991), 11.

18. Cole, *Selling the Holocaust,* 116.

19. Dwork and van Pelt, *Auschwitz,* 362.

20. Julie S. Dermansky and Georg Steinboeck, "Artists' Statement for 'At Auschwitz' Show at Hebrew Union College–Jewish Institute of Religion," unpublished, unnumbered page.

21. Rudolf Hoss, Pery Broad, and Johann Paul Kremer, *KL Auschwitz Seen by the SS* (Oswiecim, Germany: Auschwitz-Birkenau State Museum, 1994), 166.

THE TRIUMPH OF THE SHILL

1. In Don DeLillo's novel *White Noise* (a satire of academia, among other things), protagonist Jack Gladney chairs the Department of Hitler Studies, a discipline he pioneered.

2. See D. B. Holt, *How Brands Become Icons: The Principles of Cultural Branding* (Boston: Harvard Business School Publishing, 2004).

3. Quoted in "Origins of the Swastika," *BBC News Magazine,* January 18, 2005, http://news.bbc.co.uk. In his canonical biography *Hitler,* the historian Joachim Fest claims that Hitler is revising history here. According to Fest, the swastika had been popular with German and Austrian ultranationalists and anti-Semites since the Aryan supremacist Lanz von Liebenfels raised it over his Austrian castle in 1907, if not earlier. Hitler's design genius lay not in brainstorming the crooked cross out of thin air, as the Führer liked to claim, but in grasping its iconic power, Fest contends: "In *Mein Kampf* Hitler pretended that the swastika flag was his invention. In fact, one of the party members, the dentist Friedrich Krohn, had designed it for the founding meeting of the Starnberg *Ortsgruppe* (local party group) in May of 1920. . . . Once again, Hitler's own contribution consisted, not of the original idea, but of the instant perception of the symbol's psychological magic. He therefore raised it to the status of a party emblem and made it obligatory." See Joachim Fest, *Hitler* (Orlando, Fla.: Harcourt, 1974), 128. Steven Heller gives a design-literate account of Hitler's role in the Nazi appropriation—rebranding?—of

the swastika in his fascinating study *The Swastika: Symbol beyond Redemption?* (New York: Allworth Press, 2000).

4. Rick Poynor, e-mail interview with the author, December 18, 2002.

5. Susan Sontag, "Fascinating Fascism," in *Under the Sign of Saturn: Essays* (New York: Picador, 2002), 99.

6. Holt, *How Brands Become Icons*, 37.

7. Aldous Huxley, *Brave New World Revisited* (New York: HarperPerennial Modern Classics, 2006), 42.

8. "Who's Afraid of the Big, Bad Wolf?": Robert Waite, *The Psychopathic God: Adolph Hitler* (Cambridge, Mass.: Da Capo Press, 1993), 27.

9. Quoted in Emily Woodward, "Revisiting Disney's Dumbo," undated review, PopMatters, http://www.popmatters.com.

10. Kevin Crosby, "Disney, Hoover, and Reno," undated essay, SkewsMe.com, http://www.skewsme.com.

11. Umberto Eco, *Foucault's Pendulum* (Orlando, Fla.: Harcourt Brace Jovanovich, 1989), 463–64.

12. This publication has vanished from the Web. However, "Our Defence of Prince Harry" can be found at the OZ—The "Other" Side of the Rainbow blog, reposted by the "Wizard of 'Oz'" under the title "Harry, Harry, Harry . . . ," January 13, 2005, http://othersiderainbow.blogspot.com.

13. Mary S. Lovell, *The Sisters: The Saga of the Mitford Family* (New York: W. W. Norton, 2003), 516.

14. Ibid.

15. Christopher Hitchens, "Churchill Didn't Say That: *The King's Speech* Is Riddled with Gross Falsifications of History," Slate, January 24, 2011, http://slate.com.

16. Gore Vidal, *Palimpsest: A Memoir* (New York: Penguin Books, 1996), 206.

17. Entry on "Edward VIII of the United Kingdom," Wikipedia, http://en.wikipedia.org. There are more such juicy morsels in this thoroughly researched entry.

ENDTIME FOR HITLER

1. Don DeLillo, *White Noise* (New York: Viking Penguin, 1985), 63.

2. Sheldon Rampton, "Book Review: Stuart Ewen's *PR! A Social History of Spin*," *PR Watch* 3, no. 4 (1996), http://www.prwatch.org.

3. Stuart Ewen, *PR! A Social History of Spin* (New York: Basic Books, 1996), 446.

4. Joachim Fest, *Hitler* (Orlando, Fla.: Harcourt, 1974), 128.

5. Ibid., 518.

6. Ron Rosenbaum, *Explaining Hitler* (New York: HarperPerennial, 1999), 86.

7. Fest, *Hitler*, 530.

8. Ibid., 517–18.

9. "Since 2006": Jamie Dubs and Olivia G., "*Downfall*/Hitler Reacts," *Know Your Meme.com*, http://knowyourmeme.com.

10. All quotes from *Downfall* remixes are my own transcriptions from videos found online, most of them on YouTube. Since users who upload these parodies are frequently the subjects of takedown notices from the film's production company, they play a cat-and-mouse game with authorities, rendering pointless the citation of any URLs for the videos mentioned in this essay.

11. Fest, *Hitler*, 741.

12. Martin Gilbert, *The Holocaust: A History of the Jews of Europe during the Second World War* (New York: Henry Holt, 1985), 442.

13. "With Comedy, We Can Rob Hitler of His Posthumous Power," unbylined interview with Mel Brooks, *Der Spiegel*, March 16, 2006, http://www.spiegel.de.

14. Ibid.

15. Entry on Werner Finck, *Wikipedia*, http://en.wikipedia.org.

16. Lynn Rapaport, "Humor as Political Opposition against the Nazi Regime," in *Gray Zones: Ambiguity and Compromise in the Holocaust and Its Aftermath*, ed. Jonathan Petropoulos and John K. Roth (New York: Berghahn Books, 2006), 254.

17. Adam LeBor and Roger Boyes, *Seduced by Hitler: The Choices of a Nation and the Ethics of Survival* (Naperville, Ill.: Sourcebooks, 2001), 36.

18. Rapaport, "Humor as Political Opposition," 256.

19. Ibid., 257.

20. Ibid., 259.

21. Fest, *Hitler*, 442.

22. Rosenbaum, *Explaining Hitler*, 70.

23. Ibid.

24. Fest, *Hitler*, 464.

25. Steven Lehrer, *Wannsee House and the Holocaust* (Jefferson, N.C.: McFarland, 2000), 65.

WORLD WIDE WONDER CLOSET

1. "The Sea Organization: The Religious Order of Scientology," at WhatIs Scientology.org, http://www.whatisscientology.org/html.

2. See Kevin Sites, "What Happened in the Fallujah Mosque: NBC Correspondent Writes about the Killing of an Injured Iraqi," originally published on November 22, 2004; archived at MSNBC.com, http://www.msnbc.msn.com.

3. Rob Walker, "Inside the Wild, Wacky, Profitable World of Boing Boing," *Fast Company*, November 30, 2010, http://www.fastcompany.com/magazine.

4. Jason Epstein, *Book Business: Publishing Past, Present, and Future* (New York: W. W. Norton, 2001), 4.

(FACE)BOOK OF THE DEAD

1. Algernon Charles Swinburne, "The Garden of Proserpine" (1866), archived at The Poetry Foundation, www.poetryfoundation.org.

2. Susan Sontag, "Notes on 'Camp,'" in *Against Interpretation, and Other Essays* (New York: Picador, 2001), 275.

3. Raymond Chandler, "The Simple Art of Murder," in *Later Novels and Other Writings* (New York: Library of America, 1995), 990.

4. Charles Burns, *Black Hole* (New York: Pantheon Books, 2005), front jacket flap copy.

5. Edward Champion, "Interview with Charles Burns," Edward Champion's "Reluctant Habits," January 22, 2008, http://www.edrants.com.

6. Erik Davis, "Teenage Head: Confessions of a High School Stoner," originally published in the *Village Voice*, June 22, 1993, http://www.techgnosis.com.

7. Burns, *Black Hole*, unnumbered page.

8. Hal Niedzviecki, "Facebook in a Crowd," *New York Times*, October 24, 2008, http://www.nytimes.com.

9. Kurt Opsahl, "Updated: Facebook Further Reduces Your Control over Personal Information," Deeplinks Blog, Electronic Frontier Foundation (EFF) website, April 19, 2010, https://www.eff.org.

10. See "FOIA: Social Networking Monitoring," under "Our Work," EFF website, https://www.eff.org.

11. Rubenr (Ruben Rodrigues), "Facebook's Anti-privacy Monopoly," DeObfuscate, May 3, 2010, http://www.deobfuscate.org.

12. LibraryThingTim (Tim Spalding), Twitter, May 1, 2010, 11:04 p.m., http://twitter.com/librarythingtim/status/13226541303.

13. W. James Au, Comment 20 in Xeni Jardin, "Infographic: Facebook's 'Anti-privacy Monopoly,'" Boing Boing, May 3, 2010, 7:02 p.m., http://www.boingboing.net/2010/05/03/infographic-facebook.html#comment-776892.

14. See Tom Hodgkinson, "With friends like these ...," *The Guardian*, January 14, 2008, http://www.guardian.co.uk.

15. Maxwell Salzberg, "Decentralize the Web with Diaspora," Kickstarter.com, http://www.kickstarter.com.

16. Raymond Chandler, *The Raymond Chandler Papers: Selected Letters and Nonfiction, 1909-1959,* ed. Tom Hiney and Frank MacShane (New York: Atlantic Monthly Press, 2000), 125.

17. Ibid., 101.

18. Ibid., 243.

19. Ibid., 84.

STRAIGHT, GAY, OR BINARY?

1. Arthur C. Clarke, *2001: A Space Odyssey* (New York: New American Library, 1968), 97.

2. Andrew Hodges, *Alan Turing: The Enigma* (New York: Simon & Schuster, 1983), 488.

3. Clarke, *2001,* 169, 148.

4. Ibid., 149.

5. Steven Levy, *Hackers: Heroes of the Computer Revolution* (New York: Dell, 1984), 83.

6. Vivian Sobchack, "The Virginity of Astronauts: Sex and the Science Fiction Film," in *Alien Zone: Cultural Theory and Contemporary Science Fiction Cinema,* ed. Annette Kuhn (New York: Verso, 1990), 103.

7. Rosalind W. Picard, "Does HAL Cry Digital Tears? Emotions and Computers," in *HAL's Legacy: "2001's" Computer as Dream and Reality,* ed. David G. Stork (Cambridge: MIT Press, 1997), 280, 296.

8. Quoted in Hodges, *Alan Turing,* 540.

9. A. M. Turing, "Computing Machinery and Intelligence," in *The Mind's I,* ed. Douglas R. Hofstadter and Daniel C. Dennett (New York: Bantam Books, 1981), 60.

10. Ibid., 54.

11. Hillel Schwartz, *The Culture of the Copy* (New York: Zone Books, 1996), 360.

12. Hodges, *Alan Turing,* 426.

13. Ibid., 426, 518.

14. Schwartz, *The Culture of the Copy,* 362.

15. Vincent LoBrutto, *Stanley Kubrick: A Biography* (New York: Donald I. Fine, 1997), 279.

16. Clarke, *2001,* 104.

17. Sobchack, "The Virginity of Astronauts," 108.

18. Ibid.

19. Arthur C. Clarke, "Foreword: The Birth of HAL," in Stork, *HAL's Legacy*, xiv.

20. Tim Brooks and Earle Marsh, *The Complete Guide to Prime Time Network TV Shows, 1946–Present*, 4th ed. (New York: Ballantine Books, 1988), 419.

21. Clarke, "Foreword," xiii.

22. My account of Clarke's comments at the University of Illinois Cyberfest '97 is based on an e-mail sent to me by Paula Treichler on March 24, 1997. Treichler's question was inspired by an earlier version of this essay, delivered the day before at the university's "Open the Pod Bay Doors: Critique, Control, and Computers" conference.

23. Toby Johnson, "In Honor of Sir Arthur C. Clarke," undated, TobyJohnson. com, http://www.tobyjohnson.com.

24. Michael Moorcock, "Brave New Worlds: Michael Moorcock Fondly Remembers His Friend Arthur C. Clarke, the Ego, Visionary and Gentleman," *The Guardian*, March 22, 2008, http://www.guardian.co.uk.

25. Johnson, "In Honor of Sir Arthur C. Clarke."

WORD SALAD SURGERY

1. Bruce Sterling, "The Flowers of Evil," Beyond the Beyond, December 28, 2003, 6:24:43 p.m., http://blog.wired.com.

2. George Johnson, "That Gibberish in Your In-Box May Be Good News," *New York Times*, January 25, 2004, http://www.nytimes.com.

3. Catalog listing, undated, Apollinaire's Bookshoppe website, http://www. apollinaires.com.

SLASHING THE BORG

1. "Sonnets from the Borgugese": *Science Friction*, no. 2, May 1993, 14. "Heart-stoppingly explicit illustrations" and "plastic splash guard cover": undated advertising flyer for *Science Friction*.

2. Henry Jenkins, *Fans, Bloggers, and Gamers: Exploring Participatory Culture* (New York: New York University Press, 2006), 47.

3. Constance Penley, "Brownian Motion: Women, Tactics, and Technology," in *Technoculture*, ed. Constance Penley and Andrew Ross (Minneapolis: University of Minnesota Press, 1991), 153–54.

4. Ibid., 158.

5. Penley discusses this story in "Brownian Motion."

6. "The Best of Both Worlds" (Part 2), *Star Trek: The Next Generation*, original airdate September 24, 1990. Episode transcript archived at *Chrissie's Transcripts Site*, http://www.chakoteya.net.

7. J. M. Dillard, *Star Trek/Deep Space Nine #1: Emissary* (New York: Pocket Books, 1993), 3.

8. Glenn Mielke, "Beamed on Borg," *Science Friction*, no. 2, May 1993, 11.

9. Tom of Finland is a gay erotic cartoonist whose obsessive, fetishized renderings of highway patrolmen, sailors, and other macho men servicing each other have earned him a devoted following among gay porn aficionados.

10. Susan Sontag, "Fascinating Fascism," in *Under the Sign of Saturn: Essays* (New York: Picador, 2002), 103.

11. Gigi the Galaxy Girl (Nancy Johnston), "Locutus," *Science Friction*, no. 1, July 1992, 17.

12. Frank Browning, *The Culture of Desire: Paradox and Perversity in Gay Lives Today* (New York: Crown, 1993), 80.

13. Ibid., 105.

14. Randy Shilts, *And the Band Played On: Politics, People, and the AIDS Epidemic* (New York: St. Martin's Press, 2007), 24.

15. Susan Sontag, "The Pornographic Imagination," in *A Susan Sontag Reader* (New York: Vintage Books, 1983), 218.

16. Browning, *The Culture of Desire*, 90.

17. Ibid., 103.

18. Gigi the Galaxy Girl, "Locutus," 15-16.

19. Ibid., 16.

20. Ibid., 17.

21. Ibid.

22. Ibid., 18.

23. John Giorno, *You Got to Burn to Shine* (London: High Risk/Serpent's Tail, 1994), 71.

24. Ibid., 74.

THINGS TO COME

1. Regrettably, you can't. Both the Neck Brace Appreciation Klub and Big-Gulp websites are now defunct, an incalculable loss to fans—and fans of fans—of fringe fetishes.

2. Quoted in Craig Bicknell, "Does the Smut Stop Here?," *Wired*, December 6, 1999, http://www.wired.com.

3. Susie Bright, "Pornographic Futures," in *Mommy's Little Girl: On Sex, Motherhood, Porn, and Cherry Pie* (Santa Cruz, Calif.: Bright Stuff, 2008), 77.

4. For a brief, informal, and not necessarily fact-checked history of *bukkake*, see http://www.asianbukkakeshowers.com. Also see the equally dubious http://www.4-bukkake.com.

5. Formerly at http://www.japan-bukkake.com, the site appears to be offline.

6. Like virtually every other site mentioned in this essay, PrivateGold is history. *Ars longa, vita brevis,* but the life of a porn site, poignantly, is briefest of all.

7. Arthur Kroker, "Panic Penis," in Arthur Kroker, Marilouise Kroker, and David Cook, *Panic Encyclopedia: The Definitive Guide to the Postmodern Scene* (New York: St. Martin's Press, 1989), 180–81.

8. Quoted in John Tierney, "Porn, the Low-Slung Engine of Progress," *New York Times,* January 9, 1994, sec. 2 (Arts and Leisure), 1.

9. Quoted in David Edelstein, "The Matrix: Marshalling Art and FX," *The Age,* May 25, 2003, http://www.theage.com.au.

TRIPE SOUP FOR THE SOUL

1. Industry valuation based on research by Marketdata Enterprises, cited in Daniel McGinn, "Living the Self-Help Life," *Newsweek,* January 10, 2000, http://www.newsweek.com.

2. Anthony Robbins, *Awaken the Giant Within: How to Take Immediate Control of Your Mental, Emotional, Physical, and Financial Destiny!* (New York: Simon & Schuster, 1991), 112.

3. John B. Watson, "Psychology as the Behaviorist Views It," *Psychological Review* 20 (1913): 158–77, archived at Classics in the History of Psychology website, http://psychclassics.yorku.ca.

4. Jean Baudrillard, *America* (London: Verso, 1988), 34.

5. Dale Carnegie, *How to Win Friends and Influence People* (1936; repr., New York: Simon & Schuster, 2009), 70.

6. Ibid., 73.

7. "Simple yet scientific system" and "Ten times each day": Norman Vincent Peale, *The Power of Positive Thinking* (1952; repr., New York: Fireside, 2003), xiii, 13.

8. Robbins, *Awaken the Giant Within,* 101.

9. Lauren Slater, "The Trouble with Self-Esteem," *New York Times Magazine,* February 3, 2002, http://www.nytimes.com.

10. Andrew Boyd, *Daily Afflictions: The Agony of Being Connected to Everything in the Universe* (New York: W. W. Norton, 2002), 91–93.

11. Ibid., xxvi–xxvii.

12. Ibid., 91.

13. Ibid., xvii.

14. Ibid., 39, 53, 84.

PONTIFICATION

1. Elaine Sciolino and Daniel J. Wakin, "Procession for Pope Draws Thousands; Viewing Begins," *New York Times,* April 5, 2005, http://www.nytimes.com.

2. Thomas Cahill, "The Price of Infallibility," *New York Times,* April 5, 2005, http://www.nytimes.com.

3. Quoted in James Likoudis, "The Degradation of Catholic Worship: How Others See Us," James Likoudis' Page, http://credo.stormloader.com.

4. See "Crystal Cathedral (Connecting You to God Wherever, Whenever, However™)," Crystal Cathedral website, http://www.crystalcathedral.org.

5. Patti Smith, "Wave," *Wave* (Arista Records, 1979).

6. Patti Smith, "Babelogue," *Easter* (Arista Records, 1978).

7. Ken Dilanian, "Centuries-Old Rituals in Modern Media Glare: The Internet and 24-Hour News Help Make an Event of Pope John Paul II's Death and the Selection of His Successor," Philly.com, April 6, 2005, http://articles.philly.com.

8. Katha Pollitt, "Is the Pope Crazy?" *The Nation,* November 3, 2003, http://www.thenation.com.

9. Marc Cooper, "Holy Shit!" April 5, 2005, http://marccooper.typepad.com.

THE PROPHET MARGIN

1. See Jack T. Chick, *Who, Me?* (Chino, Calif.: Chick Publications, 1998), unnumbered page.

2. Daniel K. Raeburn, e-mail to the author, March 11, 1999.

3. Daniel K. Raeburn, "The Holy Book of Chick," *The Imp,* no. 2 (1998): 21–22.

4. Quoted in R. Laurence Moore, *Selling God: American Religion in the Marketplace of Culture* (New York: Oxford University Press, 1994), 21.

5. Quoted in ibid., 22.

6. Jack T. Chick, *Who, Me?,* inside back cover.

7. Richard Preston, *The Hot Zone* (New York: Anchor Books, 1995), 85.

8. Quoted in Raeburn, "The Holy Book of Chick," 9.

9. This estimate is Bob Fowler's, given in a phone conversation with the author. Fowler, a Chick obsessive, is the author of *The History of the World According to Jack T. Chick* (San Francisco: Last Gasp, 2001).

10. Moore, *Selling God,* 51.

11. "Biography of Jack Chick," Chick Publications website, http://www.chick
.com.

12. Jack T. Chick, *Who, Me?*, unnumbered page.

13. Raeburn, "The Holy Book of Chick," 2.

14. Ibid., 4.

15. Ibid.

16. Ibid., 29.

2012

1. "Production Notes" for *2012*, 2011, archived at *Cinema Review*, http://www
.cinemareview.com.

2. Daniel Pinchbeck, "Evolver Spores: 2012 or, How I Learned to Stop Worrying and Love the Dimensional Shift," Reality Sandwich, November 11, 2009, http://
www.realitysandwich.com.

3. Quoted in Benjamin Anastas, "The Final Days," *New York Times*, July 1,
2007, http://www.nytimes.com.

4. "42 percent of Republicans": Elyse Siegel, "Birther Poll: 42 Percent of Republicans Believe Obama Not Born in U.S.," Huffington Post, September 24, 2009,
http://www.huffingtonpost.com. "10 percent of the nation's voters": Daniel Burke,
"Poll: 1 in 10 Think Obama Is Muslim," *USA Today*, April 1, 2008, http://www
.usatoday.com. "61 percent of the population": "The Religious and Other Beliefs
of Americans: More People Believe in the Devil, Hell, and Angels than Believe in
Darwin's Theory of Evolution," Business Wire, November 29, 2007, http://www
.businesswire.com.

5. Erik Davis, "Galactic Games 1: The Dreamspell Calendar," Reality Sandwich, July 13, 2007, http://www.realitysandwich.com.

6. Xeni Jardin, e-mail to the author, November 10, 2009, 1:50 p.m.

7. Jardin, e-mail to the author, November 10, 2009, 1:33 p.m.

8. Ibid.

9. Jardin, e-mail to the author, November 10, 2009, 1:38 p.m.

THE VAST SANTANIC CONSPIRACY

1. See *Random House Dictionary* and *American Heritage Dictionary* definitions for "Kriss Kringle" at Dictionary.com, http://dictionary.reference.com.

2. Clement Clarke Moore, "A Visit From St. Nicholas," in *An American Anthology, 1787–1900*, ed. Edmund Clarence Stedman (Boston: Houghton Mifflin, 1900),
archived at Bartleby.com, http://www.bartleby.com.

3. Ibid.

4. Mark Twain, *The Adventures of Huckleberry Finn* (San Francisco: Ignatius Press, 2009), 16.

5. Quoted in Tom Dooley, "Narcissism Nation: My Country 'Tis of Me," Eclectica 12, no. 1 (January/February 2008), http://www.eclectica.org.

6. Of course, there's a hitch: "If you will be faithful and do what God is asking you to do," Osteen preaches, "God will do His part." What God is asking you to do, naturally, is drop a horse-choking wad of unmarked bills in the collection plate. Osteen rakes in more than $43 million a year in church donations and another $30 million-plus by mail, according to The Merge. See Eric Wright, "Joel Osteen and Money," The Merge, December 3, 2007, http://www.themergeblog.com. By contrast, all Santa asks is that you sacrifice a cookie in his name. And some milk.

7. Front-page tagline, The Cutting Edge, http://www.cuttingedge.org.

8. "Encroaching mind-control of the Illuminati": "Global Mind Control and the Rapture of the Church—Part 2 of 3," The Cutting Edge, 2009, http://www.cuttingedge.org. "Genetic scientists": "News Alert & Bookstore Bulletin," The Cutting Edge, August 28, 2009, http://www.cuttingedge.org.

9. "Jesus Christ vs. Santa Claus: Santa Truly Has Been Created to Be a Counterfeit Jesus to the Secular World!," The Cutting Edge, undated, http://www.cuttingedge.org.

10. All facts and quotes in this paragraph are gleaned from Terry Watkins, "Santa Claus: The Great Pretender," BibleBelievers.com, http://www.biblebelievers.com.

11. See Jeremy Seal, *Nicholas: The Epic Journey from Saint to Santa Claus* (New York: Bloomsbury, 2005).

12. Jeremy Seal, interviewed by Renée Montagne, "The Story of Saint Nicholas," National Public Radio, original airdate December 23, 2005, archived at http://www.npr.org.

13. Gerry Bowler, *Santa Claus: A Biography* (Toronto: McClelland & Stewart, 2005), 142, 124.

14. See Stephen Nissenbaum, *The Battle for Christmas* (New York: Alfred A. Knopf, 1996).

15. Ibid., 54.

16. Ibid., 55.

17. Ibid., 10.

18. See Phyllis Siefker, *Santa Claus, Last of the Wild Men* (Jefferson, N.C.: McFarland, 1997).

19. Ibid., 40.

20. Ibid., 65.

21. Ibid., 71.

22. Ibid., 6.

23. David Sedaris, "SantaLand Diaries," in *Holidays on Ice: Stories* (New York: Little, Brown, 1997), 22.

OPEN WIDE

1. See Dr. Damon Jenkins, "Questions," DentalFear.com, http://www.dental fear.com.

2. Edgar Allan Poe, *Complete Stories and Poems of Edgar Allan Poe* (New York: Doubleday, 1984), 175.

3. Cited in Roger Forclaz, "A Source for 'Berenice' and a Note on Poe's Reading," *Poe Newsletter* 1, no. 2 (October 1968): 25–27, archived at http://www.eapoe .org.

4. Richard Zacks, *An Underground Education: The Unauthorized and Outrageous Supplement to Everything You Thought You Knew about Art, Sex, Business, Crime, Science, Medicine, and Other Fields of Human Knowledge* (New York: Anchor, 1999), 205.

5. E. Fontana, P. Tristi, and A. Piatelli, "Freeze-Dried Aura Mater for Guided Tissue Regeneration in Post-extraction Dental Implants: A Clinical and Histologic Study," *Journal of Periodontology* 65 (1994): 658 (abstract), in *Western Society of Periodontics Clinical Studies* 2 (1995), http://www.dent.ucla.edu.

6. Both items are listed in the online catalog for JT's Stockroom, http://www .stockroom.com.

GRAY MATTER

1. "Skin diseases": See Charles Hilton Fagge, *Catalogue of the models of diseases of the skin in the Museum of Guy's Hospital* (London: J. & A. Churchill, 1876); "Occult origins": See William Adams, *Disquisition of the Stone and Gravel: And Other Diseases of the Bladder, Kidneys, &c.; The Occult Causes of the Stone Assign'd, Its Principles Explain'd with the Manner of Its Accumulation, and by What Means a Nucleus is First Form'd, Which Generates the Stone* (London: Shatwell, 177?), title page.

2. *Sublime of flagellation* was published sometime in the 1700s; the exact date and, for that matter, place of publication are hazy. The earliest edition in the NYAML collections is a reprint, listed as published in London, in "18—?," by an unknown publisher. The catalog adds that it is a "reprint of the [17—?] ed. published by G. Peacock, London."

3. "History of the NYAM Library," NYAM website, http://www.nyam.org.

4. J. G. Ballard, "Project for a Glossary of the 20th Century," in *A User's Guide to the Millennium* (New York: Picador, 1996), 277, 182.

5. "Dead on the floor" and "elderly man": Both accounts in Robert R. Hazelwood, Park Elliott Dietz, and Ann Wolbert Burgess, *Autoerotic Fatalities* (Lexington, Mass.: Lexington Books, 1983), 118 and 115–16, respectively.

6. P. E. Dietz and Ronald O'Halloran, "Autoerotic Fatalities with Power Hydraulics," *Journal of Forensic Sciences* 38, no. 2 (March 1993): 359–64, quoted in Brent Turvey, "An Objective Overview of Autoerotic Fatalities," Knowledge Solutions Library, June 1995, Forensic Solutions Library section of Forensic Solutions website, http://www.corpus-delicti.com.

7. J. C. Rupp, "The Love Bug," *Journal of Forensic Sciences* 18 (1973): 259–62, reprinted in *Amok Journal*, ed. Stuart Swezey (Los Angeles: Amok Books, 1995), 30–33.

8. Ibid.

9. Tom Wolfe, "Stalking the Billion-Footed Beast: A Literary Manifesto for the New Social Novel," *Harper's Magazine*, November 1989, 55.

10. Ibid., 50.

11. Ibid., 49.

12. J. G. Ballard, "Introduction to the French Edition of *Crash*," in *Crash* (1973; repr., New York: Vintage Books, 1985), 1.

13. Ibid., 5–6.

THIRTEEN WAYS OF LOOKING AT A SEVERED HEAD

1. "Only child": For the first ten years of my life, until my parents adopted my sister, an infant at the time.

2. In the world after 9/11, when "all Americans . . . need to watch what they say," as then-White House press secretary Ari Fleischer helpfully reminded us, cultural critics who wonder aloud how the president's head would look in a basket are asking for an all-expenses-paid stay in a reeducation camp or a midnight knock from the Secret Service. Then, too, threatening POTUS is a class D felony under U.S. law. Thus this disclaimer: My remark that former President George W. Bush looks as if he deserves to lose his head is politically incorrect whimsy only. It is not intended as a threat to, nor as an incitement to violence against, any actual person, living, dead, or illegitimately enthroned by a jackleg judiciary. Paranoia? Perhaps. Still, better to err on the side of caution, in light of news stories such as this Reuters item: "Officials See Threat in Bush Cartoon: The Secret Service is studying as a possible threat a pro-Bush cartoon in the *Los Angeles Times* that showed

the president with a gun to his head, officials said Monday." Archived by "critic" at L.A. IndyMedia as "L.A. Times Cartoonist Investigated by the Secret Service," July 22, 2003, http://la.indymedia.org.

3. See Daniel Gerould, *Guillotine: Its Legend and Lore* (New York: Blast Books, 1992), 54–56.

4. Quoted in ibid., 54.

5. Quoted in Robert Wilde, "Does the Head of a Guillotined Individual Remain Briefly Alive?," About.com, 2001, http://europeanhistory.about.com.

6. Quoted in ibid.

7. See "Mike's Story," undated, MikeTheHeadlessChicken.org, http://www.miketheheadlesschicken.org.

8. "Headless Reporter Continues Work," Futurefeedforward.com, March 4, 2005, http://www.futurefeedforward.com.

9. Ibid.

10. Ibid.

11. The fetish site CuddlyNecrobabes is a clearinghouse for amateur snuff-fetish porn, some of it involving decapitation. "One of the largest collections of original artwork, stories, retouches, and collections from contributors," the site offers a "wide, diversified range of erotic, necrotic *[sic]* material that is sure to please everyone's particular tastes." See CuddlyNecrobabes.com, http://www.cuddlynecrobabes.com/promo2/home02d.html.

12. The Fantasy Decapitation Channel and its sister site the Fantasy Hanging Channel are defunct.

13. Marquis, "A Rolling Head Gathers No Moss," Chez Marquis, http://darkstoriesarchive.net78.net/~marquis/decap.html.

14. Ibid.

15. Marquis, "Giving Head." This story is no longer available online.

16. R. Crumb, "A Bitchin' Bod," in *The R. Crumb Coffee Table Art Book* (New York: Little, Brown, 1997), 233.

17. "American Hogarth": Robert Hughes, "An X Cartoon," *Time,* May 22, 1972, http://www.time.com.

18. Sigmund Freud, "Medusa's Head," in *The Life and Work of Sigmund Freud,* vol. 5, ed. James Strachey (New York: Basic Books, 1959), 105.

19. Quoted in John Toland, *Adolf Hitler,* vol. 1 (Garden City, N.Y.: Doubleday, 1976), 143.

20. See Gerould, *Guillotine,* 240.

21. Robert G. L. Waite, *The Psychopathic God: Adolf Hitler* (New York: Basic Books, 1977), 157.

22. Sigmund Freud, "The 'Uncanny,'" in *On Creativity and the Unconscious* (New York: Harper & Row, 1958), 137–38. For more on the case of the purportedly missing testicle, see Waite, *The Psychopathic God*, 18–22; and Ron Rosenbaum, *Explaining Hitler: The Search for the Origins of His Evil* (New York: HarperCollins, 1998), 140–50. For my money, Rosenbaum conclusively debunks the Single-Ball Theory.

23. Waite, *The Psychopathic God*, 157.

24. Ibid.

25. Gerould, *Guillotine*, 182.

26. See ibid., 99.

27. Quoted in ibid., 183.

28. Ibid., 182.

29. Regina Janes, "Beheadings," in *Death and Representation*, ed. Sarah Webster Goodwin and Elizabeth Bronfen (Baltimore: Johns Hopkins University Press, 1993), 255.

30. Photo caption, image for the calendar page for October, in *The Mütter Museum 2000 Calendar* (Philadelphia: College of Physicians of Philadelphia, 2000).

31. See Georges Bataille, *The Tears of Eros* (San Francisco: City Lights Books, 1989), 204–6.

32. Norman Kempster, "Oil-Hungry U.S. Ignores Human Rights Abuses of Saudi Arabia," *Los Angeles Times*, March 28, 2000, reprinted at CommonDreams.org, http://www.commondreams.org.

33. Susan Candiotti, "Botched Execution Prompts More Electric-Chair Scrutiny," CNN.com, March 26, 1997, http://www.cnn.com.

34. Alison Motluk, "Execution by Injection Far from Painless," *New Scientist*, April 14, 2005, http://www.newscientist.com.

35. Ibid.

36. Quoted in Gerould, *Guillotine*, 109–11.

BEEN THERE, PIERCED THAT

1. Quoted in Stephen Lemons, "Apocalypse Culture Vulture," Salon.com, September 20, 2000, www.salonmag.com.

2. Ibid.

3. Quoted in Michael Collins, "Adam and Evil: Hollywood Is Sinking Its Fangs into Adam Parfrey's Bloody Books," *Los Angeles Magazine*, January 1998, 20-21 (available on the Web via Google Books).

4. "Nascent mass murderer": contributor's bio for Joe Coleman in *Apocalypse Culture*, ed. Adam Parfrey (New York: Amok Press, 1987), unnumbered page.

5. "Necrocard," in *Apocalypse Culture II*, ed. Adam Parfrey (Venice, Calif.: Feral House, 2000), 276.

6. This site, which in the '90s stirred up controversy by offering one-stop shopping to Websurfers with an appetite for emetic, is now part of the Web's fossil record, its contents either offline or lost for all time. In other words, you'll have to trust me on this one.

7. Quoted in Scott Timberg, "Prince of Darkness: Adam Parfrey, Publisher of the Troublemaking Press Feral House, Has Made It His Life's Work to Propagate the Apocalypse," *New Times L.A.*, August 26–September 1, 1999, 19.

8. "My articles and investigations": Adam Parfrey, e-mail to the author, November 9, 2000, 5:53 p.m. "To cull Boyd Rice": Parfrey, e-mail to the author, November 10, 2000, 12:41 p.m.

9. Parfrey, e-mail to the author, November 9, 2000, 5:53 p.m.

DEATH TO ALL HUMANS!

1. Chris Korda, private e-mail to the author, May 26, 1999.

2. "Church of Euthanasia FAQ," Church of Euthanasia website, February 2004, http://www.churchofeuthanasia.org.

3. "E-sermon #14," undated, archived on the Church of Euthanasia website, http://www.churchofeuthanasia.org.

4. "Church of Euthanasia FAQ."

5. Quoted in David Grad, "Eat Me: Rev. Chris Korda Dines for Our Sins," *New York Press*, March 6–12, 1996, 22.

6. Quoted in "Church News: Lydia Eccles Interviews Rev. Chris Korda," *Snuff It: The Journal of the Church of Euthanasia*, no. 4, undated, unpaginated, archived on the Church of Euthanasia website, http://www.churchofeuthanasia.org.

7. Korda, private e-mail to the author, June 1, 1999.

8. "Contacts," *Snuff It: The Journal of the Church of Euthanasia*, no. 4, undated, unpaginated, archived on the Church of Euthanasia website, http://www.churchofeuthanasia.org.

9. Randall Phillip, "Shit from the Womb," *Fuck*, no. 11, undated, 7.

10. Jim Goad, "You Turn Me Off," in *Answer Me! The First Three*, ed. Jim and Debbie Goad (San Francisco: AK Press, 1994), 31.

11. Korda, private e-mail to the author, June 2, 1999.

12. Ibid.

13. William Hazlitt, "Malthus and the Liberties of the Poor," in *Hazlitt Painted by Himself*, presented by Catherine Macdonald Maclean (London: Temple, 1948), archived by Peter Landry at BluPete.com, http://www.blupete.com.

14. Quoted in Amanda Macintosh, "Who's Afraid of Population Growth?," *Living Marxism*, no. 71 (September 1994): 28, archived at http://classic-web.archive.org.

15. George Orwell, "Marrakech," in *Facing Unpleasant Facts: Narrative Essays* (Orlando, Fla.: Harcourt, 2008), 44–45.

GREAT CAESAR'S GHOST

1. "Onuphrio Muralto" and "an ancient Catholic family": Horace Walpole, *The Castle of Otranto: A Gothic Story* (New York: Oxford University Press, 2009), title page and 6, respectively.

2. Richard Davenport-Hines, *Gothic: Four Hundred Years of Excess, Horror, Evil, and Ruin* (New York: North Point Press, 1999), 31–32.

3. Ibid., 33–34.

4. Frances K. Barasch, "Introduction," in Thomas Wright, *A History of Caricature and Grotesque in Literature and Art* (New York: Frederick Ungar, 1968), xxv.

5. Rinaldo Cordovani, *The Capuchin Cemetery: Historical Notes and Guide* (Rome: Roman Province of Friars Minor Capuchin, 2009), 17.

6. Ibid., 26.

7. Ibid.

8. Nathaniel Hawthorne, *The Marble Faun* (New York: Oxford University Press, 2008), 150–51.

9. Mark Twain, *The Innocents Abroad* (New York: Penguin Books, 2002), 218.

10. Ibid., 221.

11. Quoted in Davenport-Hines, *Gothic*, 37.

APHRODITES OF THE OPERATING THEATER

1. David Cronenberg, interview with the author, circa 1995.

2. For a detailed description of ceroplastic technique and a lively account of the origins of La Specola and Joseph II's patronage of Fontana, see Felix Gonzalez-Crussi, *Suspended Animation: Six Essays on the Preservation of Bodily Parts* (New York: Harcourt Brace, 1995), 70–74. All of the historical facts in these two paragraphs, from the sentence beginning "The ceroplastic process" through the sentence ending "where the survivors repose to this day" were gleaned from Gonzalez-Crussi's book.

3. Nahoko Kametsu, "The Museum Called 'La Specola,'" in Akira Sato, *Anatomia Barocca* (Tokyo: Treville, 1994), unnumbered page.

4. Hillel Schwartz, *The Culture of the Copy: Striking Likenesses, Unreasonable Facsimiles* (New York: Zone Books, 1996), 107.

5. This quote is taken from a typescript copy of Michael Sappol's essay "Anatomy Out of Gear: Popular Anatomy at the Margins in Late 19th-Century America," sent to me by the author circa 1997–98. Although the essay informed Sappol's book *A Traffic of Dead Bodies: Anatomy and Embodied Social Identity in 19th-Century America* (Princeton, N.J.: Princeton University Press, 2002), the passage quoted here does not appear verbatim in the finished book.

6. Schwartz, *The Culture of the Copy*, 107.

7. McKenzie Wark, "Everybody Knows," published on Nettime, a closed, moderated electronic mailing list, on January 12, 1997, http://www.desk.nl/~nettime.

8. Ian Buruma, *Behind the Mask: On Sexual Demons, Sacred Mothers, Transvestites, Gangsters, Drifters, and Other Japanese Cultural Heroes* (New York: New American Library, 1984), 12.

9. Quoted in *Re/Search #13: Angry Women*, ed. Andrea Juno and V. Vale (San Francisco: Re/Search Publications, 1991), 34.

10. J. G. Ballard, *The Kindness of Women* (New York: Farrar, Straus & Giroux, 1991), 71.

11. Ibid., 82.

12. Ibid., 85.

13. Ibid., 86.

14. Quoted in *The World of Leonardo 1452-1519*, ed. Robert Wallace and the Editors of Time-Life Books (New York: Time-Life Books, 1966), 140.

15. Gonzalez-Crussi, *Suspended Animation*, 87.

GOODBYE, CRUEL WORDS

1. "Lady Lazarus," in Sylvia Plath, *Ariel* (New York: Harper & Row, 1965), 7.

2. Statistics taken from "Suicide in the United States," a fact sheet available online at the website of the Centers for Disease Control and Prevention, http://www.cdc.gov.

3. Ibid.

4. Quoted in Marc Etkind, . . . *Or Not to Be: A Collection of Suicide Notes* (New York: Riverhead Books, 1997), 51.

5. See Kay Redfield Jamison, *Night Falls Fast: Understanding Suicide* (New York: Alfred A. Knopf, 1999), 133–34.

6. For lists of types of suicide notes, see Etkind, . . . *Or Not to Be*, 12; George Howe Colt, *November of the Soul: The Enigma of Suicide* (New York: Summit Books, 1991), 239; and Alec Wilkinson, "Notes Left Behind: The Language of Suicide," *New Yorker*, February 15, 1999, 47.

7. "Merry Christmas": quoted in Jamison, *Night Falls Fast*, 73; "I'm done with life" and "Good-bye, suckers": quoted in Colt, *November of the Soul*, 242, 239.

8. Quoted in Jamison, *Night Falls Fast*, 77.

9. Quoted in Colt, *November of the Soul*, 240.

10. Quoted in Etkind, . . . *Or Not to Be*, 9.

11. Quoted in ibid., 13.

12. Quoted in Wilkinson, "Notes Left Behind," 49.

13. Quoted in Etkind, . . . *Or Not to Be*, 13.

14. Quoted in Wilkinson, "Notes Left Behind," 49.

15. Quoted in Etkind, . . . *Or Not to Be*, 79.

16. Quoted in Jamison, *Night Falls Fast*, 96.

17. Quoted in Colt, *November of the Soul*, 240.

18. Quoted in Jamison, *Night Falls Fast*, 74.

19. Quoted in Etkind, . . . *Or Not to Be*, introduction, unnumbered page.

20. Quoted in Colt, *November of the Soul*, 123.

21. See Howard Rheingold, *The Virtual Community: Homesteading on the Electronic Frontier* (Cambridge: MIT Press, 2000), 18–22.

CORTEX ENVY

1. A. J. Jacobs, *The Know-It-All: One Man's Humble Quest to Become the Smartest Person in the World* (New York: Simon & Schuster, 2004), 16.

2. "Where No Man Has Gone Before," *Star Trek*, original airdate September 22, 1966, transcript of dialogue archived at Chrissie's Transcripts Site, http://www.chakoteya.net.

3. Loosely defined, the Cronus complex is the psychodynamic in which a father emulates the tyrannical behavior of his father, "devouring" (i.e., psychically dominating) his children—specifically, his male children—to forestall any challenges to his patriarchal authority. Franco Fornari defines the Cronus complex as "the inverse of the Oedipus Complex. It consists primarily in the father's unconscious hostility and rivalry in relation to his sons, and in his unconscious wish to castrate, humiliate, and annihilate them." Franco Fornari, *The Psychoanalysis of War* (Garden City, N.Y.: Anchor Press, 1974), 13. The complex takes its name from the Greek Titan who, envious of his father's powers as ruler of the universe, castrated and deposed him. Terrified by a prophecy that his own son would follow his patricidal example, Cronus ate his offspring as soon as they emerged from the womb. See Rachel Bowlby, "The Cronus Complex," in *Freudian Mythologies: Greek Tragedy and Modern Identities* (New York: Oxford University Press, 2007), 146–68;

Warren Colman, "Tyrannical Omnipotence in the Archetypal Father," *Journal of Analytical Psychology* 45, no. 4 (2000): 521–39; and John W. Crandall, "The Cronus Complex," *Clinical Social Work Journal* 12, no. 2 (June 1984): 108–17.

4. Letter to the author from his stepfather (name concealed to protect his privacy), August 21, 1996.

5. "Gifted children': An oddly Christian name for America's panic-button response to Russia's launch of *Sputnik*. A federal initiative, the program prioritized math and science, in early education, in order to recapture the techno-scientific beachhead. The government front-burnered the program in response to the 1972 Marland Report to Congress, which urged "differential educational programs and/ or services" for "gifted and talented children" to enable them to "realize their contribution to self and the society." Quoted in *Handbook of Psychosocial Characteristics of Exceptional Children*, ed. Vicki L. Schwean and Donald H. Saklofske (New York: Kluwer Academic/Plenum, 1999), 403. To this ex-Protestant's ear, "gifted" is uncomfortably evocative of the "gifts of the spirit" described in Corinthians. The implication is clear: academic excellence, rather than being the fruit of hard work, is bestowed by a capricious divinity on an undeserving child who, but for the grace of God, might just as easily have been consigned to the short bus.

6. E-mail to the author from his stepfather, February 27, 2009, 4:01 a.m.

7. "Me or the kid": Bearing in mind that the WAIS is normed for age group, and allowing for the precipitous decline, with age, in mental acuity.

8. Quoted in Raymond E. Fancher, *The Intelligence Men: Makers of the IQ Controversy* (New York: W. W. Norton, 1985), 117.

9. "So-called" because, as critics of the very idea of IQ testing point out, the WAIS and other tests like it may assess specialized cognitive skills—such as, say, IQ test taking—rather than true intelligence, the definition of which is still launching doctoral dissertations. "Most widely used": According to Randy W. Kamphaus, *Clinical Assessment of Child and Adolescent Intelligence* (New York: Springer Science + Business Media, 2005), 292.

10. David Wechsler, *The Measurement of Adult Intelligence* (Baltimore: Williams & Wilkins, 1939), 229.

11. David S. Tulsky, Donald H. Saklofske, Gordon J. Chelune, and Robert K. Heaton, eds., *Clinical Interpretation of the WAIS-III and WMS-III* (San Diego, Calif.: Academic Press, 2003), 70. This user's guide to the WAIS contains detailed descriptions of each of the subtests, placing them in the context of their historical origins as well as, in some cases, their strenuously debated revisions.

12. The formula for calculating an examinee's IQ is as follows: examinee's mental age—the chronological age implied by the score received, based on the average score for a given age—divided by actual age, then multiplied by one hun-

dred to eliminate the decimal point, a concept Terman borrowed from the German psychologist Wilhelm Stern. This formula works well enough when comparing children to children, but is notably less reliable for adults, since intelligence plateaus in adulthood. For that reason, today's intelligence tests have retired the IQ formula and are normed for age group. Nonetheless, the term *IQ* persists, unkillable as a termite. Or, if you will, Termanite.

13. Stephen Murdoch, *IQ: A Smart History of a Failed Idea* (Hoboken, N.J.: John Wiley & Sons, 2007), 91–92.

14. "Which is prettier?": See Clarence J. Karier, "Testing for Order and Control in the Corporate Liberal State," in *The IQ Controversy,* ed. N. J. Block and Gerald Dworkin (New York: Pantheon Books, 1976), 352–53.

15. Lewis Madison Terman, *The Measurement of Intelligence* (1915; repr., Charleston, S.C.: BiblioBazaar, 2008), 118.

16. "Sixty thousand Americans": Edwin Black, "Eugenics and the Nazis—the California Connection," *San Francisco Chronicle,* November 9, 2003, http://www.sfgate.com.

17. Karier, "Testing for Order and Control," 344.

18. Lewis M. Terman, *The Measurement of Intelligence: An Explanation of and a Complete Guide for the Use of the Stanford Revision and Extension of the Binet-Simon Intelligence Scale* (New York: Houghton Mifflin, 1916), 91–92.

19. For more on this subject, see Stefan Kuhl's excellent *The Nazi Connection: Eugenics, American Racism, and German National Socialism* (New York: Oxford University Press, 1994).

20. Quoted in "Hitler's Debt to America," an excerpt from Edwin Black's *War against the Weak, The Guardian,* February 6, 2004, http://www.waragainsttheweak.com.

21. "Gardnerian model": As in Howard Gardner, the Harvard professor of psychology who propounded the theory of multiple intelligences, defined on his website as "a critique of the notion that there exists but a single human intelligence that can be adequately assessed by standard psychometric instruments." See "Multiple Intelligences" page at HowardGardner.com, http://www.howardgardner.com.

22. Quoted in Mitchell Leslie, "The Vexing Legacy of Lewis Terman," *Stanford Magazine,* July/August 2000, http://www.stanfordalumni.org.

23. Walter Lippmann, "A Future for the Tests," in Block and Dworkin, *The IQ Controversy,* 28.

24. Quoted in N. J. Block and Gerald Dworkin, "IQ, Heritability, and Inequality" in Block and Dworkin, *The IQ Controversy,* 425.

25. Walter Lippmann, "The Measure of the 'A' Men," in Block and Dworkin, *The IQ Controversy,* 11.

Publication History

"Dead Man Walking: What Do Zombies Mean?" was originally published in trueslant.com, March 17, 2010.

"Gun Play: An American Tragedy in Three Acts" was originally published in thoughtcatalog.com, January 19, 2011.

"Mysterious Stranger: Grandpa Twain's Dark Side" was originally published in trueslant.com, July 16, 2010.

"Aladdin Sane Called. He Wants His Lightning Bolt Back: On Lady Gaga" was originally published in trueslant.com, April 20, 2010.

"Jocko Homo: How Gay Is the Super Bowl?" was originally published in trueslant.com, February 9, 2010.

"Wimps, Wussies, and W.: Masculinity, American Style" was originally published in the *Los Angeles Times,* May 3, 2007.

"Stardust Memories: How David Bowie Killed the '60s, Ushered in the '70s, and, for One Brief Shining Moment, Made the Mullet Hip" was originally published in *Las Vegas Weekly,* December 16, 2009.

"When Animals Attack! An Aesop's Fable about Anthropomorphism" was originally published in trueslant.com, May 21, 2010.

"Toe *Fou*: Subliminally Seduced by Madonna's Big Toe" was originally published in shovelware.com, February 7, 2005.

"Shoah Business" was originally published in gettingit.com, November 8, 1999.

"The Triumph of the Shill: Fascist Branding" was originally published in shovelware.com, January 26, 2005.

"Endtime for Hitler: On the *Downfall* Parodies and the Inglorious Return of Der Führer" was originally published in trueslant.com, April 27, 2010.

"World Wide Wonder Closet: On Blogging" was originally published in Portuguese in *Revista Cult*, no. 114 (June 2007).

"(Face)Book of the Dead" was originally published in *Cabinet*, no. 36 (Winter 2009/2010).

"Straight, Gay, or Binary? HAL Comes out of the Cybernetic Closet" was originally published in suck.com, May 1997.

"Word Salad Surgery: Spam, Deconstructed" was originally published in Spanish in elniuton.com, May 24, 2007.

"Slashing the Borg: Resistance Is Fertile" was originally published in *21C Magazine*, no. 4 (1996).

"Things to Come: Xtreme Kink and the Future of Porn" was originally published in nerve.com, August 11, 2003.

"Tripe Soup for the Soul: The Daily Affirmation" was originally published in *Bookforum*, Summer 2002.

"Pontification: On the Death of the Pope" was originally published in shovelware.com, April 5, 2005.

"The Prophet Margin: Jack Chick's Comic-Book Apocalypse" was originally published in *The Village Voice*, April 13, 1999.

"2012: Carnival of Bunkum" was originally published in *H+ Magazine*, November 12, 2009.

"The Vast Santanic Conspiracy" was originally published in *Las Vegas Weekly*, December 24, 2009.

"Open Wide: Dental Horror" was originally published in shovelware.com, January 4, 2005.

"Gray Matter: The Obscure Pleasures of Medical Libraries" was originally published in *Village Voice Literary Supplement*, October 9–15, 2002.

"Thirteen Ways of Looking at a Severed Head" was originally published in *Cabinet*, no. 10 (Spring 2003).

"Been There, Pierced That: *Apocalypse Culture* and the Escalation of Subcultural Hostilities" was originally published in *The Village Voice*, December 2000.

"Death to All Humans! The Church of Euthanasia's Modest Proposal" was originally published in gettingit.com, August 2, 1999.

"Great Caesar's Ghost: On the Crypt of the Capuchins" was originally published in boingboing.com, August 10, 2009.

"Aphrodites of the Operating Theater: On La Specola's Anatomical Venuses" was originally published in boingboing.com, August 15, 2009.

"Goodbye, Cruel Words: On the Suicide Note as a Literary Genre" was originally published in *Bookforum*, Summer 2003.

"Cortex Envy: Bringing Up Baby Einstein" was originally published in *Cabinet*, no. 34 (Summer 2009).

MARK DERY is a cultural critic best known for his writings on the politics of popular culture in books such as *The Pyrotechnic Insanitarium: American Culture on the Brink, Escape Velocity: Cyberculture at the End of the Century, Flame Wars,* and *Culture Jamming.* He has been a professor of journalism at New York University, a Chancellor's Distinguished Fellow at the University of California, Irvine, and a visiting scholar at the American Academy in Rome. www.markdery.com.

BRUCE STERLING is a science fiction writer and a founder of the cyberpunk movement. His novels include *Distraction, Zeitgeist, Holy Fire,* and *The Caryatids,* and he is editor of the collection *Mirrorshades: A Cyberpunk Anthology.*